French Women Playwrights
before the
Twentieth Century

French Women Playwrights before the Twentieth Century

A Checklist

Compiled by
CECILIA BEACH

Bibliographies and Indexes in Women's Studies, Number 22

GREENWOOD PRESS
Westport, Connecticut • London

Library of Congress Cataloging-in-Publication Data

Beach, Cecilia.
    French women playwrights before the twentieth century : a
checklist / compiled by Cecilia Beach.
       p. cm.—(Bibliographies and indexes in women's studies,
ISSN 0742–6941 ; no. 22.)
    Includes bibliographical references and index.
    ISBN 0–313–29174–8
    1. French drama—Women authors—Bibliography. 2. Women and
literature—France—Bibliography. I. Title. II. Title: French
women playwrights before the 20th century. III. Series.
Z2174.D7B43   1994
[PQ509]
016.842008′09287—dc20   94–28703

British Library Cataloguing in Publication Data is available.

Library of Congress Catalog Card Number: 94–28703
ISBN: 0–313–29174–8
ISSN: 0742–6941

First published in 1994

Greenwood Press, 88 Post Road West, Westport, CT 06881
An imprint of Greenwood Publishing Group, Inc.

Printed in the United States of America

The paper used in this book complies with the
Permanent Paper Standard issued by the National
Information Standards Organization (Z39.48–1984).

10 9 8 7 6 5 4 3 2

For my parents

Contents

Preface

Women playwrights are one of the groups of authors most neglected by French literary criticism and history. Critics and historians have written extensively on male authors of all genres, a certain amount on women novelists and, to a lesser degree, poets. Yet, until recently, French women playwrights had received almost no critical attention and their works were for the most part completely unknown. When I mentioned that I was writing my thesis of French women playwrights, the most common reaction was simply: "Are there any?" Ironically then, those women who chose to write for the theater, the most *public* genre, and who were often criticized for making a spectacle of themselves, have been condemned to near oblivion. Often, when their names are not entirely unfamiliar, it is because they also wrote novels or poetry, and have been remembered primarily, if not exclusively, as novelists or poets (not to mention those who were actresses).

When I began my doctoral research, no full-length study had been published on French women playwrights. There were no bibliographies or lists of any kind that I could consult to choose the plays I wished to analyze in my dissertation. I was therefore obliged to conduct extensive bibliographical research prior to determining my corpus. The resulting bibliography expanded over the years and eventually became the present checklist. During the past few years, the situation has improved. Several important studies have since appeared on French women playwrights, sessions have been devoted to the subject at major conferences, and an anthology of plays written between 1650 and 1750 has recently been published[*]. A number of anthologies of plays from

---

[*] Gethner, Perry, comp. and ed. Femmes dramaturges en France: 1650 - 1750 (Paris, Seattle, Tubingen: Biblio 17, 1993).

different periods are also currently being prepared. Yet, the history and criticism of women playwrights in France is still far behind its equivalent in England and in the United States. I hope that this checklist will further help to bring this important group of authors and their works out of obscurity, both facilitating research on the subject and, perhaps, inciting theater professionals to revive some of these long forgotten works.

This bibliography will consist of two volumes: (1) French Women Playwrights before the Twentieth Century, and (2) French Women Playwrights of the Twentieth Century**. It is designed to be as comprehensive as possible***, including plays written by women that were either published and/or performed in France during the specified periods, as well as some unperformed works in manuscript form. The genres represented range from tragedy to à propos, from opera to vaudeville, and the playwrights from unknown authors to more canonical writers like Marguerite de Navarre and George Sand. The decision to include the less well known authors and "minor" genres was based on several factors. First, feminist research involves breaking down the limits of the canon which has traditionally had a tendency to exclude women authors. Many women writers who were considered important in their day have been erased from literary history, particularly from the history of theater. While George Sand, for example, published over thirty plays, most of which were produced in major Parisian theaters (Comédie Française, Odéon, etc.), how many people think of her as a prolific playwright? Furthermore, omitting the less well known writers would amount to telling only part of the story. The majority of women dramatists, like their male counterparts, were not canonical writers, yet acknowledging their existence, individually and as a group, is essential to understanding the history of theater and of women's literature during a given period of time. Finally, we cannot predict the research interests of those who may wish to consult the checklist. I have found in my own research, for example, that a *saynète* performed in a private residence may be more revealing of the status of women at a given period than a tragedy performed at the Comédie Française.

I have not included authors who only wrote translations of foreign plays even when their production was important as in the case of Madame Dacier's seventeenth-century translations of the classics, or, in the eighteenth century, the numerous translations of English plays by Mme de Vasse and her

---

** Cecilia Beach, <u>French Women Playwrights of the Twentieth Century: A Checklist</u> (Westport, CT: Greenwood Press, forthcoming 1995).
*** I cannot, however, claim this checklist to be exhaustive (nor my research to be finished), since a certain number of authors and plays have undoubtedly been omitted. Such omissions are entirely unintentional.

sister, Marie Wouters.   Similarly, I have not included authors whose only dramatic works were adaptations of works in another genre (most frequently the novel). I have, however, listed some adaptations when the adapter was either a prolific playwright or also author of the original work. Finally, I have not included plays written in French by non-French women that were neither published nor performed in France. This is the case, for example, of Elisabeth Craven, daughter of the count of Berkeley and then lady margrave of Anspach, wrote numerous plays in French that were performed in Anspach, Germany. On the other hand, a certain number of the plays of Catherine II, Empress of Russia during the eighteenth century, were not only written and performed in French at the Théâtre de l'Hermitage in St. Petersburg, but were also published in Paris. These works are therefore included in the bibliography, as are the plays of other foreign women published or performed in France.

One of the difficulties I encountered in carrying out this research was the multiplicity of women's names. I had to take into account not only spelling variations and pseudonyms (common also to research on men), but also frequent name changes due to marriages. A glance through the list will give the reader an idea of the extent of the problem.   The situation is further complicated by varying practices in catalogues, bibliographies and biographical dictionaries. Often a women author is not listed by the name with which she signs her works, but rather by the name of her latest husband. I have tried, when possible, to list all variants (maiden name, married name(s), and pseudonyms) with cross-references. If a work is published under a female name and I have no evidence that the author is *not* a woman, I have included it in the checklist. Further studies may, therefore, prove some of these authors to be men with female pseudonyms.   I regret any such errors that may have occurred.

An additional difficulty I encountered during my research was the fact that most Parisian libraries have vast collections of manuscripts and printed works that have never been catalogued. This is the case, for example, at the library of the Société des Auteurs et Compositeurs Dramatiques and at the Bibliothèque de l'Arsenal. Thanks to the help of librarians at both institutions, I have been able to locate some of the uncatalogued works, but others are certainly still left to be discovered. The absence of a call number for a given work could have several other interpretations. First, the play may not really have ever existed. It may have only been a project never completed or a simple error on the behalf of one of my sources. Similarly, some works written by another playwright may have been falsely attributed to one of the authors listed here. I have tried to indicate my doubts in such cases (e.g. attribution highly uncertain), but I have inevitably perpetuated some such errors.   Others plays may have been lost or destroyed. And still others may be preserved in other libraries or in private collections. I am still hopeful that I will some day find a number of the plays not yet located and others whose very existence I ignore to date.

While I have tried to be as complete as possible, my primary exigency was not to indicate every copy available in Paris, but rather to indicate *at least one*. Therefore, the fact that I have not indicated that the play can be found at a given library does not necessarily mean that it is not there. Furthermore, with some exceptions, I have not indicated multiple copies within the same institution. The Bibliothèque de l'Arsenal, for example, has many different collections from various sources and often with separate catalogues (Th.N., GD, B.L. etc.). It would be conceivable to find a copy of a given play in each of these collections. Yet, with the exception of manuscripts and the Rondel collection which I have listed separately, I have only indicated one call number even if several copies are available there.

The listings in this volume are organized in four sections corresponding to the four centuries covered. Within each century, the entries are listed alphabetically by author. When an author's production spanned two centuries, her works are listed in the dominant period. When she wrote an approximately equal numbers of works in both centuries, I have placed her in the earlier period. The same is true for authors who wrote both in the nineteenth and twentieth centuries. When the majority of an author's plays were produced and/or published in the twentieth century, her name only appears as a cross-reference in this volume; her works will be listed in the volume of twentieth-century playwrights (e.g. Sarah Bernhardt, Rachilde).

I have included the following information about the authors whenever possible:

(1) Author's name (additional names -- maiden name, married name(s) -- in parentheses).

(2) Pseudonym(s).

(3) Place and date of birth and death.

(4) Other professions or activities for which the author is known (e.g. actress, teacher) and other genres practiced by the author (e.g. novelist, poet).

The plays are listed under the author's name in chronological order (I have used the first date, whether it be the date of publication or the date of performance). Each entry includes the following information about the play whenever possible:

(5) Title (and variants when appropriate).

(6) Genre, number of acts, and prose or verse (if known). In some cases, when the term does not have a precise translation in English (e.g. féerie, à propos, bluette) or when it is very specific (e.g. drame-légende du temps des croisades, comédie nationale, opéra héroï-comique), I have chosen to leave the genre in French.

(7) Co-author(s) and/or composer(s) (when appropriate).

(8) Place and date of publication (day-month-year). In most cases, I have only listed the first edition.

(9) Place and date of first performance (day-month-year).

(10) Coded references to Parisian libraries or archives (see list of codes) where the play can be found in either published or manuscript form, followed by the call numbers.

Sample entry :

1)   **GIRARDIN** (Delphine GAY, Mme Emile de).
2)   Pseudonyms: Vicomte de LAUNAY, Léon LESPES.
3)   Aix-la-Chapelle, 1804 - Paris, 1855.
4)   Journalist, poet and novelist.

5-7)   Judith (tragedy, 3 acts).
8)   Paris: Tresse, 1843.
9)   Paris, Théâtre français, 24-4-43.
10)   [BN 4° Yth 2239, RON Rf. 42.892, ARS GD 8° 42462, BHVP in-16 118467, TF 1 JUD Gir, AN F^{18}675, TF ms. 765].

According to this entry, the tragedy, Judith by Mme de Girardin was published in Paris by Tresse in 1843 and performed at the Théâtre Français on April 24 of the same year. The published version is available at a number of libraries: the Bibliothèque Nationale, the Bibliothèque de l'Arsenal (both in the Rondel collection and at least one other collection), the Bibliothèque Historique de la Ville de Paris, and the library of the Théâtre Français. Unpublished manuscripts can also be found in the censorship archives at the Archives Nationales and at the library of the Théâtre français.

When more than one play can be found within a given volume, I have indicated the title of the anthology (underlined) followed by the titles of the individual plays in quotation marks. In some cases, notably when the anthology contains a great number of plays, I have only listed those works which I know to have been performed.

Finally, I would like to acknowledge a certain number of people who helped me through the preparation of this checklist. First, I would like to thank the Association of University Women and the French government for their generous financial support while I was completing my dissertation and carrying out the research for this book. I would also like to thank the librarians at the Société des Auteurs et Compositeurs Dramatiques, the Bibliothèque de l'Arsenal and the Bibliothèque Municipale de Tours for their help in locating texts; Marcia Parker and Perry Gethner for sharing their information respectively on Mme de Chabrillan and playwrights of the seventeenth century; Gabrielle Verdier and Danielle Haase-Dubosc for their continual encouragement; and Aline, Christine and Laurent for their help in proofreading.

Codes for Library References

AN F^{18}   Censorship archives at the Archives Nationales (primarily manuscripts).

ARS   Bibliothèque de l'Arsenal.

BHVP   Bibliothèque Historique de la Ville de Paris.

BL   British Library, London.

BN   Bibliothèque Nationale.

ms.   Indicates that the copy is in manuscript form.

OP   Bibliothèque de l'Opéra.

RON   Rondel Collection, Bibliothèque Nationale, Départment des Arts du Spectacle, located at the Bibliothèque de l'Arsenal.

SACD   Bibliothèque de la Société des Auteurs et Compositeurs Dramatiques.

TF   Bibliothèque du Théâtre Français.

VER   Bibliothèque Municipale de Versailles.

French Women Playwrights
before the
Twentieth Century

Sixteenth Century

DES ROCHES (Mme Madeleine, née NEVEU, later Dame de LAVILLÉE) and (Mlle Catherine).
>   Poitiers, c.1520 - *id.*, 1587; Poitiers, 1542 - *id.*, 1587.
>   Mother and daughter; both poets; literary salon in Poitiers.

>   Panthée (tragedy, 5 acts, verse), 1571. Attribution highly uncertain. Probably by Caye Jules de Guerens.

>   Tobie (tragi-comédie, 1 act, verse) by Catherine des Roches, 1570.
>>   In Oeuvres de Mesdames des Roches.
>>   Paris: A. l'Anglier, 1579.
>>   [BN Rés. Ye 522, RON Rf. 1220, SACD Rés.].

>   Bergerie (bergerie, verse) by Mme des Roches, 1583.
>>   In Les Secondes oeuvres de Mesdames des Roches.
>>   Poitiers: N. Courtoys, 1583.
>>   [BN Rés. p. Ye. 410, RON Rf. 1221].

>   Oeuvres. Ed. Anne R. Larsen.   Includes "La Tragicomedie [*sic*] de Tobie" by Catherine des Roches.
>>   Geneva: Droz, 1993.
>>   [BN 16° Z 738 (428), ARS 16° Z 8112].

MARGUERITE DE NAVARRE (née d'ANGOULÊME).
Angoulême, 1492 - Odos (Bigorre), 1549.
Poet and author of l'Heptameron; Duchess of Alençon, then Queen of Navarre; daughter of Charles d'Orléans and sister of François 1er.

Le Malade (farce), 1535.
[BN ms. fr. 12485].

L'Inquisiteur (farce), 1536.
[BN ms. fr. 12485].

Les Marguerites de la Marguerite des Princesses.
Volume II includes: "Comédie de la nativité de Jésus Christ", "Comédie de l'adoration des trois roys à Jésus Christ", "Comédie des innocents", "Comédie du désert".

Volume IV includes: "Les Quatre dames et les quatre gentilzhommes [*sic*]" (1542), "Comédie", "Farce de Trop, Prou, Peu, Moins" (1544).
Lyons: J. de Tournes, 1547; Geneva: Slatkine Reprints, 1970 (facsimile edition).
[BN Fol. Ye. 206, RON Rf. 1370, BN ms. fr. 12485].

Comédie sur le trépas du Roy (comedy), 1547.
[BN ms. fr. 24298].

Comédie de Mont-de-Marsan (comedy).
Performed at Mont de Marsan, 1547.
[BN ms. fr. 24298].

La Comédie de la nativité de Jésus-Christ (sacré, verse), 1547.
Paris: Boivin, 1939.
[BN 8° Z 28359 (5)].

Comédie du parfait amant (comedy), 1549.
[BN ms. fr. 883].

Deux farces inédites: "La Fille abhorrant mariage", "La Vierge repentie".
Paris: A. Aubry, 1856.
[BN 8° Yth 4845, RON Rf. 1375, BHVP 8° 21280].

Epîtres et comédies inédites. Includes an untitled comedy.
Paris: H. Champion, 1927.
[BN 8° Ye pièce 9570, BHVP 8° 129006].

Oeuvres. Comédies. Includes: "La Nativité de Jésus Christ", "L'Adoration des troys roys [sic]", "Les Innocents", "Comédie du désert", "Comédie sur le trespas [sic] du roy", "Comédie jouée au Mont de Marsan".
Strasburg: Heitz, [c.1922].
[BN m. 8° Z 21186 (295-299), BHVP in-24 613 105].

Théâtre profane. Ed. V.L. Saulnier. Includes: "Le Malade", "L'Inquisiteur", "Comédie des quatre femmes", "Trop, Prou, Peu, Moins", "Comédie sur le trépas du roy", "Comédie de Mont-de-Marsan", "Comédie du parfait amant".
Geneva: Droz; Paris: Minard, 1963.
[BN 16° Yf. 632].

ROHAN (Catherine de PARTHENAY-L'ARCHEVÊQUE, dame de SOUBISE, then baronne de PONT, and finally vicomtesse de).
Parc-Soubise, 1554 - Poitou, 1631.
Famous calvinist imprisoned after the siege at La Rochelle; friend of Madame, sister of Henri IV.

Holopherne (tragedy, verse)
Performed at La Rochelle during the siege, 1574.

Baletz representez devant le roy à la venue de Madame à Tours 1593.
Contains three ballet-comedies: "AV balet de Madame", "AV balet de Madame de Rohan", "Autre balet représenté devant Madame à Pau le 23 jour d'Aoust 1592".
Tours: Mettayer, n.d. Published anonymously.
[BN microfilm m. 1764].

Ballets allégoriques en vers, 1592-1593. Ed. Raymond Ritter.
Reprints the same three ballets using as original an annotated copy at the Bibliothèque Municipale de Tours which has since been destroyed.
"Balet représenté devant Madame",
    Performed for Madame (Catherine de Bourbon) at the
    Château de Pau, 23-8-1592;
"Balet de Madame",
    Performed for Henri IV at the Palais de l'Archevêché de
    Tours, March 1593;
"Autre Balet de Madame de Rohan",
    Performed for Henri IV and Catherine de Bourbon at the
    Palais de l'Archevêché de Tours, March 1593.
Paris: Edouard Champion, 1927.
[BN 8° Yf. 2281, BHVP 8° A.R.T. 626 142].

Comédies-Ballets représentées en l'honneur de Madame, soeur du Roi Henri IV. Ed. Marcel Paquot. Most accurate reproduction of the same three ballets.

In Revue belge de philologie et d'histoire X.4 (1931); Paris: Droz, 1932.

[BN 8° Z. 22159].

Seventeenth Century

BEDACIER (Catherine) (née DURAND).
   ? - Paris, 1736.
   Novelist and poet; received an award for poetry from the Académie
   Française in 1701.

   Comédies en proverbes. Collection of 10 proverbs: "Tel maître, tel
   valet", "A bon chat, bon rat", "On ne connaît pas le vin au cercle",
   "Qui court deux lièvres, n'en prend point", "Pour un plaisir, mille
   douleurs", "Il n'est point de belles prisons, ni de laides amours", "Les
   Jours se suivent, & ne se ressemblent pas", "A laver la tête d'un asne
   [*sic*], on y perd la lessive", "Bonne renommée vaut mieux que ceinture
   dorée", "Oisiveté est mere [*sic*] de tout vice".
         In Voyage de campagne by Madame la comtesse de M***
         [Murat], tome II.
         Paris: Vve de C. Barbin, 1699.
         Probably performed privately.
         [BN Y^2 73823].

   Adraste (opera, 5 acts, verse).
         In Oeuvres, vol. V.
         Paris: Prault père, 1737.
         [BN Y^2 31565-31576, RON Rf. 82.798].

BERNARD (Catherine).

Rouen, 1662 - Paris, 1712.

Poet and novelist; honored three times each by the Jeux Floraux de Toulouse and the Académie française; member of the Ricovrati Academy in Italy; possibly a relative of Corneille and Fontanelle.

Laodamie, reine d'Epire (tragedy, 5 acts, verse).
In Théâtre français ou Recueil des meilleurs pièces de théâtre, Tome V.
Paris: Ribou, 1935; Paris: P. Gandouin, Nyon père, Valleyre, Huart, Nyon fils, Clousier, 1737.
Comédie Française, 11-2-1689.
[BN microfiche Yf 5159].

Brutus (tragedy, 5 acts, verse). Possibly co-authored by Fontanelle.
Paris: la Vve Gontier, 1691; Paris: Ribou, 1730.
Comédie Française, 18-12-1690.
[BN 8° Yth 2363; ARS 8° B 13.513 (5); RON Rf. 5487; SACD Rés., TF 1 BRU Ber; TF ms. 22].

Bradamante (tragedy, 5 acts, verse). Generally attributed to Thomas Corneille.
Paris: Brunet, 1695.
Théâtre Français, 1695.
[BN Yf. 8792].

Théâtre. Contains Ribou editions of "Brutus" and "Laodamie, reine d'Epire".
[ARS 8° B.L. 13879].

COMEIGE (Mme de).

Mahomet.

COSNARD (Marthe).

Sées (Ornes), c. 1614 - id., after 1659.
Poet.

Les Chastes martyrs (tragédie sacrée, 5 acts, verse). Adaptation of Agathonphile (1621) by Camus de Belley.
Paris: Courbé, 1650; Paris: N. et J. de la Coste, 1650; Rouen: Société des Bibliophiles Normands, 1888.
Possibly performed in 1650.
[BN Rés. Yf. 239, ARS 4° B.L. 3634].

Two other plays have been attributed to Marthe Cosnard, but most likely erroneously:

Le Martyre de St. Eustache (tragedy). Probably by des Fontaines. Paris: T. Quinet et N. de Sercy, 1643. [BN Yf. 4835];

Le Martyre de Ste Catherine (tragedy). Probably by l'abbé Hédelin d'Aubignac. Caen: E. Manglant, 1649 [BN Yf. 4836].

CROY (Dorothée de) (Duchesse douairière de Croy et d'Arschot).
    1580 (or 1588?) - 1660.
    Author of religious and profane songs.

    Cinnatus et Camma (tragi-comédie, 3 acts, verse). 1637.
        [BN ms. fr. 9282].

DESHOULIERES (Antoinette, née du LIGIER DE LA GARDE).
    Paris, 1637 - id., 1694.
    Poet, received pension from Louis XIV in 1688; member of the Ricovrati Academy in Italy in 1684 and the Academy of Arles in 1689.

    Genseric, Roi des Vandales (tragedy, 5 acts).
        Paris: C. Barbin, 1680.
        Théâtre de l'Hôtel de Bourgogne, 20-1-1680.
        [BN 8° Yth 7885, RON Rf. 6010, ARS GD 8° 11083, BHVP 8° 20481].

    Oeuvres de Mme et de Mlle Deshoulières.
    Tome II includes "Genseric" (see above) and fragments of "Zoroastre et Sémiramus" (opera) and "Jules Antoine" (tragedy).
        Paris: Vve Dabo, 1721.
        [BN Ye 30378 (18), RON Rf. 6007].

    Les Eaux de Bourbon (comedy), incomplete.

DESHOULIERES (Antoinette Thérèse, Mlle).
    Rocroi, 1659 (or Paris, 1662) - Paris, 1718.
    Poet; daughter of above; received a prize from the Académie française in 1687; also received a royal pension.

    Oeuvres de Mme et de Mlle Deshoulières.
    Tome II includes "La Mort de Cochon" (comedy), 1688.
        Paris: Vve Dabo, 1721.
        [BN Ye 30378 (18), RON Rf. 6007].

La Mort de Cochon (comedy).
In Les Amours de Grisette.
Paris: Sansot, 1906.
[BN 8° Ye 6952].

DESJARDINS (see VILLEDIEU).

DURAND (Catherine) (see BEDACIER).

LA CHAPELLE (de) or **DELACHAPELLE**.
Nun.

L'Illustre philosophe, ou l'Histoire de Ste Catherine d'Alexandrie (tragédie sacrée, 5 acts). Dedicated to "M. le Prieur, son frère".
Autun: Blaise Simonnet, 1663.

LA ROCHE-GUILHEM or **GUILHEN** (Anne de).
Rouen, 1644 - London, 1707.
Novels and translations from Spanish; protestant, she lived in exile in London from 1687 until her death.

Rare-en-tout (comedy-ballet, 3 acts, verse).
London: Jacques Magnes & Richard Bentley, 1677.
London, Whitehall, 29-5-1677.
[BL 11736.e.9].

Le Plus grand charme est l'amour (comedy, 3 acts). Attribution uncertain. Listed in Bibliothèque Dramatique de Soleinne (3582).

LONGCHAMP (Mme Pitel de).
Actress and prompter at the Comédie Française, called La Longchamp; wife and mother-in-law of actors, Henry Pitel, sieur de Longchamp, and J.B. Raisin.

Le Voleur, ou Titapapouf (comedy, 1 act, prose).
Unpublished.
Théâtre Français, 4-11-1687.

MAINTENON (Françoise d'AUBIGNÉ, Dame SCARRON, then marquise de).
Niort, 1635 - St.-Cyr, 1719.
Responsible for the education of the children of Madame de Montespan; married Louis le Grand in 1685; patron of the arts; founded l'École de St.-Cyr.

Proverbes inédits de Madame la marquise de Maintenon. Collection of 40 dramatic proverbs written c. 1690-1710.
Paris: Blaise, 1829.
[BN Yf. 9996, SACD 105 P3].

PASCAL (Françoise).
Lyons, 1632 - Paris, 1680.
Poet, painter and musician.

Agathonphile martyr (tragi-comédie, 5 acts, verse).
Lyons: C. Petit, 1655.
[BN Rés. Yf 4579, ARS GD 8° 4783].

La Mort du grand et véritable Cyrus (tragedy, 5 acts, verse). Published anonymously and tentatively attributed to F. Pascal in Bibliothèque Dramatique de Soleinne (1281).
Lyons: J. Montenat, 1655.

L'Endymion (tragi-comédie, 5 acts, verse).
Lyons: C. Petit, 1657.
[ARS GD 8° 526].

Diverses poésies de Mademoiselle Pascal. Includes:
"L'Amoureux extravagant" (comedy, 1 act, verse);
"L'Amoureuse vaine et ridicule" (comedy, 1 act, verse).
Lyons: S. Matheret, 1657.
[ARS Rés. 8° B.L. 14087].

Sésosiris (tragi-comédie, 5 acts, verse).
Lyons: Antoine Offray, 1661.
[ARS GD 8° 1594].

Le Vieillard amoureux, ou l'Heureuse feinte (comedy-farce, 1 act, verse).
Lyons: A. Offray, 1664.
[ARS Rés. 8° B. 14086].

PASCAL (Jacqueline).
1625 - 1661.
Blaise Pascal's sister; entered Port-Royal under the name of Jacqueline de Sainte-Euphémie; author of poetry, as well as *pensées* on the death of Christ and a book of regulations for novices at Port-Royal.

[Play] (5 acts). Co-authored by Anne and Catherine Saintot.
Unpublished.
Performed privately in 1636.

ROCHE-GUILHEM (see LA ROCHE-GUILHEM).

SAINCTONGE or **SAINTONGE** (Louise-Geneviève de GILLOT de BEAUCOUR, dame de).
Paris, 1650 - *id,*. 1718.
Poet, translator.

Didon (tragedy-opera, 5 acts, verse). Music by Desmarets.
Paris: C. Ballard, 1693.
Académie Royale de Musique, 11-9-1693 (and 18-7-1704).
[BN Rés. Yf. 10961, ARS GD 8° 88, BHVP 8° 12567 (3),
OP LIV. 17/R4 (11)].

Circé (opera or tragédie lyrique, 5 acts, verse). Music by Desmarets.
Paris: l'Académie, 1694.
Académie Royale de Musique, 1694.
[BN Rés. Yf. 1169, BHVP in-4° 61252 (1), OP LIV. 17/R4 (14)].

Les Charmes des saisons (ballet, verse).
In Poésies galantes.
Paris: J. Guignard, 1696.
[BN Ye. 8829].

Enée et Didon (tragédie lyrique or opera, 3 acts). Music by le sieur des Marais.
[BN ms. fr. 2207].

Théâtre de Madame de Saintonge. Includes "L'Intrigue des concerts" and "Griselde, ou la Princesse de Saluces".
N.p., n.d.
[ARS 8° B.L. 13.106].

Poésies diverses. Includes:
"Les Charmes des saisons" (ballet, 1 act, verse);
"Diane et Endymion" (pastoral-comedy, 1 act, verse),
        Performed for the Duc de Lorraine [SACD Rés.];
"L'Intrigue des concerts" (comedy, 1 act, verse),
        Performed in Dijon, 1714;
"Griselde, ou la Princesse de Saluces" (comedy, 5 acts, verse),
        Performed in Dijon, 1714.
        Dijon: A. de Fay, 1714.
        [BN Ye. 8831-8828, ARS GD 8° 2500, SACD].

SAINT-BALMON(T) (Alberte-Barbe d'ERNECOURT, comtesse de).
La Neuville-en-Verdunois, 1607 (or 1608) - Bar-le-Duc, 1660.
Known for her military exploits.

Les Jumeaux martyrs, ou Marc et Marcellin (tragédie sacrée, 5 acts, verse).
        Paris: A. Courbé, 1650.
        Possibly performed in 1650.
        [BN Yf. 491, ARS GD 8° 23480, TF 3. SAI Jum 1650].

La Fille généreuse (tragi-comédie, 5 acts, verse), 1650. Anonymous.
Attribution highly contested.
        [BN ms. fr. 9301].

SAINTOT (Anne and Catherine) (see Jacqueline PASCAL).

ULRICH (Mme).
Daughter of one of the King's violin players.

La Folle enchère (comedy, 1 act, prose). Usually attributed to Dancourt.
        Paris: Vve de L. Gontier, 1691.
        Comédie Française, 30-5-1690.
        [BN Yf. 7306, BHVP in-12 611855, TF ms. 20].

VILLEDIEU (Marie-Catherine-Hortense DESJARDINS, called Mme de).
St. Rémi du Plain (or Paris?), 1632? (different sources give birth dates ranging from 1631 to 1640) - Clinchemaure (near Alençon), 1683. Poet and novelist; received a pension from Louis XIV; member of the Ricovrati Academy in Italy.

Manlius (tragi-comédie, 5 acts, verse).
    Paris: C. Barbin, 1662.
    Hôtel de Bourgogne, 1662.
    [BN Yf. 6856, ARS 8° N.F. 4616 (I), RON Rf. 7362, SACD, TF 3 DES Man 1662].

Nitetis (tragedy, 5 acts, verse).
    Paris: C. Barbin, 1663.
    Hôtel de Bourgogne, 1663.
    [BN 8° Yth 1292, ARS GD 8° 14875bis, SACD].

Oeuvres de Mademoiselle Desjardins: "Manlius", "Nitetis".
    Paris: G. Quinet, 1664.
    [BN Rés. p. Ye. 2097, RON Rf. 7359, TF 2 DES O 1664].

Le Favory (tragi-comédie, 5 acts, verse).
    Paris: L. Billaine, 1665.
    Versailles, 14-1-1665.
    [BN Rés. Yf. 3740, ARS 8° B 30.558 (5), SACD, TF 3 DES Fav 1665].

Triomphe de l'Amour sur l'enfance (ballet). Written for the Dauphin.

Tragédies de Mme de Villedieu: "Manlius", "Nitetis", "Le Favory".
    Paris: M.E. David, [1720].
    [BN Yf. 12103].

Oeuvres de Madame de Villedieu. 12 tomes.
Tome II includes "Manlius", "Nitetis", "Le Favori [sic]".
    Paris: Barbin, 1720; Geneva: Slatkine Reprints, 1971.
    [BN Fol. Y^2 1076 (1)].

Four other plays are attributed to Mme de Villedieu by Cioranescu, but their attribution is undoubtedly erroneous: Mariane (tragedy, 5 acts, verse), 1669; Pausanias (tragedy, 5 acts, verse), 1669 (there is a play with the same title by Quinault in the same year); Virginie (tragedy, 5 acts, verse), 1683 and Alcibiade (tragedy, 5 acts, verse), 1686 (plays with the same titles by Jean Galbert de Campistron in the same years).

Eighteenth Century

ARCONVILLE (see THIROUX D'ARCONVILLE).

AUFRESNE or **AUFRÈNE** (Mlle E. or J.).
Probably related to Jean Rival Aufresne, actor at the Comédie Française, then at St. Petersburg between c. 1776 and 1804.

L'Officier suffisant ou le Fat puni (proverb, 1 act, prose).
In Théâtre de l'Hermitage, volume II.
Paris: Buisson, an VII.
Performed in St. Petersburg, Théâtre de l'Hermitage, 1787 or 1788, in the presence of the Catherine II.
[BN Yf 4570 (2)].

BARBIER (Marie-Anne) (or Mlle A.M.).
Orléans, 1670 - Paris, 1745.

Arrie et Pétus (tragedy, 5 acts, verse).
Paris: M. Brunet, 1702.
Comédie Française, 3-6-1702.
[BN 8° Yth 1222, ARS GD 8° 5566, BHVP 611 198 (3), SACD, TF 1. ARR Bar].

Cornélie, mère des Gracques (tragedy, 5 acts, verse).
Paris: P. Ribou, 1703.
Comédie Française, 5-1-1703.
[BN Yf 3160, ARS GD 8° 19883, SACD, TF 1 COR Bar].

Thomyris (tragedy, 5 acts, verse).
    Paris: P. Ribou, 1707.
    Comédie Française, 23-11-1706.
    [BN 8° Yth 17367, ARS GD 8° 22470, SACD, TF 1 TOM Bar].

La Mort de César (tragedy, 5 acts, verse).
    Paris: P. Ribou, 1710.
    Comédie Française, 26-11-1709.
    [BN Yf 8162, ARS GD 8° 21362, SACD, TF 1 MOR Bar].

Les Fêtes de l'été or Les Soirées d'été (ballet-opera). Possibly co-authored by Pellegrin. Music by Montéclair.
    Paris: P. Ribou, 1716.
    Académie Royale de Musique, 12-6-1716.
    [BN Rés. Yf. 1131, ARS GD 8° 40, BHVP 612 534 (1), OP LIV. 18/R28 (7), SACD Rés.].

Le Jugement de Pâris (ballet-opera or pastoral). Co-authored by l'abbé Pellegrin. Music by Bertin.
    Paris: P. Ribou, 1718.
    Académie Royale de musique, 14-6-1718.
    [BN m. 1329, ARS GD 8° 40, BHVP 612 534 (5), OP LIV. 18/R29 (10)].

Le Plaisir de la campagne (ballet-opera). Co-authored by l'abbé Pellegrin. Music by Bertin.
    Paris: Vve de P. Ribou, 1719.
    Académie Royale de Musique, 10-8-1719.
    [BN Rés. Yf. 1167, ARS GD 8° 40, BHVP 612 534 (8), OP LIV. 18/R32 (4), SACD Rés.].

Le Faucon (comedy, 1 act, verse).
    Paris: Vve de P. Ribou, 1719.
    Comédie Française, 1-9-1719.
    [BN Yf 81633, ARS GD 8° 10143, SACD, TF ms. 87].

Joseph (tragedy, verse). Unpublished.

Panthée (tragedy). Unpublished.

La Capricieuse (comedy, 1 act, verse).
    [BN ms. fr. 9248].

L'Inconstant (comedy, 3 acts, pr). Possibly co-authored by Pellegrin.
[BN ms. fr. 9248].

Les Tragédies et autres poésies. Contains: "Arrie et Pétus", "Cornélie",
"Thomyris" and "La Mort de César".
Leide: B.J. Vander Aa, 1719.
[BN Yf 3703].

Théâtre de Mademoiselle Barbier. Contains: "Arrie et Pétus",
"Cornélie", "Thomyris", "La Mort de César" and "Le Faucon".
Paris: Brisson, 1745.
[BN Yf 3650, BHVP 919 431, SACD 17 P1, TF 2. BAR O
1745].

BEAUHARNAIS (Marie-Françoise (*Fanny*) MOUCHARD, comtesse de).
Paris, 1737 - *id.*, 1813.
Important literary salon; poet and novelist; member of the Académie
de Lyon and the Académie des Arcades (Rome).

La Fausse inconstance, ou le Triomphe de l'honnêteté (comedy, 5 acts,
prose).
Paris: Lesclapart, 1787.
Théâtre Français, 31-1-1787 (interrupted at the third act).
[BN 8° Yth 6571, RON Rf. 7898, ARS GD 8° 10223, BHVP
611 235, SACD PC 230, TF 1 FAU Bea].

Mélange de poésies fugitives et de prose sans conséquence. Includes:
"La Haine par amour" (féerie, 1 act, prose);
"Le Rosier parlant" (féerie, 1 act, prose).
Private performance, 1773.
Amsterdam, Paris: Delalain, 1776.
[BN Ye. 10215, ARS Rés. 8 B.L. 15989, SACD 12 P7].

Le Somnambule. Includes "La Veuve et le célibataire" (scène), "Les
Illuminés" (comedy, 1 act, prose).
Paris: F. Didot, 1786.
[BN microfiche m. 8621, RON Rf. 7897, ARS GD 8° 1004].

BENOI(S)T (Françoise-Albine PUZIN de la MARTINIÈRE, Mme).
Lyons, 1724 - 1809.
Novelist; often published anonymously or under the intitial B.;
member of the Académie des Arcades (Rome).

La Supercherie réciproque (comedy, 1 act, prose).
Amsterdam, Paris: Durand, 1768.
[BN Yf 7661, ARS GD 8° 22297].

Le Triomphe de la probité (comedy, 2a, prose). Imitation of Goldoni's
L'Avvocato veneziano.
Paris: Le Jay, 1768.
[BN Yf 7691, ARS GD 24060, BHVP 611 300 (1)].

L'Officieux (comedy, 3 acts, prose). Attribution uncertain, generally
attributed to A. N. P. de la Salle d'Offremont.
Paris, 1780.
Théâtre Italien, 18-8-1780.
[BN 8° Yth 12956].

BISSON DE LA COUDRAYE (Jeanne).

Le Martyre ou la Décollation de Saint Jean (tragedy, 5 acts, verse).
Caen: J.-J. Godel, 1703; Rouen: Laurent Machuel, n.d.
Rouen, 1702 or 1703.
[RON Rf. 5503, ARS 8 B.L. 13960].

BOUILLON (Marie-Anne MANCINI, duchesse de).
Rome, 1646 - 1714.

Mustapha et Zeangir (tragedy, 5 acts, verse). Attribution uncertain.
Primary author is François Belin. Bouillon may have been a co-author.
Paris: P. Ribou, 1705.
Comédie Française, 20-1-1705.
[BN Yf. 6567, SACD PC430, TF ms. 59].

BOURDIC (see VIOT).

BOURETTE (Mme Charlotte REYNIER, dame CURÉ, then Mme) (called La Muse Limonadière).

> Paris, 1714 - *id.*, 1784.
>
> Ran the *Café allemand* in Paris which doubled as a literary salon and *théâtre de société*; poet.

> La Coquette punie (comedy, 1 act, verse).
> > Paris et Versailles: J.F. Bastien, 1779.
> > Théâtre de Maestricht, 1779; also performed in her café.
> > [BN 8° Yth 4023, ARS GD 8° 8089, RON Rf. 8276].

BUJAC (Madame).

> Les Persans à Paris (comédie nationale, 2 acts, prose).
> > Bordeaux: Labothière, 1791.
> > Bordeaux, Théâtre de la Nation, 22-6-1791.
> > [ARS GD 8° 15859].

CANDEILLE (Amélie-*Julie*) (Mme Nicolas DELAROCHE, then Mme SIMONS, and later Mme PÉRIÉ DE SENONVERT) (also listed as SIMONS-CANDEILLE and PÉRIÉ-CANDEILLE).

> Paris, 1767 - *id.*, 1834.
>
> Musician (singer, pianist, composer); actress at the Comédie Française until 1790, then at the Théâtre des Variétés du Palais-Royal; novelist, essayist; school teacher (1803-1813).

> Catherine ou la Belle fermière (comedy, 3 acts, prose). Original title La Fermière de qualité.
> > Paris: Maradan, 1793.
> > Théâtre de la République (Comédie Française), 27-11-1792 (Candeille played the leading role); Théâtre Français, 7-8-1799.
> > [BN 8° Yth 2783, ARS GD 8° 19761, RON Rf. 17206, BHVP 61097, TF 1 CAT Can].

> Bathilde ou le Duo (prose).
> > Unpublished.
> > Performed 16-09-1793.

> Le Commissaire (comedy, 2 acts).
> > Paris: Maradan, an III.
> > Théâtre de l'Egalité, 7 frimaire an 3 (27-11-1794).
> > [BN 8° Yth 3766, ARS GD 8° 110, RON Rf. 17.211, BHVP 611162].

La Bayadère ou le Français à Surate (comedy, 4 acts, verse).
Unpublished.
Théâtre de la République, 24-02-1795.

Ida, ou l'Orpheline de Berlin (comic opera, 2 acts).
Unpublished.
Opéra-comique (Théâtre Favart), 19-5-1807.

Louise ou la Réconciliation (comedy, 5 acts, prose).
Unpublished.
Théâtre Français, 14-12-1808.
[TF ms. 481].

CATHERINE II (Sophie-Auguste-Frédérique d'ANHALT-ZERBST).
Stettin, 1729 - Tsarskoïe Selo, 1796.
Empress of Russia; author in variety of genres (poetry, essays, tales, plays).

Recueil des pièces de l'Hermitage. 3 volumes. Includes:
"A quelque chose malheur est bon" (proverb, 1 act, prose);
"Il n'y a point de mal sans bien" (proverb, 1 act, prose);
"Le Flatteur et les flattés" (proverb, 1 act, prose);
"La Rage aux proverbes" (proverb, 1 act, prose);
"Un Tiens vaut toujours mieux que deux tu l'auras" (proverb, 1 act, prose);
"Les Voyages de M. Bontems" (proverb, 1 act, prose).
        St. Petersburg: n.p., n.d.
        All performed in St. Petersburg, Théâtre de l'Hermitage, 1787-88.

Théâtre de l'Hermitage de Catherine II, Impératrice de Russie. 2 volumes. Includes:
Volume I. "Le Tracassier" (proverb, 1 act, prose), "La Rage aux proverbes", "Le Flatteur et les flattés".

Volume II. "Les Voyages de M. Bontems", "Il n'y a point de mal sans bien", "Imitation de Schakespear [sic], scène historique, sans observation d'aucune Règle de Théâtre, tirée de la Vie de Rurick" (5 acts, prose).
        Paris: Buisson, an VII.
        All performed at St. Petersburg, Théâtre de l'Hermitage, 1787-1788.
        [BN Yf. 4569 (1) -4570 (2)].

CAVELIER (see LEVESQUE).

CHALLE(S) (Sophie).
Wife of the King's painter/illustrator (according to handwritten note on manuscript).

Les Morts tragiques (tragédie burlesque, 1 act, verse).
Unpublished.
Théâtre des Grands-Danseurs (Nicolet).
[OP ms. LIV. M. 238].

CHARRIÈRE (Isabelle Agnès Elisabeth van TUYLL van SEROOSKERKEN van ZUYLEN, dame de).
Holland, 1740 - Colombier (canton of Neuchâtel), 1805.
Novelist and musician; author of political essays; correspondence.

L'Emigré (comedy, 3 acts).
Neuchâtel: n.p., 1794 (new edition in 1906).
Performed at Neuchâtel, 15-1-1906.
[BN 8° Yth 31576].

Les Phéniciennes (tragédie lyrique, 3 acts, verse).
Neuchâtel: impr. de la Société Typographique, 1788.

Oeuvres complètes. Tome VII: "Théâtre 1764-1801". Ed. Jeroom Vercruysse. 25 plays (many incomplete) including:
"La Famille d'Ornac" (comedy, 1 act, prose), 1784; "Monsieur Darget" (comedy, 1 act, prose), 1785; "Les Phéniciennes" (see above); "Comment la nommera-t-on ?" (comedy, 5 acts, prose), 1788; "Les Femmes" (comic opera, 2 acts), 1790; "L'Auteur embarrassé et la jeune lingère" (comedy, 2 acts); "L'Emigré" (see above); "La Parfaite liberté ou les Vous et les toi" (comedy, 3 acts); "Elise ou l'université" (comedy, 3 acts), 1794; "Les Modernes caquets" (comedy, 1 act), 1794; "L'Extravagant" (comedy, 3 acts), 1795; "L'Enfant gâté ou le fils et la nièce" (comedy, 5 acts), 1800.
Amsterdam: G.A. Van Oorschot, 1979.
[BN 16° Z 22394 (7), ARS 16° Z 1529 (7), mss. at Bibliothèque de Neuchâtel].

CHASSIGNET (Mlle Marie-Charlotte).
Actress at the Théâtre Patriotique.

La Veillée (comic opera, 2 acts, verse), 1787.
[BN ms. 9274].

Les Deux jumelles (comic opera, 3 acts, prose). Music by Guglielmi.
Paris: Imprimerie de Monsieur, 1790.
Théâtre de Monsieur, 29-5-1790.
[SACD PC 175, BN ms. 9274].

CHAUMONT (Mme) (see FALCONNET).

CLARET DE FLEURIEU (Aglaé Deslacs d'ARCAMBAL, dame) (later dame
Bacconnière de SALVERTE).
? - 1826 or 1828.
Author of a novel published anonymously.

Le Rival par amitié, ou Frontin Quakre (comedy, 1 act, verse) by
Madame de F***.
In Siècle des ballons. Ballopolis, Paris: Cailleau, 1784; and
In Recueil des pièces qui ont eu le plus de succès sur les
théâtres de la rue de Richelieu... Paris: Bein, Valade, 1791.
Théâtre de l'Ambigu-Comique, 17-5-1784.
[BN Ye 33225, RON Rf. 10160, ARS GD 8° 21964, BHVP
in-32 18 656 (5), SACD].

Pauline (comedy, 2 acts, verse) by Mme de F***.
Paris: impr. 13, rue de la Monnoie, 1791.
Théâtre de la Nation (Théâtre Français), 2-7-1791.
[BN Yf 11248, RON Rf. 10162, ARS GD 8° 21587, OP LIV.
18/892, BHVP 8° 611689].

CLEMENT-HEMERY (Albertine) (Mme Clément HEMERY).
Author of a variety of genres including poetry, geography books and a
treatise defending women's right to read.

L'Intrigue de Province ou l'Auteur sifflé (3 acts, prose), after 1789.
[BN ms. 9246].

Les Arts et l'amitié (vaudeville, 1 act, verse).

COLLEVILLE (Mlle Anne-Hyacinthe de SAINT-LEGER, dame de).
Paris, 1761 - *id.*, 1824.
Novelist.

Les Deux soeurs (comedy, 1 act, prose).
Paris: Vve Ballard et fils, 1783.
Variétés-amusantes, 14-6-1783.
[BN 8° Yth 5043, ARS GD 8° 8853, RON Rf. 13481, BHVP
613 157 (9), OP LIV. 18/1021].

Le Bouquet du père de famille (divertissement, 1 act, prose).
Paris: Mérigot l'aîné, 1783.
[ARS GD 8° 6544, BHVP 611 848 (3), SACD PC 84].

Sophie et Derville (comedy, 1 act, prose).
Paris: Brunet, 1788.
Comédie Italienne, 8-1-1788.
[RON Rf. 13488, OP LIV. 18/2141].

La Famille réunie (comedy, 1 act, with ariettes).
[OP ms. LIV.M. 288].

DALIBARD (Françoise-Thérèse AUMERLE de ST. PHALIER, dame).
Paris, c. 1722 - *id*, 1757.
Author of historical letters, poetry and a novel.

La Renaissance des arts (ballet).

La Rivale confidente (comedy, 3 acts, prose).
Paris: Mérigot, 1753.
Théâtre Italien, 12-12-1752.
[ARS 8 GD. 21969].

DELAUNAY (Mlle) (see STAAL).

DELAVIGNE (Mme)

Le Prince bienfaisant (comedy, 2 acts).
Chambéry: M.-F. Gorrin, 1785.
Performed in Chambéry, August 1783.

DELHORME(S) (Mmes)

La Rupture, ou le Malentendu (comedy, 1 act, verse). Also attributed to
Legrand.
> Paris: Vve Duchesne, 1777.
> Théâtre Français, 23-11-1776.
> [ARS GD 8° 17429, SACD 534, TF 1 RUP Del].

DENIS (Marie-Louise MIGNOT, Madame).
> Paris, 1712 - id. 1790.
> Voltaire's niece; held a literary salon in Paris; correspondence.

Alceste (tragedy, 3 acts, verse).

L'Etranger persécuté (comedy, 5 acts, verse).

La Coquette punie (comedy, 5 acts, verse).

Paméla (comedy, 3 acts, prose).

DEZÈDES (Florine).
> 1766 - ?
> Musician.

Les Mérardines ou la Fête du village ("bouquet présenté à Mlle
Mérard").
> Private performance, 24-11-1767.

DORCEY (Mme).
French actress at the Comédie Française in 1763 and later in Vienna.

Niza et Bêkir (comedy, 2 acts, prose).
> Vienna: J. T. de Trattnern, 1771; Nantes: Vatar fils aîné, 1771.
> Vienna, Burgtheater, 26-12-1770; Paris, Ambigu-Comique,
> 17-11-1790.
> [ARS GD 8° 14882].

DORFEUILLE (Jeanne-Louise) (veuve VIAT-ROSELLY).
1754 - 1795.
Directed the Théâtre de Bordeaux in *an III*; imprisoned in 1793-4;
wife or mistress of actor and director Dorfeuille.

Le Retour du Prince d'Orange, ou les Pêcheurs de Schevelinge
(comedy, 2 acts, prose).
The Hague: l'auteur, 1787
[BN 8° Yth 15407].

DU BOC(C)AGE (Anne-Marie LEPAGE, dame FIQUET).
Rouen, 1710 - Paris, 1802.
Poet; held a literary salon; member of the academies of Rome,
Bologna, Padua, Lyons and Rouen.

Les Amazones (tragedy, 5 acts, verse).
Paris: Mérigot, 1749.
Comédie Française, 24-7-1749.
[BN Yf 6207 (1), RON Rf. 9444, ARS GD 8° 5078, TF 1.
AMA Dub, TF ms. 192].

DU DEFFAND (Marie-Anne de VICHY-CHAMROND, marquise de).
Chamrond, 1697 - Paris, 1780.
Held a literary salon; correspondence.

Ines de Castro en Mirlitons (vaudeville, 1 act, verse).
In Pièces intéressantes et peu connues pour servir à l'histoire.
Tome II. Ed. Pierre de La Place.
Brussels, Paris: Prault, 1781-90.
[BN Rés. 8 L^{45} 37].

Le Bel esprit du temps ou l'Homme de bel air (comedy, prose). Also
attributed to Forcalquier.
In La Comtesse de Rochefort et ses amis by L. de Loménie.
Paris, 1870; Geneva: Slatkine Reprints, 1971.
Aux Porcherons, 1740 (3 acts); Hôtel de Bracas, 1741 (1 act).
[BN 8° Ln^{27} 25733].

DUFRÉN(O)Y (Adélaïde-Gillette BILLET, Mme PETIT-).
Nantes (or Paris), 1765 - Paris, 1825.
Author of poetry and children's books.

L'Amour exilé des cieux (comedy, 1 act, verse).
Théâtre Français, 18-11-1788.
[TF ms. 363].

DUHAMEL (Mlle Marie Catherine) (Mlle l'aînée).
Actress/entertainer and mime with Nicolet's company.

Agnès (divertissement, 1 act, prose and verse).
Paris: C. Hérissant, 1763.
Théâtre des Boulevards (Théâtre Nicolet), 26-4-1763.
[RON Rf. 9681, ARS GD 8° 4773, OP LIV. 18/1554, SACD PC 11].

DURAND (Catherine) (see Seventeenth Century).

DU REY (Mlle) (dame or veuve Maréchal).

Adélaïde ou l'Heureux stratagème (comedy, 3 acts, prose).
Paris: d'Hourey, 1778.
[BN 8° Yth 176, RON Rf. 9687, ARS GD 8° 4719, SACD PC5].

FALCON(N)ET (Françoise-Cécile de CHAUMONT, then dame).
Nancy, 1758 - Paris, 1816 (or 1819).
Held a literary salon.

L'Heureuse rencontre (comedy, 1 act, prose). Co-authored by Mme Rozet.
Paris: Vve Duchesne, 1771.
Théâtre Français, 7-3-1771.
[BN 8° Yth 8503, ARS GD 8° 20779, RON Rf. 9809, TF 1 HEU Roz, TF ms. 274].

L'Amour à Tempé (pastorale érotique, 2 acts, prose).
Paris: Vve Duchesne, 1773.
Comédie Française, 3-7-1773.
[BN 8° Yth 698, RON Rf. 9810, ARS GD 8° 19477, SACD PC 25].

FAVART (Marie-*Justine*-Benoîte Cabaret du RONCERAY, Mme).
Avignon, 1727 - Belleville, 1772.
Actress at the Comédie Italienne; responsible for important costume reforms.

Compliment de clôture (compliment).
Théâtre Italien, 18-3-1752.

Compliment de rentrée (compliment).
Théâtre Italien, 10-4-1752.

Les Amours de Bastien et Bastienne (parody, 1 act, verse). Parody of Le Divin du Village. Co-authored by M. Harny.
Paris: Delormel, Foin et Preault fils, 1753.
Théâtre Italien, 26-9-1753.
[BN 8° Yth 816, RON Rf. 10.108, ARS GD 8° 5189, BHVP 8° 610609, OP LIV 18/1882, SACD PC 29, SACD ms].

Fêtes d'amour, ou Lucas et Colinette (comedy, 1 act, verse). Possible co-authors: Guerin, Harni, Chevalier, M. Favart.
Paris: Vve Delormel, 1754.
Théâtre Italien, 5-12-1754.
[BN 8° Yth 6913, RON Rf. 10116-120, ARS 8 B.L. 13.655].

Les Ensorcelés, ou Jeannot et Jeannette (parody, 1 act, prose). Parody of Surprises de l'amour by Gentil-Bernard. Co-authored by Guérin, Harny and possibly Favart.
Paris: Vve Delormel, 1758.
Théâtre Italien, 1-9-1757.
[BN 8° Yth 6022, RON Rf. 10121, ARS GD 8° 9764, OP LIV 18/2396, SACD PC 212, ARS ms. Douay 71-72].

La Fille mal-gardée, ou le Pédant amoureux (parody, 1 act). Parody of La Provinçale. Co-authored by Lourdet de Santerre.
Paris: N.B. Duchesne, 1758.
Théâtre Italien, 4-3-1758.
[BN 8° Yth 7151, RON Rf. 10127, OP Liv 18/1897, SACD].

Annette et Lubin (comedy, 1 act, verse). Co-authored by Lourdet de Santerre, Marmontel and possibly M. Favart.
> Paris: Duchesne, 1762.
> Théâtre Italien, 15-2-1762.
> [BN 8° Yth 974, RON Rf. 10130, ARS GD 8° 5358, OP LIV. 18/1915, SACD, ARS ms. Douay 1825].

La Fortune au village (parody, 1 act). Parody of Eglé. Co-authored by Bertrand and possibly M. Favart.
> Paris: Duchesne, 1761.
> Théâtre Italien, 8-10-1760.
> [BN 8° Yth 7476, ARS GD 8° 10835, BHVP in-16 948 396 (5)].

Parodie d'Annette et Lubin (parody, 1 act).
> Bagatelle, 1762.
> [BHVP N.A. ms. 230].

Théâtre de M. et Mme Favart. 10 tomes in 5 volumes. Tome V "de Madame Favart" includes:
"Les Amours de Bastien et Bastienne", "La Feste d'Amour ou Lucas & Colinette", "Les Ensorcelés ou Jeannot & Jeannette", "La Fille mal gardée ou le Pédant amoureux", "La Fortune au village", "Annette et Lubin".
> Paris: Duchesne, 1763-1772; Geneva: Slatkine Reprints, 1971.
> [BN 8° Yf 3322 (3)].

FLEURIEU (see CLARET de FLEURIEU).

FLEURY (la citoyenne).
Possibly the actress at the Comédie Française from 1784 to 1807: Marie Anne Florence Bernady-Nanes, then Mme Chevetel, called Mlle Fleury (Anvers, 1766 - Orly, 1818).

Adélaïde, ou l'Heureux coupable (drame, 3 acts, prose), 1794.
> [BN ms. fr. 9263].

GALLOIS (Mme)

La Religieuse malgré elle (comedy, 3 acts, prose).
> Théâtre des Variétés, 28-3-1791.

GENLIS (Caroline-Stéphanie-Félicité du Crest de ST. AUBIN, marquise de SILLERY, comtesse de).
Champcéry (near Autun), 1746 - Paris, 1830.
Literary salon; lady in waiting of the duchesse de Chartres (1772); responsible for the education of the Orléans children (1777); received a pension during the Empire and the July Monarchy; author of novels and short stories, essays, and memoirs.

La Montagne des deux amants (comedy).
      Performed in Vaudreuil, 1770.

Les Deux sultanes (comic opera, 3 acts, prose).
      Performed in Vaudreuil, 1770.

Le Bailli (comedy).
      Private performance at the home of the author, 1776.

Théâtre à l'usage des jeunes personnes. 7 volumes.
Volume I:
"La Mort d'Adam" (tragedy, 3 acts, prose). Translated from English;
"Agar dans le désert" (comedy, 1 act, prose) [SACD ms.];
"Isaac" (comedy, 2 acts, prose). Translated from Italian;
"Joseph reconnu par ses frères" (comedy, 2 acts, prose);
"Ruth et Noémi" (comedy, 2 acts, prose);
"La Veuve de Sorepta" (comedy, 1 act, prose);
"Le Retour du jeune Tobie" (comedy, 1 act, prose).

Volume II:
"L'Enfant gâté" (comedy, 2 acts, prose);
"L'Ile heureuse" (comedy, 2 acts, prose);
"La Belle et la bête" (comedy, 2 acts, prose),
      Théâtre des Jeunes Personnes, 1785;
"La Colombe" (comedy, 1 act, prose);
"La Curieuse" (comedy, 5 acts, prose);
      Théâtre des Petits Comédiens du Bois de Boulogne, 29-10-
      1779 (2 acts version);
"Les Dangers du monde" (comedy, 3 acts, prose),
      Performed in Moscow, 1780;
"Les Flacons" (comedy, 1 act, prose).

Volume III:
"Cécile ou le Sacrifice de l'amitié" (comedy, 1 act, prose);
"L'Aveugle de Spa" (comedy, 1 act, prose),
    Théâtre de Spa, 3-9-1789;
"L'Intrigante" (comedy, 2 acts, prose);
"La Bonne mère" (comedy, 3 acts, prose);
"Les Ennemies généreuses" (comedy, 2 acts, prose).

Volume IV:
"Le Bal d'enfants ou le Duel" (comedy, 2 acts, prose),
    Collège de Parthenay, 1787;
"Le Magistrat" (comedy, 3 acts, prose);
"Le Voyageur" (comedy, 2 acts, prose);
"Les Faux amis" (comedy, 2 acts, prose);
"Vathek" (comedy, 2 acts, prose).

Volume V:
"La Lingère" (comedy, 2 acts, prose);
"La Marchande de modes" (comedy, 1 act prose);
"La Rosière de Salency" (comedy, 2 acts, prose);
"Le Libraire" (comedy, 1 act, prose);
"Le Portrait ou les Rivaux généreux" (comedy, 3 acts, prose);
"Le Vrai sage" (comedy, 2 acts, prose).

Volume VI:
"L'Amant anonyme" (comedy, 5 acts, prose);
"La Cloison" (comedy, 1 act, prose);
"La Mère rivale" (comedy, 5 acts, prose);
"La Tendresse maternelle" (comedy, 1 act, prose).

Volume VII:
"Le Méchant par air" (comedy, 5 acts, prose);
"La Curieuse" (comedy, 5 acts, prose),
    Théâtre de la Cité, 1-8-1793 [OP LIV. 18/1159];
"Les Fausses délicatesses" (comedy, 3 acts, prose);
"Zélie ou l'Ingénue" (comedy, 5 acts, prose).
    Paris: M. Lambert, 1779-1780 (4 volumes); 1785 (7 volumes
    including 5 volumes of "Théâtre de l'éducation" and 2
    volumes of "Théâtre de Société").
    [BN Yf 5975-5981, ARS 8 B.L. 13.385 (1-4), BHVP in-18
    919451, SACD 5 P9].

Le Club des Dames ou le Retour de Descartes (comedy, 1 act, prose).
    Paris: au bureau de la Bibliothèque des romans, 1784.
    [BN 8° Yth 3558].

Le Club des Dames ou les Deux partis (comedy, 2 acts, prose).
>   Avignon: n.p., 1787.
>   [BN 8° Yth 3563].

Nouveau théâtre sentimental à l'usage de la jeunesse. Signed Mme la
contesse de S. [Sillery]. Contains:
"La Journée de Titus, ou le Bon prince" (drame, 1 act);
"La Fête du village" (comedy, 2 acts);
"Les Séances de Melopène et de Thalie à la rentrée de la Comédie
françoise" (comedy, 1 act);
"Le François à Amsterdam" (comedy, 3 acts);
"L'Intendant comme il y en a peu, ou les Folies du luxe réprimées"
(comedy, 3 acts).
>   [BN Z Rothschild 4655].

Jean-Jacques Rousseau dans l'île de Saint-Pierre (5 acts, prose).
>   Théâtre Français, 15-12-1791 (1 performance).

Le Libraire (comedy, 1 act).
>   N.p., 1798.
>   [BN 8° Yth 21187].

Le Voyage de Paris, ou la Colombe (comedy, 2 acts).
>   [ARS ms. Douay 1847].

L'Enfant gâté
>   In Théâtre du XVIIIe siècle, t. II.
>   Paris: Gallimard (La Pléiade), 1974.
>   [BN 16° Z. 15297 (241)].

GLEON (Geneviève SAVALETTE, marquise de).
Paris, c. 1732 - Vicence (in the State of Venice), 1795.
Known for her acting in the *théâtre de salon* of her uncle, Savalette de
Magnanville, in the Château de la Chevrette.

L'Henriette (comedy).
>   Théâtre de la Chevrette, 1775.

L'Enlèvement (comedy).
>   Théâtre de la Chevrette, 1775.

Recueil de comédies nouvelles. Includes: "L'Ascendant de la vertu ou
la Paysanne philosophe" (comedy, 5 acts, prose), "La Fausse
sensibilité" (comedy, 5 acts, prose), "Le Nouvelliste provincial"
(comedy, 1 act).
>   Paris: Prault, 1787.
>   All performed at Théâtre de la Chevrette.
>   [BN Yf. 4521, ARS 8 B.L. 13.700, RON Rf. 10353, SACD 9 P9].

GOMEZ (née Madeleine Angélique POISSON, dame Gabriel de).
Paris, 1684 - St. Germain-en-Laye, 1770.
Daughter of an actor; professional writer in a number of genres:
poetry, historical novels; best known for a series of *nouvelles* published
under the title, Cent nouvelles nouvelles (8 volumes).

Sémiramis (tragedy, 5 acts, verse).
>   Paris: 1707; Utrecht: E. Neaulme, 1737.
>   Comédie Française, 1-2-1716.
>   [ARS GD 8° 17728 (1737), SACD, TF 1. SEM Gom (1707)].

Habis (tragedy, 5 acts, verse).
>   Paris: Ribou, 1714; Utrecht: E. Neaulme, 1732.
>   Comédie Française, 17-4-1714.
>   [BN 8° Yth 20383, ARS GD 8° 11338, RON Rf. 10.358, OP
>   LIV. 18/343, SACD, TF 1. HAB Gom, TF ms. 72].

Marsidie, reine des Cimbres (tragedy, 5 acts, verse).
>   Utrecht: E. Neaulme, 1735.
>   Possibly performed in 1716.
>   [ARS Rf. Rec. 10^4, SACD].

Cléarque, tyran d'Heraclée (tragedy, 5 acts, verse).
>   Paris: Ribou, 1717; Utrecht: E. Neaulme, 1733.
>   Comédie Française, 26-11-1717.
>   [TF 1. CLE Gom (1733), SACD, TF ms 82].

Oeuvres mêlées de Madame de Gomez. Contains: "Habis",
"Sémiramis", "Cléarque, tyran d'Heraclée", "Marsidie, reine des
Cimbres", "Les Epreuves" (ballet, 3 acts, verse).
>   Paris: G. Saugrin, 1724.
>   [BN Yf 4026, ARS GD 8° 1524, RON Rf. 10357, BHVP in-12
>   948 120, SACD 49 P3, TF 2. Gom. O 1724].

GOUGES (Olympe de).
Pseudonym of Marie AUBRY, née GOUZE.
Montauban, 1748 - Paris, 1793.
Active participant in the French Revolution; best known for her
Déclaration des droits de la femme et de la citoyenne (1791);
guillotined for defending Louis XVI.

Zamore et Mirza, ou l'Heureux naufrage, later called L'Esclavage des
noirs (drame, 3 acts, prose).
Paris: Cailleau, 1788; Paris: Vve Duchesne, 1792; Paris:
Côté-femmes, 1989.
Accepted by Comédie Française in 1785 but not performed
until 28-12-1789.
[BN m. 1142 (6), ARS GD 8° 688 (4), BHVP 8° 710 (4 & 8),
SACD PC 217, TF ms. 371].

Lucinde et Cardenio, ou le Fou par amour (drame, 1 act).
Unpublished; submitted to Comédie Française in the fall of
1785 but never performed.

Le Mariage inattendu de Chérubin (comedy, 3 acts, prose). Other title
Les Amours de Chérubin.
Seville, Paris: Cailleau, 1786.
Accepted by Comédie Italienne in 1784 but never performed.
[BN m. 10784, ARS GD 8° 688 (1), BHVP 8° 710 (2), SACD
P57, TF 2. GOU Mar 1786].

L'Homme généreux (melodrama, 5 acts, prose).
Paris: l'auteur, 1786.
[BN m. 1142 (21), ARS GD 8° 688 (2), BHVP 8° 710 (1),
SACD P9].

Le Mariage de Fanchette (comedy, 3 acts, prose). Also attributed to
Delon.
Geneva: n.p., 1786.
[TF I Bea BC "p" GOU].

Le Philosophe corrigé, ou le Cocu supposé (comedy, 5 acts, prose).
N.p.: 1787
[BN m. 1142 (22), ARS GD 8° 688 (3), BHVP 8° 710 (10),
TF 2. GOU Mar 1786].

Molière chez Ninon, ou le Siècle des grands hommes (pièce épiso-
dique, 5 acts, prose). Original title: La Servante de Molière.
> Paris: l'auteur, 1788.
> Refused by Comédie Française, 17-2-1788.
> [BN Z 29359, ARS GD 8° 688 (5), BHVP 710 (3), SACD
> P55].

La Bienfaisance récompensée, ou la Vertu couronnée (comedy, 1 act,
prose).
> Paris, 1788.
> [BN m. 1142(18), ARS GD 8° 464 (3)].

Oeuvres de Madame de Gouges. 3 volumes.
I: "Le Mariage inattendu de Chérubin", "Le Philosophe corrigé, ou le
Cocu supposé";
II: "L'Homme généreux";
III: "Zamore et Mirza", "Molière chez Ninon", "La Bienfaisance
récompensée".
> Paris: l'auteur et Cailleau, 1788.
> [BN m. 17994 (1-3), ARS GD 8° 464, BHVP 617 434[1],
> SACD 11 P9, TF 2. GOU O 17788].

Hypatie (drame), 1789.

Le Temps et la liberté (pièce allégorique, 2 acts), 1790.

Le Nouveau Tartuffe, ou l'Ecole des jeunes gens (drame, 5 acts).
Original title: Le Danger des préjugés, ou l'Ecole des jeunes gens.
> Submitted to the Comédie Française in December 1790.

Les Rêveries de Jean-Jacques, la mort de Jean-Jacques à Ermenonville
(3 acts).
> Refused by Comédie Française, 11-1-1791.

Le Couvent, ou les Voeux forcés (drame, 2 acts, later 3 acts). Other
titles: La Révolution des couvens [sic] and Les Voeux volontaires, ou
l'Ecole du fanatisme.
> Paris: Vve Duchesne, 1792.
> Théâtre Français, Comique et Lyrique, 21-10-1790 (42
> performances between 1790 and 1792).
> [BN m. 1142 (10), ARS GD 8° 114, BHVP 8° 941 362, SACD
> PC 152].

Le Marché des noirs (comedy, 3 acts).
    Unpublished; submitted to the Comédie Française in
    December 1790.

Les Noces de Gamache.
    [ms. listed in Bibliothèque dramatique de Soleinne (2606)].

Le Mauvais fils.
    [ms. listed in Bibliothèque dramatique de Soleinne (2661)].

L'Homme incorrigible (comedy).
    [ms. listed in Bibliothèque dramatique de Soleinne (3072)].

Les Démocrates et les aristocrates, ou les Curieux du Champs de Mars
(comedy, 1 act, prose), written in 1789.
    N.p., [1792]. Anonymous.
    [BN Lb^{39} 3777].

La Nécessité du divorce, ou le Divorce (3 acts, prose), 1790.
Erroneously attributed to Prévost. Submitted to Comédie Italienne in
1794.
    [BN ms. fr. 9280].

Mirabeau aux Champs-Elysées (dialogue politique, 1 act, 9 tableaux,
prose).
    Paris: Garnéry, [1791].
    Théâtre Italien, 15-4-1791.
    [BN m. 1142 (2), ARS GD 8° 689 (1), BHVP 8° 611178 (4)].

Oeuvres: 2 volumes, including:
"Le Couvent, ou les Vœux forcés" (see above);
"Les Aristocrates et les démocrates, ou le Curieux du Champs de
Mars" (1 act), 1789;
"L'Esclavage des nègres" (3 acts) 1789 (original title of Zamore et
Mirza) [TF ms].
    1792.

L'Entrée de Dumourier [sic] à Bruxelles ou les Vivandiers (5 acts,
prose).
    Paris: Regnaud et Le Jay, 1793.
    Théâtre de la République, 23-1-1793.
    [BN m. 1142 (1), ARS GD 8° 689 (4), BHVP 710 (9), SACD
    P9, TF 2. GOU Ent 1793].

Le Prélat d'autrefois, ou Sophie et Saint-Elme (comedy, 3 acts, prose).
Performed under the names of Pompigny and Degouges.
Paris: impr. de Cailleau, an III (1795).
Théâtre de la Cité-Variétés, 1794.
[BN 8° Yth 14596, ARS GD 8° 689 (5), BHVP 8° 611769,
SACD P9].

La France sauvée, ou le Tyran détrôné (drame historique, 5 acts,
prose), c. 1792. Incomplete manuscript.
[AN ms. W 293].

Théâtre politique. 2 volumes.
I. "Le Couvent, ou les Voeux forcés", "Mirabeau aux Champs Elysées"
and "L'Entrée de Dumouriez à Bruxelles ou les Vivandiers";

II. "L'Homme généreux", "Les Démocrates et les aristocrates, ou les
Curieux du Champs de Mars", "La Nécessité du divorce", "La France
sauvée, ou le Tyran détrôné", "Le Prélat d'autrefois, ou Sophie et
Saint-Elme".
Paris: côté-femmes, 1991-3.
[TF 2. GOU O 1991, BHVP 8° 736 386].

Oeuvres complètes. Tome I: "Théâtre".
Includes: "L'Esclavage des noirs", "Le Mariage inattendu", "L'Homme
généreux", "Le Philosophe corrigé", "Le Siècle des grands hommes ou
Ninon chez Molière", "Le Curieux du Champs de Mars", "Le
Couvent", "La Nécessité du divorce", "Mirabeau aux Champs-Elysées",
"Le Prélat d'autrefois", "L'Entrée de Dumouriez à Bruxelles ou les
Vivandiers", "Le Tyran détrôné ou la France sauvée".
Montauban: Cocagne, 1993.
[BN 4° Z 11691 (1), BHVP 8° 736 358].

Other possible titles: "L'Ami joué", "Au peuple", "Le Bénitier
renversé", "Encore Figaro", "L'Enfant de l'amour", "La Femme
misanthrope (ou la Femme persécutée?)", "Le Français à Rosette", "Le
Génie de Brutus", "Les Héritiers, ou le Mort ressuscité", "La Leçon de
bal," "Les Mariés (or Manies) du temps",, "Matanda et Juma", "La
Mère imprudente", "Monsieur le comte", "Volonterette et Colombette",
"Le Nouveau preux", "L'Orpheline et son seigneur", "Le Patriotisme
puni" [see AN W 93 n°10].

GRAF(F)IGNY (Françoise d'ISSEMBOURG d'HAPPENCOURT, Mme de).
Nancy, 1695 - Paris, 1758.
Literary salon; perhaps best known for her novel, <u>Lettres d'une Péruvienne</u>, first published anonymously in 1747; requested by Empress to write plays for the young archdukes of Austria; correspondence.

<u>Ziman et Zenise</u> (comedy, 1 act, prose).
Vienna: Jean Pierre Van Ghelen, 1749.
Performed in Vienna in October 1749 and in Berny at the home of the Comte de Clermont in 1753.

<u>Le Temple de la vertu</u> (comedy), 1750s.

<u>Cénie</u> (drame, 5 acts, prose).
Paris: Cailleau, 1751.
Comédie Française, 25-6-1750.
[BN 8° Yth 2897, ARS 8 B 13.535 (1), RON Rf. 10379, BHVP 21696, SACD PC 107, TF 1 CEN Gra].

<u>Les Saturnales</u> (comedy, 3 acts, prose).
Vienna, Burgtheater, 28-10-1752.

<u>Azor</u> (comedy).
Private performance, 1755.

<u>La Fille d'Aristide</u> (comedy, 5 acts, prose). Original title "Théonise".
Paris: N.B. Duchesne, 1759.
Comédie Française, 29-4-1758.
[BN 8° Yth 7052, ARS 8 B 13.469 (6), RON Rf. 10390, SACD PC 245, TF 1 FIL Gra].

<u>Oeuvres de théâtre de Madame de Grafigny</u>. Includes "Cénie" and "La Fille d'Aristide".
Paris: la Vve Duchesne, 1766.
[BN Yf 3856-3857, ARS GD 8° 632 (1), RON Rf. 10375-10378, SACD 51 P3, TF 2 GRA O 1766].

Oeuvres posthumes de Madame de Grafigny.
"Phaza" (comedy, 1 act, prose). Other title: "L'Education inutile".
Performed in the home of the author in 1748, in Vienna by
the Emperor's children, and in Berny at the home of the
Comte de Clermont in 1753.
"Ziman et Zenise" (see above).
Amsterdam, Paris: Marchand de Nouveautés, 1770.
[BN Yf 3855, ARS 8 B. 13309, RON Rf. 10375 (2), SACD].

Le Fils légitime (drame, 3 acts, prose). Attribution uncertain.
Lausanne: Grasset & Cie, 1771.
[RON Rf. 10391, SACD PC 250].

Other plays listed in a Catalogue of the Phillips Collection of
Manuscripts, reprinted by Sotheby & Co. in 1965 (available at the
Bibliothèque de l'Arsenal):
"Les Effets de la prévention" (comedy), "Les Défauts copiez [sic]",
"Les Guirlandes", "Celidor" (comedy), "Les Mécontens [sic]"
(comedy), "Héraclite prétendu sage".(puppet play), "Les Tuteurs"
(comedy), "L'Epouse généreuse" (drame), "Le Sentiment récompensé"
(comedy), "Azakia" (comedy), "Saïs" (tragedy), "L'Ecole des amis".
According to the Catalogue, most of these plays are fragmentary,
unpublished manuscripts; "Madame de Graffigny was correcting the
proofs at the time of her death".

GUIBERT (Mme Elisabeth).
Versailles, 1725 - c. 1787.
Received a pension from Louis XV; poetry.

Poésies et oeuvres diverses. Includes:
"La Coquette corrigée", "tragédie contre les femmes dictée par M.
Guibert, âgé de neuf ans" (1 act, verse);
"Les Rendez-vous" (comedy, 1 act, verse);
"Les Triumvirs" (tragedy, 5 acts, verse).
Performed, 5-6-1764.
Amsterdam: 1764.
[ARS 8 N.F. 4347, SACD P5].

Les Filles à marier (comedy, 1 act, verse).
Amsterdam, Paris: Vve Duchesne, 1768.
Théâtre des grands danseurs du Roi (Théâtre Nicolet), 1768.
[ARS 8 B 13.484 (2), RON Rf. 10492, SACD PC 248].

Les Ruses amoureuses ou le Valet utile (comedy, 1 act, prose), 1781.
[BN ms. 9244].

HEMERY (Mme) (see CLEMENT-HEMERY).

HUAU (Mlle).

Le Caprice de l'amour (comedy, 3 acts, prose).
The Hague: Antoine van Dole, 1739.
Performed in The Hague, 1739.
[BN 8° Yth 2656, BHVP 8° 939393].

HUS (Mme Françoise-Nicolle).
? - c. 1780.
Actress.

Plutus rival de l'amour (comedy, 1 act, prose).
Paris: Ballard, 1756.
Théâtre Italien, 2-9-1756.
[BN Yf. 7564, RON Rf. 10741, SACD PC 488].

KENNENS (Mme de)

Le Dîner au Pré Saint-Gervais (comedy, 1 act, prose). Co-authored by
J.-B. Radet.
Paris: Migneret, 1797.
Paris, Vaudeville, 19-11-1796.
[BN 8° Yth 5206].

Ida, ou Que deviendra-t-elle? (comedy-anecdote, 2 acts, prose). Co-
authored by J.B. Radet.
Paris: Barda, an X (1802).
Paris, Vaudeville, 28 frimaire, an X.
[BN microfiche m. 5285]

Les Préventions d'une femme (comedy, 3 acts, prose). Co-authored by
J.B. Radet.
Paris: n.p., 1803.

LA FITE (Marie-Elisabeth de BOUÉE, Mme de).
Paris, 1750 - London, 1794.
Wrote translations from German and educational books; wife of a protestant minister in The Hague.

Entretiens, drames et contes moraux à l'usage des enfants. Includes 5 drames: "L'Epreuve de l'amour filial", "La Glaneuse", "Le Paysan généreux", "Le Jeu des estampes", "L'Amour fraternel".
The Hague: Detune, 1778; Paris, n.p., 1801.
[BN R. 22253, SACD P15 B.L.].

LAGRANGE de RICHEBOURG (see LE GIVRE DE RICHEBOURG).

LAISSE (Mme de).
Author of *contes*.

Proverbes dramatiques mêlés d'ariettes connues. Includes 13 proverbs: "L'Innocence éclairée", "A l'amour tout est possible", "Qui possède un ami, n'a rien à désirer", "La Grandeur ne fait pas le bonheur", "Les Ridicules", "Si jeunesse savoit, si vieillesse pouvoit", "L'Or fait tout", "Le Fat puni", "La Vanité trompée, ou le François à Paris", "Le Bonheur échappe à qui croient le tenir", "La Bonne mère", "L'Heureux déguisement", "L'Apparence est trompeuse".
Amsterdam, Paris: Duchesne, 1777.
[BN 8° Yth 6528 (incomplete), ARS 8 B.L. 13.362 (1), SACD 42 P7].

Nouveau genre de proverbes dramatiques, mêlés de chants. Includes: "L'Heureux repentir" (drame), "L'Heureux recommodement" (proverb), "La Françoise aimable" (drame), "L'Amour précepteur" (proverb), "L'Agréable surprise" (proverb), "L'Erreur du moment" (proverb), "Les Deux cousines" (proverb), "Le Concert projeté" (proverb).
Amsterdam, Paris: l'auteur, 1778.
[BN Yf. 5947, ARS 8 B.L. 13.362 (1)].

LA ROCHE-GUILHEM (Anne de) (see Seventeeth Century).

LEBRUN (Mlle Denise).

Thélamire (tragedy, 5 acts, verse). Also attributed to H. L. d'Herbigny de Thibouville.
Paris: Le Breton, 1739.
Théâtre Français, 6-7-1739.
[BN Yf. 6732, TF 1 THE Thi, TF ms. 151].

LE GENDRE de RICHEBOURG (see LE GIVRE DE RICHEBOURG).

LE GIVRE DE RICHEBOURG (Mme) (her signature, Mme L. G. D. R, has also been interpreted as LAGRANGE de RICHEBOURG or LE GENDRE de RICHEBOURG).
Author of novels adapted from Spanish literature.

La Dupe de soi-mesme [*sic*] (divertissement, 1 act), Les Caprices de l'amour (divertissement, 1 act).
In La Veuve en puissance de mary [*sic*].
Paris: Prault, 1732.
[BN Y^2 72985, ARS GD 8° 18957, RON Rf. 10953].

Le Talisman (comedy, 1 act, prose).
In Aventures de don Ramire et de dona Léonore de Mendoce, volume 1.
Paris: André Cailleau, 1737.
[BN Y^2 11026].

Arlequin subdélègue l'amour (comedy, 1 act, verse).
In Aventures de don Ramire et de dona Léonore de Mendoce, volume 2.
Paris: André Cailleau, 1737.
[BN Y^2 11027, SACD ms.].

LEMARCHAND (Françoise DUCHÉ de VANCY, Mme).
Paris, ? - c. 1754.
Author of fairy tales; literary salon; published anonymously.

Le Défiant (comedy, 3 acts, prose), 1776.

Le Mystérieux (comedy, 3 acts, prose), 1776.

LESPINASSE (Julie Jeanne Eléonore de).
Lyons, 1732 - Paris, 1776.
Reader for Mme Du Deffand (1752), then established her own literary salon; correspondence.

Les Epoux sans le savoir (comedy, 1 act, prose).

LEVE(S)QUE (Louise CAVELIER, Mme) (Mme L***).
Rouen, 1703 - Paris, 1743 (or 1745).
Author of poetry, novels and *contes*.

Judith (opera, 5 acts), 1736.
Never performed.

L'Auteur fortuné (comedy, 1 act, verse) by Mme L***.
Never performed.
Paris: n.p., 1740.
[ARS 8 GD 5792, RON Rf. 11589, SACD PC 51].

LUSSAN (Marguerite de).
Paris, 1682 (or 1686?) - *id.*, 1758.
Best known for her historical novels; also wrote fairy tales.

Divertissement pour le Roi (divertissement, verse). Music by Bury.
Paris: Ballard fils, 1746.
Performed at Versailles, 19-3-1746.
[BN 8° Yth 5252, OP LIV. 18/228].

MAINTENON (see Seventeenth Century).

MARRON (Marie-Anne de CARRELET, baronne de MEILLONAZ, dame de).
Dijon, 1725 - Bourg-en-Bressse, 1778.
Artist.

Sophonisbe (tragedy, 5 acts, verse), 1767.

Childéric, Roi de France (tragedy, 5 acts, verse), 1768.

Les Héraclides, ou le Dévouement de la famille d'Hercule (tragedy, 5 acts, verse), 1768.

Le Prisonnier, ou le Conte d'Harville (drame), 1769.

Les Atrides (tragedy, 5 acts, verse), 1769.

Clarice (comedy), 1769.

La Comtesse de Fayel (tragédie de société, 5 acts, verse). Only play published.

> Lyons: les frères Périsse, 1770.
> [BN 8° Yth 3846, RON Rf. 78954, ARS GD 8° 7916].

Valérie (tragedy, 5 acts, verse), 1770.

Antigone (tragedy, 5 acts, verse), 1773.

Le Bon père, ou l'Ecole des pères (comedy, verse), 1774.

MARTINEAU (Mlle).
Nun at the convent of the Ursulines in Angers.

Impromptu (comedy, verse).
> Performed at the convent of the Ursulines in Angers, 1776.

Les Enchères (comedy, verse).
> Performed at the convent of the Ursulines in Angers, 1778.

Les Présents (comedy, verse).
> Performed at the convent of the Ursulines in Angers, 1786.

MÉRARD DE SAINT-JUSTE (Anne-Jeanne-Félicie d'ORMOY, Mme).
Pithiviers (Loiret), 1765 - c. 1830.
Novelist and poet, published anonymously.

Laurette (opera or comédie lyrique), 1765.

La Nuit tous les chats sont gris (proverb, 1 act, prose).
> In Bergeries et opuscules.
> Arcadie, Paris: Lamey, 1784.
> [BN Yf. 12267, RON Rf. 82.885, ARS GD 8° 1625].

MOLÉ-LÉGER (Mme) (see Nineteenth Century).

MONICAULT (Mlle).
? - c.1740.

Le Dédain affecté (comedy, 3 acts, prose).
Paris: Briasson, 1728.
Théâtre Italien, 26-12-1724.
[BN Yf 5855, RON Rf. 12283, ARS 8 B.L. 14.328, BHVP 12°
611315 (1), SACD].

MONNET (Marie MOREAU(D), dame) (la citoyenne Monnet).
La Rochelle, 1752 - Paris, 1798.
Author of novels, poetry and oriental tales.

Zadig, ou l'Epreuve nécessaire (comedy, 2 acts, prose).
In Lettres de Jenny Bleinmore, tome II.
Surate, Paris: Regnault, 1787.
[BN Y^2 54102].

Les Montagnards (comedy, 3 acts, prose).
Paris: Mme Toubon, an III (1795).
Théâtre National (Théâtre de l'Egalité), 24 vendémaire an II
(15-10-1793).
[BN 8° Yth 12225, ARS GD 8° 14499, BHVP 8° 611751,
SACD PC 423].

MONTANCLOS (Marie-Emilie MAYON, baronne de PRINCEN, and finally
dame de).
Aix, 1736 - Paris, 1812.
Poet; founder and director of Journal des Dames (1774).

Le Choix des fées par l'Amour et l'Hymen (comedy). Written in honor
of the birth of the Dauphin.
Paris, Brussels: Vve Duchesne, 1782.
Accepted by the Comédie Française in 1781 but never
performed.
[BN Rés. Yf 4549, ARS GD 8° 7423, RON Rf. 18.950, BHVP
8° 611847 (9), SACD PC 123].

Le Déjeuner interrompu (comedy, 2 acts, prose).
Théatre Français, 17-3-1783.
[TF ms. 326].

Le Fauteuil (comedy, 1 act, prose).
  Paris: Corbaux, 1799.
  Théâtre de Molière, 19 vendémaire an VII (10-10-1798).
  [ARS GD 8° 10233, RON Rf. 18.951, BHVP 8° 603 535,
  SACD PC 231].

Robert le bossu, ou les Trois soeurs (vaudeville, 1 act).
  Paris: Barba, 1799.
  Théâtre Montansier-Variétés, 22 pluviôse an VII (10-2-1799).
  [BN 8° Yth 15633, ARS GD 8° 17241, RON Rf. 18.951,
  BHVP 8° 613 146 (1), SACD PC 526].

Alison et Sylvain, ou les Habitans de Vaucluse (opera-vaudeville, 1
act). Music by Mengotzi.
  Paris: Barba, 1803.
  Théâtre Montansier, 13 prairial an VII (1-6-1799).
  [ARS GD 8° 19536, RON Rf. 18.955, BHVP 8° 613 162 (12),
  SACD PC 16].

Les Trois soeurs dans leurs ménages, ou la suite de Robert le bossu
(vaudeville, 1 act).
  Théâtre Montansier, an VIII.

La Bonne maîtresse, ou la Lettre trouvée (comedy, 1 act, prose).
  Paris: Hugelet, an X (1803).
  Théâtre des Jeunes Artistes (rue de Bondy), 18 messidor an
  XI (7-7-1803).
  [BN 8° Yth 2178, ARS GD 8° 3351 (1), RON Rf 18.956,
  OP LIV. 19/12a, BHVP 8° 611713 (8), SACD PC 81].

MONTESSON (Charlotte-Jeanne de BÉRAUD de la HAYE de RIOU,
marquise de).
Paris, 1738 - Romainville, 1806.
Poet and novelist; gifted artist, musician, singer and *actrice de société*;
secretly married to the duc d'Orléans in 1773, after the death of her
first husband.

Oeuvres. 8 volumes. Volumes I-VI: "Théâtre".
I. "Marianne ou l'Orpheline" (comedy, 5 acts, prose),
  Private performance at the home of the author, 5-2-1766;
"La Marquise de Sainville, ou la Femme sincère" (comedy, 3 acts,
prose).
  Private performance at the home of the author, 1776.

II. "L'Heureux échange" (comedy, 3 acts, prose),
      Private performance at the home of the author, March 1777;
"Roberts Sciaris" (comedy, 5 acts, prose),
      Private performance at the home of the author, February
      1777.
III. "L'Amant romanesque" (comedy, 5 acts, prose),
      Private performance at the home of the author, March 1778;
"L'Aventurier comme il y en a peu" (comedy, 1 act, prose),
      Private performance at the home of the author, January 1779.

IV. "L'Héritier généreux" (comedy, 5 acts, prose),
      Private performance, 1780;
"L'Homme impassible" (comedy, 5 acts, verse),
      Private performance at the home of the author, 1781.

V. "Le Sourd volontaire" (comedy, 2 acts, verse),
      Private performance at the home of the author, 1780;
"La Fausse vertu" (comedy, 5 acts, verse),
      Private performance at the home of the author, 1781.

VI. "L'Amant mari" (comedy, 5 acts, verse);
"La Comtesse de Bar" (tragedy, 5 acts, verse),
      Performed in the home of the author, 4-5-1783.

VII. "Agnès de Maranie" (tragedy, 5 acts, verse),
      Private performance at the home of the author, 1784;
"La Comtesse de Chazelle" (comedy, 5 acts, verse),
      Théâtre Français, 6-5-1785.
      Paris: Didot l'aîné, 1782-1785.
      [BN Rés. Yf. 3425-3432, RON Rf. 82.903-910].

Les Frères généreux (drame, 5 acts, prose).
      Private performance at the home of the author, 1780.

La Comtesse de Chazelle.
      Paris: Didot, 1785.
      [ARS GD 8° 41149, SACD Rés. NS C].

Ziblis (ballet, 1 act, verse). Attribution uncertain.
      [BN ms. 9293].

MONTMORT (Mlle de).

Héraclide et Démocrite (comedy, prose). Early 18th century.

NECKER (Mlle Albertine-Adrienne de SAUSSURE, dame).
 Geneva, 1766- *id.*, 1841.
 Cousin of Mme de Staël; author of translations from German.

 Les Inconvénients de la vie de Paris (comedy, 2 acts, prose).
  Château de St. Ouen, 1778.

ORMOY (Mme la présidente d') (Charlotte, née CHAUMET).
 Etampes, 1732 - Paris, 1791.
 Novelist; member of the Académie des Arcades under the pseudonym
 of Laurilla; wrote for the Journal de Monsieur 1779-1780; mother of
 Mme Mérard de Saint-Juste.

 Zelmis, ou la Jeune sauvage (comic opera, 1 act, prose).
  London, Paris: Marchands de nouveautés, 1780.
  Performed in Versailles.
  [RON Rf. 12467, ARS GD 8° 22637].

PARIGOT (Mlle Elisabeth Louise).

 Les Rivaux réunis (comedy, 1 act, prose), 1783.
  [BN ms. fr. 9245].

 Le Comte de Waltham, ou l'Amitié trahie (drame, 3 acts, prose).
  Paris: l'auteur, 1784.
  [ARS GD 8° 7896, RON Rf. 12567].

PUISIEUX (Madeleine d'ARSANT, Mme de).
 Paris, 1720 - *id.*, 1798.
 Moralist and novelist; author of works about education.

 Le Marquis à la mode (comedy, 3 acts, prose). Signed Madame de
 P***.
  London (Paris): 1763.
  [BN m. 1966, ARS GD 8° 13683, RON Rf. 12957, SACD].

RAUCOURT (Mlle).

Pseudonym of Françoise-Marie-Antoinette-Josèphe SAUCEROTTE.
Paris, 1756 - *id.*, 1815.

Actress, primarily at the Théâtre Français; protected by the Queen and later by Napoleon I; arrested as a royalist in 1793.

Henriette (drame, 3 acts, prose). Performed under the title: La Fille déserteur. Sometimes attributed to Durosoy and Monvel.
> Paris: Saugrin, 1782.
> Comédie Française, 1-3-1782 (Raucourt performed leading role).
> [ARS GD 8° 11467, RON Rf. 13002, SACD PC 284, BHVP 8° 118012, TF 1 HEN Rau, TF ms 316].

RENELLE (Mme).

La Veuve (comedy, 1 act, prose).
> Berlin: imp. Charles Louis Hartmann, n.d.
> Performed, 29-10-1790.
> [RON Rf. 82.920].

RICCOBONI (Hélène Virginie Baletti, Mme) (called *Flaminia*).
Ferrare, 1686 - Paris, 1771.
Actress at the Théâtre Italien, 1716-1732.

Le Naufrage (comedy, 5 acts, prose).
> Paris: N. Pissot, 1726; in Le Nouveau Théâtre Italien, tome V (1753).
> Théâtre Italien, 14-2-1726.
> [BN Yf. 7491, ARS GD 8° 21426, RON Rf. 13019, BHVP 12° 9482 (T.V, 1), SACD].

Abdilly, roi de Grenade (tragi-comédie, 3 acts, prose).
> Théâtre Italien, 19-12-1729.
> [BN ms. 9311].

RICCOBONI-MÉZIERES (Marie-Jeanne Laboras de MEZIÈRES, Mme).
Paris, 1713 - *id.*, 1792.
Daughter-in-law of Flaminia Riccoboni; actress at the Théâtre Italien,
1734-1760; author of epistolary novels and translations from English;
correspondence.

Compliment de clôture (compliment, verse).
    Théâtre Italien, 1735.

Compliment de clôture (compliment, verse).
    Théâtre Italien, 1739.

Compliment d'ouverture (compliment, verse).
    Théâtre Italien, 1739.

Compliment d'ouverture (compliment, verse).
    Théâtre Italien, 1744.

Le Siège de Grenade (pièce héroï-comique, 5 acts, prose). Co-authored
by Ciavarelli. Attribution uncertain (Quérard attributes this play to A.
F. Riccoboni).
    Paris: Delormel, 1745.
    Théâtre Italien, 2-1-1745.
    [ARS 8 GD. 22142, RON Rf. 13033].

Les Caquets (comedy, 3 acts, prose). Imitation of Goldoni. Co-
authored by A.F. Riccoboni.
    Paris: Ballard, 1761.
    Théâtre Italien, 4-2-1761.
    [BN 8° Yth 2672].

Sophie ou le Mariage caché (comic opera, 3 acts). Co-authored by
Biancolleli.
    The Hague: n.p., 1770.
    Théâtre Italien, 4-6-1768.
    [RON Rf. 13035-6].

Collection complète des oeuvres de Mme Riccoboni. Tomes VII and
VIII contain translations of English theater.
    Neuchâtel: impr. de la société typographique, 1780.
    [BN 8° Y^2 60187, ARS GD 8° 1651, SACD 73 P5].

ROSALINE (Mlle).

> Compliment pour la clôture de la Foire St.-Laurent.
> Paris: Duchesne, 1753.
> Performed by Mlle Rosaline, Opéra-Comique, August 1753.
> [SACD PC 136].

ROZET (Mme) (see FALCONNET).

SABET (Mlle).
Baculard Arnaud's niece.

> Le Compliment de noces (1 act, prose with vaudevilles).
> Paris: Brunet, n.d. Published anonymously.
> Société de l'Amitié, 13 or 18-1-1784.
> [ARS GD 8° 22976, SACD].

SAINCTONGE (Louise-Geneviève de) (see Seventeenth Century).

SAINT-CHA(U)MOND (Claire-Marie MAZARELLI, marquise de la VIEUVILLE de).
Paris, 1731 - *id.* in the first years of the Revolution.
Author of poetry, *éloges* and *contes*.

> Les Amants sans le sçavoir [*sic*] (comedy, 3 acts, prose).
> Paris: Monory, 1771.
> Comédie Française, 6-7-1771.
> [BN Yf. 6954, ARS 8° B.L. 13.344, RON Rf. 13421, BHVP 8°
> 613 154 (9), TF 1 AMA Sai, TF ms. 275].

SAINT-LEGER (see COLLEVILLE).

SAINT-PHALIER (see DALIBARD).

SAINT-SAUVEUR (Mme de)

> Il ne faut jurer de rien (comedy, 1 act).
> Paris: Rainville, 1799.
> [SACD PC 304].

Recueil de pièces intéressantes et morales convenables aux théâtres de société.
"L'Enfant délaissé, ou le Double hasard" (comedy, 2 acts);
"L'Habit de bal, ou Prend son plaisir où on le trouve" (comedy, 1 act).
   "Jouée sur différens [sic] Théâtres";
"Il ne faut jurer de rien" (comedy, 1 act).
   "Jouée sur différens [sic] Théâtres".
   Paris: Pigoreau, an VIII.
   [ARS GD 8° 24253].

SAL(L)É (Marie).
   1707 - 1756.
   Dancer at the Opéra de Paris.

   Ariane et Bacchus (ballet).
      London, Covent-Garden, 1734.

   Pygmalion (ballet).
      London, Covent-Garden, 1734.

   Alcina (ballet).
      London, Covent-Garden, 1735.

SALM-DYCK (Constance Marie de THÉIS, Mme PIPELET DE LEURY, and later princesse de SALM-(REIFFERSCHEID)-DYCK).
   Nantes, 1767 - Paris, 1845.
   Poet and novelist.

   Sapho (tragedy, 3 acts, verse) by la citoyenne Pipelet. Music by Martini.
      Paris: chez l'auteur, 1795; Paris: Vente, 1810.
      Théâtre des Amis de la Patrie (Théâtre Louvois), 22 frimaire an III (14-12-1794).
      [BN 8° Yth 16118, ARS GD 8° 22145, RON Rf. 19.718, BHVP 8° 939608, SACD PC 539].

   Camille, ou Amitié et imprudence (drame, 5 acts, verse).
      Théâtre Français, 9 ventôse an VIII (28-1-1800).

   Oeuvres complètes. 4 volumes. Volume II includes "Sapho".
      Paris: Firmin Didot, 1842.
      [BN Z. 59680 (2), ARS GD 8° 2894, SACD P31]

SAVALETTE (see GLEON).

SIMON (Mme).

> Les Quakers (ballet).
> > Théâtre de Valenciennes, 30-12-1780.

STAAL (Marguerite-Jeanne CORDIER, called Mlle DELAUNAY (her mother's maiden name), then baronne de).
Paris, 1684 - Gennevilliers, 1750.
Secretary of the duchesse du Maine; memoirs.

> Suite des divertissemens [sic] de Sceaux. Includes three divertissements in verse: "La Toilette", "Le Jeu", et "La Comédie".
> > Paris: Ganeau, 1725.
> > All performed at the Château de Sceaux, May 1715.
> > [BN 8° Le Senne 14040].

> Théâtre de Madame de Staal.
> "L'Engouement" (comedy, 3 acts, prose),
> > Performed at the Château de Sceaux;
> "La Mode" (comedy, 3 acts, prose),
> > Château de Sceaux, c. 1725 [BN ms.fr. 24342].
> > London: n.p., 1755.
> > [BN 8° Yth 22143-22144, ARS GD 8° 1530, RON Rf 82.940].

> Les Ridicules du jour (comedy, 3 acts, prose). Same as La Mode.
> > Théâtre Italien, 22-10-1761.

> Oeuvres complètes de Mme de Staal, contenant ses mémoires et ses comédies. 2 volumes. Volume II includes "L'Engouement" et "La Mode".
> > Maestricht: Cavelier; Paris: Barrois, 1783.
> > [BN 16 Z. 1281 (2)].

> Oeuvres de Madame de Staal. 2 volumes. Volume I includes "L'Engouement" et "La Mode".
> > Paris: A.-A. Renouard, 1821.
> > [BN Z 61147, BHVP 8° 10 525].

> La Mode (comedy, 3 acts, prose).
> > Paris: Librairie théâtrale, 1931.
> > [BN 8° Yth 39371, ARS ms. Douay 2425 (7)].

STAEL-HOLSTEIN (Anne-Louise-Germaine NECKER, baronne de).
Paris, 1766 - *id.*, 1817.
Political salon; novelist and essayist.

Sophie ou les Sentiments secrets (3 acts, prose).
N.p.: 1790; Paris: Treuttel et Würtz, 1821.
Performed in 1786.
[RON Rf. 82.940, ARS GD 8° 17998].

Jane Grey (tragedy, 5 acts, verse), written in 1787.
Paris: Desenne, 1790.
Performed in 1787.
[ARS GD 8° 12248, SACD].

Agar dans le désert (drame biblique), 1789.
Lille: maison Saint-Joseph, 1898.
[BN 8° Yf pièce 363].

Oeuvres inédites de Madame de Staël (tome III).
"Jane Grey" (tragedy, 5 acts, verse),
Performed in 1787;
"Sophie ou les Sentiments secrets" (3 acts, prose),
Performed in 1786.
Paris: Treuttel et Würtz, 1821.
[BN Smith-Lesouëf 2508, RON Rf. 82.940].

Oeuvres complètes. Volume XVI: "Essais dramatiques".
"Agar dans le désert" (scène lyrique), 1806;
"Geneviève de Brabant" (drame, 3 acts, prose), 1808;
"La Sunamite" (drame, 3 acts, prose), 1808;
"Le Capitaine Kernadec ou Sept années en un jour" (comedy, 2 acts, prose), 1810;
"La Signora fantastici" (proverb), 1811;
"Le Mannequin" (proverb, 2 acts), 1811;
"Sapho" (drame, 5 acts, prose), 1811.
Paris: Treuttel, Wurtz, 1821.
[BN Z. 30160, RON Rf. 82.940, SACD].

Oeuvres. Volume III includes "Jane Grey" and "Sophie ou les Sentiments secrets".
Paris: Lefèvre, 1838.
[BN Z. 30181].

Oeuvres posthumes de Madame la baronne de Staël-Holstein. 2 volumes. Includes:
I. "Agar dans le désert", "Geneviève de Brabant", "La Sunamite",
   Performed privately within the author's family;
"Le Capitaine Kernadec ou Sept années en un jour", "La Signora fantastici", "Le Mannequin",
   Performed privately in Geneva;
"Sapho", incomplete and never performed.

II. "Jane Gray", written in 1787;
"Sophie ou les Sentiments secrets", written in 1786.
   Paris: 1861; Geneva: Slatkine Reprints, 1967.
   [BN usuel SDT-BI-STA].

Comédies: "Le Capitaine Kernadec", "Le Mannequin".
   Paris: H. Gautier, 1890; Paris: Gedalge, 1911.
   [BN 8° Z. 10658 (199)].

THIROUX D'ARCONVILLE (Marie-Geneviève-Charlotte D'ARLUS, Mme).
   Paris, 1720 - 1805.
   Literary salon; author of poetry, essays on science and history, and translations from English.

Mélanges de littérature, de morale et de physique (anonymous). Tome VII includes 9 plays, 7 translations and 2 originals: "Les Bouquets de noce ou les Deux bouquetières" (dialogue, prose) and "Louis IX" (tragedy, 5 acts, verse).
   Amsterdam: aux dépens de la compagnie, 1775-76.

VALORY (Caroline TOCHON, comtesse de).

Céline de Saint-Albe (comedy, 2 acts, prose). Co-authored by A.L.B. Beaunoir.
   Paris: Hardouin & Gattey, 1786.
   Théâtre Italien, 20-10-1786.

VIAT-ROSELLY (veuve) (see DORFEUILLE).

VILLIERS (Mme Nicole-Mathieu).
From Burgundy.

Barra, ou la Mère Républicaine (drame historique, 3 acts, prose).
Dijon: impr. de P. Causse, an II (1794); Dijon: impr. Carré, 1889.
Théâtre de Dijon, 5 germinal an II (25-3-1794).
[BN 8° Yth 1748, RON Rf. 77051, ARS GD 8° 6114].

VIOT (Marie-Anne-Henriette PAYAN de L'ESTANG or DELESTANG, Mme la marquise d'ANTREMONT, and finally Mme de BOURDIC).
Dresden, 1746 - Ramière, 1802.
Author of poetry and essays.

La Forêt de Brama (opera, 3 acts).
Never performed.
[ms. 489 (Bibliothèque de G. M. de Pixérécourt)].

VUÏET (Caroline) (see WUÏET).

WARENS (Louise-Françoise-Eléonore de la TOUR, baronne de).
Pays de Vaud, 1699 - 1759 (or 1762).
Rousseau's patron; published correspondence and memoirs.

Les Perdrix (comedy, verse).

WUÏET OR VUÏET (Caroline) (baronne AUFFDIENER).
1766 - 1835.
Received a pension from the Queen; composer; poet.

Angélina (comedy, 3 acts, prose), 1782.

Zéphire et Flore (opera, 3 acts, verse). Signed Mlle de W***.
Brussels: impr. de l'Olympe, 1784.

Sophie (comedy, 1 act, prose).
Paris: Cailleau, 1787.
Variétés-Amusantes (Palais Royal), 29-3-1787.
[ARS GD 8° 17997, BHVP 8° 613 126 (7)].

Nineteenth Century

ACLOCQUE (Mme Elisa).
Author of a variety of works including political essays, novels and a biography.

La Fête à Pontoise (vaudeville, 1 act).
Paris: Mifliez, 1864.
Champs-Elysées, 12-9-1864.
[BN 4° Yth 1607, ARS GD 8° 46216, SACD G.C. supp.].

Deux contre deux (comedy-vaudeville, 1 act).
Paris: Mifliez, Tresse, 1864.
Théâtre de Belleville, 26-4-1864.
[BN 8° Yth 1127, ARS GD 8° 46103, SACD G.C. supp.].

Mon Oncle le Général (vaudeville, 1 act).
[SACD ms. 95].

ADAM (Juliette) (née LAMBER, Mme Alexis LA MESSINA, then Mme Edmond ADAM).
Pseudonym: Paul VASILI.
Verberie (Oise), 1836 - 1936.
Author of novels, short stories, political essays, memoirs; founder of La Nouvelle Revue (1879); also known for her salon.

Coupable (comedy, 1 act).
Paris: Librairie de la Nouvelle Revue, 1886.
Théâtre de la Porte St. Martin, 6-5-86.
[RON Rf. 49.652, ARS GD 8° 36266].

Oeuvres complètes. Volume XXI, "Mon petit théâtre":
"Le Temps nouveau" (comedy, 3 acts),
    Private performance, 18-5-95;
"Mourir" (1 act),
    Private performance, 28-5-95;
"Coupable" (see above);
"Fleurs piquées" (lever de rideau);
"Galatée" (greek drama, 3 acts),
    Théâtre des Nations, 22-12-80 [AN F^{18}740].
    Paris: Havard, 1896.
    [BN 8° Yf 837, RON Rf. 49.651, ARS GD 8° 4043, BHVP
    615 660].

Part égale (drame monténégrin, 3 acts).
    In La Nouvelle Revue, 01-01-1912.
    [RON Rf. 49.653].

ADAM-BOISGONTIER (Mme Elisa).
Pseudonym of Elisabeth-Françoise ADAM, Mme ROCHEBLAVE.
St. Malo, 1819 - 1876.
Wrote short stories adapted from works of Mme de Genlis and
Berquin.

Nouveau théâtre des demoiselles. Includes: "Les Petites filles savantes"
(comedy, 2 acts), "L'Officieuse" (comedy, 1 act), "Palmire" (comedy, 1
act), "La Colère" (drame, 3 acts), "Rosamond ou le Courage"
(vaudeville, 1 act, 2 tableaux), "Indulgence et rigueur, ou l'Ecole des
jeunes institutrices" (comedy, 1 act), "Le Couronnement de la rosière"
(comedy, 1 act).
    Paris: Fontenay & Peltier, 1851.
    [BN Yf 8314].

La Pariure [sic] de Jules-Denis (comedy, 2 acts, with songs).
    Paris: Michel Lévy fr., 1852.
    Théâtre du Gymnase, 30-9-52.
    [BN 8° Yth 10714, RON Rf. 37.130, ARS GD 8° 15594,
    BHVP 607 778 (4), AN F^{18}830].

Maître Wolff (comedy, 1 act, prose).
    Paris: Librairie théâtrale, 1858.
    Odéon, 7-9-58.
    [BN 8° Yth 10714, RON Rf. 37.132, ARS GD 8° 13279,
    BHVP 607 964 (1), AN F^{18}714].

La Course à la dot (comedy, 1 act).
In Journal des demoiselles 24 (1858).
[BN R. 611, ARS GD 8° 41090].

AGOULT (see Daniel STERN).

AIGREMONT (see ROUSSEN).

ALBENAS or **ALBANAS** (Mlle Clémence-Isaure d').

Boabdil ou les Abencerrages (tragedy, 5 acts, verse).
Paris: Goetshy fils, 1832 (dedicated to the Queen of England).
Never performed.
[ARS GD 8° 6380, SACD PC 77].

ALBERT (Mme d').

C'est la vie (comedy, 1 act).
Théâtre de l'Application (Bodinière), 3-2-98.
[AN F^{18}1300].

ALBITTE or **ALBITTE DE VALLIVON** (see MOLE-LEGER).

ALEXANDRE (see FRIEDELLE).

ALLOUARD (Mme Emma).
Wrote translations from English and novels published under
pseudonyms Emile Jouan and Jouan-Rolland.

Un Mari empoisonné (vaudeville, 1 act).
Théâtre Déjazet, 25-5-67.
[AN F^{18}1200].

Un Entresol à louer (comedy, 1 act).
Théâtre de Cluny, 15-3-73.
[AN F^{18}1020].

La Perle fausse (comedy, 1 act).
Salle Rue Blanche, 22-5-98.

ALQ (Louise d').
Pseudonym of Mme Louise ALQUIÉ DE RIEUPEYROUX.
Paris, 1840 - after 1901.
Journalist; founder of <u>Les Causeries familières</u> and <u>Paris-Charmant</u>;
author of short stories and a variety of books on *savoir-vivre* and
education, as well as translations of English novels.

<u>Comédies et monologues.</u> Collection of 16 monologues, 1 act plays and
saynètes including:
"Ce n'est pas mon jour" (comedy 1 act),
    Salle Mustel, 15-2-1900;
"L'Habit ne fait pas le moine" (comedy, 1 act). Co-authored by Mme
S.B. de Courpon.
    Théâtre Mondain, 24-6-96 [AN F^{18}1398];
    Paris: au bureau des "Causeries familières", 1898.
    [BN 8° Yf 118].

<u>Saynètes et monologues pour fillettes, jeunes filles et jeunes gens.</u>
Collection of 12 monologues, comedies and saynètes including:
"Après le bal" (saynète, 1 act),
    Salle Mustel, 15-2-1900;
"La Jeune fille fin de siècle" (monologue),
    Salle des agriculteurs de France, 15-4-94;
"Derrière la cloison" (saynète),
    Salle des Agriculteurs de France, 15-4-94.
    Paris: au bureau des "Causeries familières", n.d.
    [BN 8° Yf 1219].

ALTENHEIM (Gabrielle SOUMET, dame BEUVAIN d').
Paris, 1814 - *id.*, 1886.
Author of novels, poetry and historical essays.

<u>Jane Grey</u> (tragedy, 5 acts, verse). Co-authored by A. Soumet.
    Paris: Marchant, 1844.
    Odéon (Second Théâtre français), 30-3-44.
    [BN 8° Yth 2128, RON Rf. 23.877, AN F^{18}708, OP LIV.
    19/1267a, TF 2 SOU Jan 1844].

<u>Le Gladiateur</u> (tragedy, 5 acts). Co-authored by A. Soumet.
    Paris: H.-L. Delloye, 1841.
    Théâtre Français, 24-4-41.
    [BN Yf 11673, BHVP 118 412, TF 2 SOU O 1841, TF ms.
    742].

ALVAREZ (Manuela).

Les Inconvénients de la réputation ou Il faut mesurer tout le monde à son aune (proverb).
In La Revue Indépendante, 10-7-44.
[BN Z. 58987/59025, RON Rf. 83.918].

AMESTOY (Amélie).

Sainte Catherine d'Alexandrie (drame lyrique, 2 acts).
Paris: Haton, n.d.
[RON Rf. 85043].

La Fête de Catherine II (operetta, 2 acts).
Paris: Haton, 1896.
[BN 8° Yth 27763].

Je serai doctoresse (comedy, 2 acts).
Paris: Haton, 1896.
[BN 8° Yth 27764].

L'Héritage de la marquise (comedy, 2 acts).
paris: Haton, 1898.
[BN 8° Yth 28644].

ANCELOT (Marguerite-Louise-*Virginie* CHARDON, dame).
Dijon, 1792 - Paris, 1875.
Novelist and painter; literary salon.

Un Divorce (drame, 1 act). Attribution uncertain. Published under her husband's name: M. François Ancelot.
Paris: Barba, 1831.
Théâtre du Vaudeville, 28-6-31.
[BN 8° Yth 17920, RON Rf. 20577].

Deux jours ou la Nouvelle mariée (comedy, 3 acts). Attribution uncertain. Published under her husband's name: M. François Ancelot.
Paris: Barba, 1832.
Théâtre du Vaudeville, 28-11-31.
[BN 8° Yth 4912, RON Rf. 20.587].

Reine, cardinal et page (comedy, 1 act, with songs). Attribution
uncertain. Published under her husband's name: M. François Ancelot.
Paris: Dondey-Dupré, 1832.
Théâtre du Vaudeville, 5-12-32.
[BN 8° Yth 15234, RON Rf. 20.593].

Un Mariage raisonnable (comedy, 1 act, prose). Attribution uncertain.
Published under her husband's name: M. François Ancelot.
Paris: Marchant, 1835.
Théâtre Français, 4-11-35.
[BN Yf 443(12), RON Rf. 20.636, TF 1 MAR Anc].

Marie, ou les Trois époques (comedy, 3 acts, prose).
Paris: Marchant, 1836.
Théâtre Français, 11-10-36.
[BN Yf 447(17), RON Rf. 20.684, BHVP 611 022 (6), SACD
PC 390, TF 1 MAR Anc].

Le Chateau de ma nièce (comedy, 1 act, prose).
Paris: Marchant, 1837.
Théâtre Français, 8-8-37.
[BN Yf 451(13), RON Rf. 20.688, SACD PC 116, AN
$F^{18}674$, TF 1 CHA Anc, TF ms. 717].

Isabelle ou Deux jours d'expérience (comedy, 3 acts, prose).
Paris: Marchant, 1838.
Théâtre Français, 14-3-38.
[BN Yf 453(13), RON Rf. 20.690, BHVP 611 098 (10), TF J.
111/40, AN $F^{18}674$].

Juana ou le Projet de vengeance (comedy, 2 acts).
Paris: Marchant, 1838.
Théâtre du Vaudeville, 4-7-38.
[BN Yf 455 (2), RON Rf. 20.692, OP LIV. 19/1759a,
AN $F^{18}746^A$, TF J. 111/166].

Clémence, ou la Fille de l'avocat (comedy-vaudeville, 2 acts).
Paris: Marchant, 1839.
Gymnase dramatique, 26-11-39.
[BN 4° Yth 839, RON Rf. 20.693, BHVP 611 098 (9),
OP LIV. 19/2678a, AN $F^{18}821$, TF J. 111/252].

Les Honneurs et les moeurs ou le Même homme (comedy-vaudeville, 2 acts).
>   Paris: Marchant, 1840.
>   Gymnase dramatique, 7-5-40.
>   [BN 4° Yth 2015, BHVP 611 098 (11), OP LIV. 19/2730a, TF J. 111/276, AN F^{18}823].

Marguerite (comedy, 3 acts).
>   Paris: Marchant, 1840.
>   Théâtre du Vaudeville, 3-10-40.
>   [BN 4° Yth 2575, RON Rf. 20.696, OP LIV. 19/1804a, SACD PC 383, AN F^{18}748, TF J. 111/295].

Le Père Marcel (comedy, 2 acts).
>   Paris: Marchant, 1841.
>   Variétés, 19-1-41.
>   [BN 4° Yth 3259, RON Rf. 20.697, SACD PC 472, AN F^{18}786, TF J. 111/305].

Les Deux impératrices ou une Petite guerre (comedy, 3 acts).
>   Paris: Beck, 1842.
>   Odéon (Second Théâtre français), 4-11-42.
>   [BN 4° Yth 1147, RON Rf. 20.698, BHVP 118 452, OP LIV. 19/1155a].

L'Hôtel de Rambouillet (comedy-vaudeville, 3 acts).
>   Paris: Beck, 1843.
>   Théâtre du Vaudeville, 19-11-42.
>   [BN 4° Yth 2020, RON Rf. 20.698, BHVP 610 101 (7), RON ms. 738, AN F^{18}750].

Une Femme à la mode (comedy-vaudeville, 1 act).
>   Paris: Beck, 1843.
>   Théâtre du Vaudeville, 12-1-43.
>   [BN 4° Yth 4478, RON Rf. 20.700, AN F^{18}750].

Hermance ou Un an trop tard (comedy, 3 acts).
>   Paris: Beck, 1843.
>   Théâtre du Vaudeville, 15-4-43.
>   [BN 4° Yth 1963, RON Rf. 20.701, BHVP 610 065 (17), AN F^{18}750].

Loïsa (comedy, 2 acts).
>   Paris: Beck, 1843.
>   Théâtre du Vaudeville, 17-6-43.
>   [BN 4° Yth 2367, RON Rf. 20.702, OP LIV 19/1776a, AN F^{18}750].

Madame Roland (drame historique, 3 acts).
>   Paris: Beck, 1843.
>   Théâtre du Vaudeville, 28-10-43.
>   [BN 4° Yth 2463, RON Rf. 20.703, BHVP 118 477, OP LIV. 19/1784a, SACD PC 370].

Pierre le millionnaire (comedy, 3 acts).
>   Paris: Beck, 1844.
>   Théâtre du Vaudeville, 2-3-44.
>   [BN 4° Yth 3340, RON Rf. 20.704, BHVP 610 066 (3), AN F^{18}751].

Follette (comedy-vaudeville, 1 act).
>   Paris: Beck, 1844.
>   Théâtre du Vaudeville, 8-10-44.
>   [BN 4° Yth 1712, RON Rf. 20.705, AN F^{18}751].

Un Jour de liberté (comedy-vaudeville, 3 acts).
>   Paris: Beck, 1844.
>   Théâtre du Vaudeville, 25-11-44.
>   [BN 4° Yth 4290, RON Rf. 20.706, OP LIV. 19/1989a].

Un Souvenir (vaudeville, 1 act).
>   Théâtre des Variétés, 29-10-46.

Une Année à Paris (comedy, 3 acts).
>   Paris: Beck, 1847.
>   Odéon (Second Théâtre Français), 21-1-47.
>   [BN 4° Yth 4429, RON Rf. 20.707, BHVP 611 029 (17), OP LIV. 19/1483a, SACD P.C. 35].

Les Femmes de Paris ou l'Homme de loisir (drame, 5 acts). Co-authored by M. Delaporte.
>   Paris: Tresse, 1848.
>   Théâtre de la Gaîté, 5-10-48.
>   [BN 4° Yth 1592, RON Rf. 20.708, BHVP 611 025 (13)].

La Rue Quincampoix (drame, 5 acts, verse). Attribution uncertain. Also attributed to M. François Ancelot.
>   Paris: Beck, 1848.
>   [BN 4° Yth 3794].

Les Quenouilles de verre (féerie-vaudeville, 3 acts). Co-authored by Michel Delaporte and M. Alnoy.
>   Paris: Impr. de Mme Vve Dondey-Duprey, n.d.
>   Folies dramatiques, 13-9-51.
>   [RON Rf. 20.709, AN F^{18}992].

Théâtre. Includes: "Marie, ou les Trois époques", "Isabelle, ou Deux jours d'expérience", "Marguerite", "Un Mariage raisonnable", "Clémence, ou la Fille de l'avocat", "Le Château de ma nièce", "Georges, ou le Même homme".
>   Paris: C. Gosselin, 1841
>   [BN Yf 8036, RON Rf. 20.682, BHVP 615 284].

Théâtre complet. 4 volumes.
>   Paris: Beck, 1848.
>   [BN Yf 8037-8040, RON Rf. 20.683, SACD P27, TF 2 ANC O 1848].

APRAXIN (Julie) (see BATTHYANY).

ARBEL (Mlle).

Coeur brisé (pantomime, 1 act).
>   Bouffes-Parisiens, 17-12-90.

ARLEMONT (Suzanne d').

Catherine est innocente (comédie-bouffe, 1 act).
>   Darm: Nathan, n.d.
>   [ARS GD 8° 30091].

ARNAUD (Simone).
Pseudonym of Mlle de LAGE, Mme Anne COPIN-ALBANCELLI.
Limoges, 1850 - Gargilesse, 1901.

Mademoiselle de Vigean (comedy, 1 act, verse).
>   Paris: Ollendorff, 1883.
>   Théâtre Français, 28-6-83.
>   [BN 8° Yth 21090, RON Rf. 50.269, BHVP 119 860, SACD PC 370, TF 1 MAD Arn, AN F^{18}684].

1802 (à propos, verse) (written for the 84th anniversary of the birth of
Victor Hugo).
        Paris: Ollendorff, 1886.
        Odéon, 26-2-86.
        [BN 8° Yth 22354, RON Rf. 50.271, BHVP 119 958, TF 1
        APO Del, AN $F^{18}724$].

Les Fils de Jahel (drame, 5 acts, verse).
        Paris: Ollendorff, 1886.
        Odéon , 14-10-86.
        [BN 8° Yth 22262, RON Rf. 50.272, BHVP 609 536, AN
        $F^{18}724$].

L'Oiseau bleu (fantaisie poétique or drame lyrique, 2 acts, 3 tableaux,
verse). Music by Coquard.
        Paris: Ollendorff, 1894.
        Théâtre de l'Application, 8-3-94.
        [BN 8° Yth 26610, RON Rf. 50.275, BHVP 120 631, OP Rés.
        2073, SACD PC 446, AN $F^{18}1298$].

La Jacquerie (drame lyrique, 4 acts). Co-authored by E. Blau. Music by
E. Lalo and A. Coquard.
        Paris: C. Lévy, 1895.
        Monte-Carlo, 9-3-95; Opéra-Comique, 23-12-95.
        [BN 8° Yth 227424, RON Rf. 50.276, BHVP 120 829, AN
        $F^{18}701$].

Jeanne d'Arc (drame, 5 acts, verse).
        Paris: Ollendorff, 1895.
        [BN 8° Yth 27009, RON Rf. 50.279].

Médéia (drame, 4 acts, verse).
        Paris: Ollendorff, 1898.
        [BN 8° Yth 28745].

Jahel (drame lyrique, 4 acts, 5 tableaux). Co-authored by Louis Gallet.
Music by A. Coquard.
        Paris: Ollendorff, 1899.
        [BN 8° Yth 28708, RON Rf. 50.274, BHVP 121 619].

Myrdihm (opéra-légende, 4 acts). Music by Bourcault-Ducoudray.
  Paris: Société française d'impr. et libr., 1912.
  Grand Théâtre, 30-3-1912.
  [BN 8° Yth 34353, RON Rf. 50.280, BHVP 123 723, OP ms.
  Rés. 519 (1-3)].

ASTOUD-TROLLEY (Louise).

Pauvres petits enfants (étude, verse).
  Paris: 45 rue de Sèvres, 1878.
  Théâtre du Vaudeville, 10-3-78.
  [BN Ye. 37606].

AUDOUARD (Olympe) (née de Jouval).
  Marseille or Aix?, 1830 - Nice, 1890.
  Feminist novelist, essayist and orator; author of travel narratives.

Il n'y a pas d'amour sans jalousie et de jalousie sans amour (comedy, 1
act, prose).
  Paris: Dentu, 1863.
  [BN 8° Yth 8860, ARS GD 8° 34329].

AULNAY (Louise d') (see GOURAUD).

AUNET (Léonie d') (Mme BIARD).
  Novelist; director of La Revue des Modes et de l'Industrie.

Une Place à la cour (comedy, 1 act).
  Poissy: Arbieu, 1854.
  [BN 8° Yth 18566].

Silvère (1 act).
  In Théâtre des Inconnus 6 (15-6-1873).
  [BN Yf 1345 (6), ARS GD 8° 46708].

Jane Osborn (drame, 4 acts).
  Paris: Taride, n.d.
  Porte St. Martin, 30-1-1855.
  [BN 4° Yth 2129, ARS GD 8° 49240, BHVP 90 374 (12)].

AVRIL (Mme J).

Un Stage (comedy, 1 act).
  Salle d'Athènes, 21-4-95.

B. (Mme de).

Zuma ou le Serment des Indiens (melodrama, 3 acts).
Théâtre de la Porte Saint Martin, 29-1-18.
[AN F^{18}600^B].

BADERE (Clémence DELAUNAY, Mme).
Vendôme, 1813 - after 1891.
Author of novels, short stories and poetry.

L'Anneau du diable (comedy-vaudeville, 2 acts).
Paris: Dentu, 1866.
Never performed.
[BN 8° Yth 968, ARS GD 8° 38315].

BALLEY (Berthe PRAQUIN de SAINT-MAXIME, Mme F.)
Author of novels and poetry.

Triple rendez-vous (comedy, 1 act, prose).
Salle Charras, 5-5-95.
[AN F^{18}1357].

BANET-RIVET (Joséphine).

La Mort de Lincoln (poème dramatique).
Paris: Librairie des auteurs, 1867.
[BN Ye 3650, RON Rf. 37.029].

La Dame de la Roche Guyon ou le Refus de serment (tragedy, 5 acts).
Paris: Editions 33 rue des Tournelles, 1871.
[RON Rf. 37.527].

BARBÉ (Hortence de CÉRÉ, dame) (also CÉRÉ-BARBÉ).
Author of religious poetry and translations from English.

Maximien (tragedy, 5 acts).
Paris: Germain-Mathiot, Poulet, 1813.
Accepted by the Théâtre Français in 1809 but never
performed.
[BN 8° Yth 11414, RON Rf. 21.712, BHVP 611 260 (7),
SACD PC 401, SACD ms. 91].

BARBIER (Mme Marie).
1827 - 1897.

La Petite soeur (comedy, 1 act).
Paris: C. Lévy, 1881.
Théâtre du Vaudeville, 4-5-81.
[BN 8° Yth 24720, ARS GD 8° 34908, RON Rf. 50.624,
BHVP 607 727 (2), AN F^{18}771].

Not' Claire (comedy, 1 act).
Paris: C. Lévy, 1895.
Odéon, 1-4-95.
[BN 8° Yth 27283, ARS GD 8° 34459, RON Rf. 50.625,
BHVP 608 016 (4), AN F^{18}727].

BARTHELEMY-HADOT (Marie-Adèle RICHARD, Mme)
Troyes (Aube), 1763 - Paris, 1821.
Novelist.

L'Ivrogne et sa femme (comedy-parody, 1 act). Imitation of a fable by
La Fontaine. Co-authored by J. Ernest (Clouard) and Armand (Mme
Barthélémy-Hadot).
Paris: Allut, 1803.
Paris, Cité-Variétés, 1802.
[BHVP 611 618 (4)].

Balthazard, ou le Bon commissionnaire (comedy, 1 act, prose).
Paris: Huguelet, an XII (1804).
Théâtre du Marais, an II; Théâtre des Jeunes Auteurs, 22-8-
03.
[BN 8° Yth 1666, RON Rf. 27.365, BHVP 611 725].

Zadig ou la Destinée (melodrama, 3 acts). Adaptation of Voltaire's
novel. Music by Tobie.
Paris: Fages, an XII (1804).
Théâtre de la Gaîté, 25-8-04.
[BN 8° Yth 19439, RON Rf. 27.366, ARS GD 8° 19336].

Zamilo et Zélia, ou le Dévouement filial (melodrama, 3 acts, prose).
Théâtre du Marais, 4-10-04.

Maclovie, comtesse de Warberg ou la Peine de Talion (historical melodrama, 3 acts). Music by Tobie.
>Paris: Fages, 1804.
>Théâtre de la Gaîté, 27-12-04.
>[BN 8° Yth 10468, RON Rf. 27.367, ARS GD 8° 13079, SACD PC 367].

L'Homme mystérieux (melodrama, 3 acts, prose). Music by Taix.
>Paris: Huet-Masson, 1806.
>Théâtre de la Gaîté, 24-4-06.
>[BN 8° Yth 8634, RON Rf. 27.368, ARS GD 8° 11662, SACD PC 296].

Jean Sobieski, Roi de Pologne ou la Lettre (melodrama, 3 acts, prose).
>Paris: Huet-Masson, 1806.
>Théâtre de la Gaîté, 22-5-06.
>[BN 8° Yth 9410, RON Rf. 27.369, ARS GD 8° 20874, SACD PC 325].

Jules ou le Toit paternel (melodrama, 3 acts). Co-authored by de Rougemont. Music by Bianchi.
>Paris: G. Bruet, 1806.
>Théâtre des Jeunes Élèves (rue de Thionville), 5-7-06.
>[BN 8° Yth 9879, RON Rf. 27.370, ARS 8° 12623, BHVP 609 978 (4), OP LIV. LIV 19/139a, SACD PC 340].

Alméria, ou l'Ecossaise fugitive (melodrama, 3 acts, prose). Music by Bianchi. Ballet by Berton.
>Paris: Ducrocq, 1806.
>Théâtre des jeunes élèves (rue de Thionville), 8-12-06; Théâtre du Petit-Lazari, 10-5-42?.
>[BN 8° Yth 440, RON Rf. 27.371, ARS GD 8° 4923, BHVP 611 650 (5), OP LIV. 19/114a, AN F^{18}605^A].

Alphonse et Adèle ou le Retour désiré (vaudeville, 1 act).
>Théâtre des Jeunes Comédiens, 18-4-07.

Amélie ou le Protecteur mystérieux (melodrama, 3 acts). Music by Taix.
>Paris: Hénée & Dumas, 1807.
>Théâtre de la Gaîté, 11-6-07.
>[RON Rf. 27.372, SACD PC 22].

Aldegonde (vaudeville, 1 act).
    Théâtre des Nouveaux Troubadours, 22-6-07.

Cosme de Médicis (melodrama, 3 acts, prose). Co-authored by R.
Périn. Music by Quasain and Piccini.
    Paris: Fages, 1809.
    Théâtre de l'Ambigu-Comique, 21-12-08.
    [BN 8° Yth 4093, RON Rf. 27.373, ARS GD 8° 19904].

L'Amazone de Grenade (melodrama, 3 acts). Co-authored by R. Perin.
Music by Taix.
    Paris: Barba, 1812.
    Théâtre de la Gaïte, 27-2-12.
    [BN 8° Yth 595, RON Rf. 27.374, ARS GD 8° 5077, BHVP
    611 195 (5), SACD PC 21].

Clarice, ou la Femme précepteur (melodrama, 3 acts). Co-authored by
R. Périn. Music by Taix.
    Paris: Barba, 1812.
    Théâtre de la Gaïte, 30-5-12.
    [BN m. 17876, RON Rf. 27.375, ARS GD 7533, BHVP 609
    988 (8)].

Charles Martel (historical melodrama, 3 acts). Co-authored by
Laroche.
    Unpublished.
    Théâtre de la Gaîté, 9-2-14.

L'Honneur ou l'Échafaud (melodrama, 3 acts). Co-authored by
Laroche. Music by Huel.
    Paris: Barba, 1816.
    Théâtre de la Gaîté, 20-4-16.
    [RON Rf. 27. 376, ARS GD 8° 11700, SACD PC 298, AN
    F[18]598].

Les Deux Valladomir (melodrama, 3 acts). Co-authored by Victor
Ducange. Music by Quasain.
    Paris: Fages, 1816.
    Théâtre de L'Ambigu-Comique, 25-9-16.
    [RON Rf. 27.377, ARS GD 8° 8882, AN F[18]599].

BASSAUME (Mme).

Les Aventures d'un garçon (drame, 5 acts).
Théâtre Beaumarchais, 14-5-87.
[AN F^{18}1134].

BATTHYANY (Mme la comtesse Julie).
Pseudonyms: Julie APRAXIN and Eiluj NIXARPA.
Novelist.

Un Rêve d'artiste (comedy, 1 act).
Théâtre des Jeunes Artistes, 24-3-64.

BAUER (Mme Louise).

Un Malheur, S.V.P. (vaudeville, 1 act). Co-authored by L. Fréville.
Délassements Comiques, 12-9-62.
[AN F^{18}1061].

Jaloux comme un tigre (vaudeville, 1 act).
Théâtre Déjazet, 20-12-65.

La Prestidigitomanie (vaudeville, 1 act).
Théâtre Déjazet, 20-8-66.

Les Ecarts de Rocantin (vaudeville, 1 act). Co-authored by Emile
Lorrain.
Folies Marigny, 21-5-70.

Spectres et phantômes [*sic*] (folie-vaudeville, 2 tableaux). Co-authored
by Jallais.
Délassements comiques, 1863.
[AN F^{18}1062].

BAWR (Alexandrine-Sophie COURY DE CHAMPGRAND, Mme ST.-
SIMON, then baronne de).
Pseudonym: François.
Paris, 1773 - 1860.
Novelist and historian.

La Matinée du jour.
Théâtre de Louvois.

Argent et adresse, ou le Petit mensonge (comedy, 1 act, prose).
Paris: Barba, an XIII (1804).
Théâtre de Louvois, 19 germinal an 10 (9-4-1802); Théâtre de l'Ambigu-Comique, April 1820.
[BN 8° Yth 1089, RON Rf. 21.793, ARS GD 8° 19562, BHVP 613 164 (10), OP LIV 19/195a, AN F^{18}587].

Le Rival obligeant (comedy, 1 act, prose).
Paris: Barba, an XIII (1804).
Ambigu-Comique, 16 messidor an 11 (5-7-03).
[RON Rf. 21.794, ARS GD 8° 21963, BHVP 613 203 (6), SACD PC 525].

Les Chevaliers du lion (mélodrame à grand spectacle, 3 acts).
Paris: Fages, an XII (1804).
Ambigu-Comique, 15 prairial an XII (4-6-04).
[RON Rf. 21.795, ARS GD 8° 19861, BHVP 608 935, OP LIV. 19/2462a, SACD PC 121].

L'Oncle rival et confident.
Paris: Pillet, 1811.
Théâtre de la rue Vieille du Temple, 1-11-05.

L'Argent du voyage, ou l'Oncle inconnu (comedy, 1 act, prose).
Paris: A. Garnier, Martinet, 1809.
Odéon (Second Théâtre Français), 1-5-09.
[RON Rf. 21.798, OP LIV. 19/1055a, SACD NS A].

Le Double stratagème (comedy, 1 act, prose).
Paris: Barba, 1813.
Ambigu-Comique, 23-7-11.
[BN 8° Yth 5418, RON Rf. 21.799, ARS GD 8° 9312, SACD PC 191].

Léon ou le Château de Montaldi (mélodrame à grand spectacle, 3 acts).
Paris: Barba, 1811.
Ambigu-Comique, 22-10-11.
[BN 8° Yth 10135, RON Rf. 21.800, ARS GD 8° 12855, SACD PC 355, AN F^{18}599^A].

La Suite d'un bal masqué (comedy, 1 act, prose).
Paris: Vente, 1813.
Théâtre Français, 9-4-13.
[BN 8° Yth 16871, RON Rf. 21.801, ARS GD 8° 22256,
BHVP 610 918 (2), TF 1. SUI Baw, TF ms. 505].

La Méprise (comedy, 1 act, prose).
Paris, 1815.
Théâtre Français, 22-11-15.

La Correspondance (comedy, 1 act).
Unpublished.
Théâtre Français, 16-2-25.
[AN F^{18}592].

L'Ami de tout le monde (comedy, 3 acts, prose).
Unpublished.
Théâtre Français, 6-10-27.
[AN F^{18}589, TF ms. 615].

Charlotte Brown (comedy, 1 act, prose).
Paris: Librairie parisienne, 1835.
Théâtre Français, 7-4-35.
[BN 8° Yth 3088, ARS GD 8° 7280, BHVP 118 288, SACD
PC 114, TF 1. CHA Baw, TF ms. 697].

Le Petit commissionnaire (comedy, 1 act, prose).
In Les Jours de congé ou les Matinées du grand oncle, vol. 2.
Paris: chez Postel fils, 1838.
[BN R. 39688, ARS GD 8° 15912, SACD PC 474].

BEAUDOUX (Mme Clarice-L. or Claire).
Author of a book about the education of girls.

Théâtre de jeunes personnes.
Paris: Maison, 1837.
[BN Yf 11903, ARS GD 8° 3233].

Théâtre des familles.
Paris: Maison et Didier, 1838.
[BN Yf 8229].

BEAUFORT DE HAUTPOUL (Anne-Marie de MONGEROULT, c^{esse} de).
Paris, 1763 - l'Abbaye-au-Bois, 1837.
Author of poetry, novels and educational books; director of
L'Almanach des dames, wrote for Le Dimanche with Mmes de Genlis
and Dufrénoy, and participated in the Bibliothèque française.

Charades mises en action, mêlées de couplets et de vaudevilles, ou
Nouveau théâtre de société. 2 volumes.
> Paris: Vernarel et Tenon, 1823.
> [BN Yf 9568-9569, ARS GD 8° 3412, SACD 14 P9].

BEAUVOIR (Mme A. R. de) (see DOZE).

BÉGON (Fanny de) (see STOLZ).

BELFEUIL (Raymond de) (see POLI).

BELFORT (Mme or Mlle).

> L'Amour exilé sur la terre.
>> Théâtre des Jeunes Auteurs, 17 messidor an X.

> Ne jugez pas sur l'apparence (vaudeville, 1 act).
>> Paris: Fages, 1804.
>> Théâtre de L'Ambigu-Comique, 1800.
>> [RON Rf. 16.985, ARS GD 8° 14788, BHVP 611 728 (6),
>> SACD PC 434].

> L'Artémise française ou les Heureux effets de la paix (comedy, 1 act,
> prose).
>> Paris: Fages, 1801.
>> Théâtre de l'Ambigu-Comique, 30 ventôse an IX (21-3-01).
>> [RON Rf. 16.987, ARS GD 8° 5594, BHVP 611 764 (6),
>> SACD P.C. 45].

> Zamor, ou les Deux fils (melodrama, 3 acts, prose). Co-authored by F.
> Levasseur.
>> Théâtre des Jeunes Élèves, 22-7-06.

> Hommage à Louis XVIII (scène lyrique, prose).
>> Montpellier: Félix Avignon, 1814.

BELLE (Florence).

L'Indécis (comedy, 1 act).
Théâtre du Vaudeville, 16-11-89.
[AN F^{18}773].

BELLEMENT (Mme).
Actress at the Théâtre de la Porte St. Martin and the Cirque Olympique.

Arsène ou le Génie maure (pantomime). Co-authored by Franconi.
Paris: Barba, 1813.
Cirque Olympique, 30-1-13.
[BN 8° Yth 1231, BHVP 609 973 (19), SACD PC 45].

BELLIER (Mme Marie) (Née KLECKER) (also BELLIER-KLECKER).

Cendrillon.
Bordeaux, Grand-Théâtre, 1886.

Théâtre du jeune âge. 3 volumes of 64 comedies or saynètes, including:
"Papa Maman !" (comedy, 1 act),
Théâtre Mondain, 17-12-96;
"Tous musiciens" (comedy, 3 acts),
Théâtre Mondain, 17-12-96;
"Monsieur l'Hiver" (comedy, 1 act),
Théâtre Mondain, 2-1-97;
"L'Enfant prodigue" (comedy, 3 acts),
Théâtre Mondain, 28-2-97;
"Le Plus beau pays" (comedy, 1 act),
Bouffes du Nord, 17-3-98;
"Les Surprises de Noël" (comedy, 3 acts),
Bouffes-Parisiens, 2-12-96;
"La Cigale et la fourmi" (dialogue, 1 act),
Salle des Agriculteurs, 25-5-98;
"Voyage au Tyrol" (vaudeville, 1 act),
Bouffes du Nord, 22-2-98.
Paris: Ollendorff, 1895.
[BN 8° Yf. 796, RON Rf. 85141].

La Naissance de l'enfant Jésus (mystery play, 1 act).
Paris: Ollendorff, 1896.
Théâtre Mondain, 24-12-96.
[BN 8° Yf Pièce 372, ARS GD 8° 32778].

L'Etoile de Catherine (saynète historique, 5 acts, with songs and dances).
>   Paris: Ollendorff, 1896.
>   [BN 8° Yth 27905, RON Rf. 85146, ARS GD 8° 2662, SACD].

La Petite cantinière de la 35e (comedy, 2 acts).
>   Paris: Ollendorff, 1897.
>   Théâtre Mondain, 17-12-96.
>   [RON Rf. 85147, ARS GD 8° 34940].

La Belle au bois dormant (saynète-opérette, 4 acts).
>   Paris: Ollendorff, 1897.
>   [RON Rf. 85144].

Les Contes de fées à la scène. Six fairy tales adapted for the stage, including:
"Le Chat botté" (operetta, 4 acts),
>   Bordeaux (Société Protectrice de l'enfance), March 1889;
>   Bouffes-Parisiens, 2-12-96;
"Le Petit chaperon rouge" (operetta, 4 acts),
>   Bordeaux, Grand-Théâtre, 1887; Théâtre Mondain, 18-1-97;
"La Pantoufle de Cendrillon" (operetta, 4 acts),
>   Bordeaux, Grand-Théâtre, Feb. 1896 (for the Société Protectrice de l'enfance); Théâtre Mondain, 28-2-97;
"Petit Poucet" (saynète),
>   Bordeaux, Grand-Théâtre, 22-02-1909;
"La Belle au bois dormant",
>   Bordeaux, Société Protectrice de l'enfance, February 1888.
>   Paris: Ollendorff, 1898.
>   [RON Rf. 85143, SACD].

Théâtre du jeune âge. 19 comedies or saynètes, including:
"Les Etrennes de mon parrain" (comedy, 3 acts).
>   Théâtre Mondain, 18-1-97.
>   Paris: Ollendorff, 1900.
>   [RON Rf. 85142].

Mozart (saynète-opéra, 4 acts).
>   Paris: Société d'édition littéraire et artistique, 1905.
>   [OP LIV. 920].

Les Deux fleurs de Savoie (drame-légende du temps des croisades, 4 acts).
>　Paris: Ollendorff, 1906.
>　[RON Rf. 85145].

Saint-Maurice, Primicier de la Légion thébienne (drame, 4 acts, 2 tableaux). Signed Mme Bellier-Klecker.
>　Paris: Roblot (Théâtre du patronage), n.d.
>　Patronage St. Joseph, 10-6-1914.
>　[RON Rf. 85148].

BELLOT-LEPRIEUR (Mme) (voir LE PRIEUR DE BLAINVILLIERS).

BENELLI (Mlle).

La Robe de bal ou les Amies de pension (comedy, 4 tableaux, prose), manuscript dated 7-6-1861.
>　[SACD ms. 124].

BENOIT (Célestine) (see VADIER).

BENOIT (Valentine).
Author of poetry and one novel.

Peintre et notaire (vaudeville, 1 act).
>　Private performance, 30-3-98.

BERNARD (Mme).

Le Petit chemin de Potsdam, ou quelques anecdotes de la vie de Frédéric II (comedy, 1 act).
>　Paris, Toulouse: n.p., an XI.
>　Porte St. Martin, 28-3-03.
>　[RON Rf. 17.000].

BERNHARDT (Sarah) (see Twentieth Century volume).

BERNOUX (see PERRONNET).

BERTHEROY (Jean).

Pseudonym of Berthe-Clorinne LE BARILLIER, Mme ROY DE CLOTTE, then CZERNICKI.

Bordeaux, 1868 (or 1860) - Le Cannet, 1927.

Novelist and poet; chevalier de la Légion d'Honneur; member of the first jury for the Prix Fémina.

Aristophane et Molière (à propos, 1 act, verse).
Paris: Colin, 1891.
Théâtre Français, 15-1-97.
[BN 8° Yth 2777, RON Rf. 3.894, ARS GD 8° 30978, BHVP 120944, TF 1 ARI Ber, TF ms. 1355].

Un Vrai ami (comedy, 1 act). Co-authored by Brandimbourg.
Grand Guignol, 25-11-97.

Cocu, ou la Femme de M. Duveau (vaudeville, 1 act). Co-authored by Habrekon and De Pawlowsky.
Divan Japonais, 16-9-99.

BERTON (Caroline, née SAMSON).

Author of children's books and short stories.

La Clause testamentaire (comedy, 1 act, prose).
Paris: Mévrel, 1835.
[BN 8° Yth 3469, RON Rf. 38.280, ARS GD 8° 7556].

Une Recette du mariage (proverb).
Théâtre du Palais Royal, 6-5-51.

Les Philosophes de vingt ans (proverb, 1 act).
Paris: Giraud & Dagneau, 1851.
Gymnase, 1-8-51.
[BN 8° Yth 14160, RON Rf. 38281, ARS GD 8° 16080, BHVP 607 776 (2), AN F^{18}829].

Qui perd, gagne (vaudeville, 1 act).
Théâtre du Vaudeville, 9-5-52.

La Diplomatie du ménage (proverb, 1 act). Original title: "Une Recette de ménage ou Mieux vaut douceur que violence" (corrected on manuscript).
>   Paris: Giraud et Dagneau, n.d.
>   Théâtre Français, 6 or 7-1-52.
>   [BN 8° Yth 5227, RON 38.284, ARS GD 8° 9105, BHVP 607 620 (1), TF 1 DIP Ber, TF ms. 908, AN F^{18}676].

L'Escapade (proverb, 1 act).
>   Salle Herz, 11-4-53 (benefit performance for orphans).

La Grande tante (comedy-proverb, 1 act, prose).
>   In Théâtre des salons. Ed. E. Rasetti.
>   N.p.: Impr. Jouast, 1859.
>   Spectacle Deburou, 2-6-58.
>   [BN Yf 11919, RON Rf. 84.454, SACD PC 274].

Faute d'une épingle (vaudeville, 1 act).
>   Folies dramatique, 1-9-58.

Pour être aimé (prologue, 1 act).
>   Théâtre des Jeunes Artistes, 4-12-63.

Le Jugement de la nourrice (vaudeville, 1 act).
>   Folies dramatiques, 21-1-64.

Les Deux masques (comedy, 1 act, verse).
>   In Le Bouquet d'un pauvre jardin.
>   Paris: Librairie des auteurs, 1868.
>   Porte Saint Martin, 30-11-73; Cluny, 1-3-74.
>   [RON Rf. 38.286].

BEZANÇON (Henriette) (see Twentieth Century volume).

BIANIC (Fanny).
>   Actress.

La Chaîne éternelle (drame, 5 acts). Co-authored by Albert Lacroix.
>   Paris: A. Lacroix, (1876).
>   [BN 8° Yth 24606, RON Rf. 38.304].

BLACKE (see JULIA).

BOIS-HEBERT (Mme de) (see Marie-Anne de BOVET).

BORNET (Anna).
   Besançon, 1841 - ?
   Poetry.

   Nicole et Perrine (comedy, 1 act, verse).
      Paris: Librairie centrale, 1868.
      [BN 8° Yth 12648, RON Rf. 38.503].

   Les Petits protecteurs (comedy, 3 acts, verse). Possibly co-authored by
   Jacques et Louise Bornet.
      In Les filles de la terre.
      Marseille: impr. de Vve M. Olive, 1864.
      [BN Yf 8385].

   Si mon père avait su ! (comedy, 1 act, verse).
      In Les filles de la terre.
      Marseilles: impr. de Vve M. Olive, 1864.
      [BN Yf 8385].

BORNEY (Mme H. de).

   Monsieur Campois (comedy).
      Théâtre Mondain, 1896.
      [AN F^{18}1358].

BOURDON (Mathilde LIPPENS, dame FROMENT, then).
   Pseudonym: Mathilde TARWELD.
   Gand, 1817 - Bailleul (Nord), 1888.
   Author of novels for children, historical narratives, religious works.

   Chacun son métier (proverb).
      Lille: L. Lefort, 1850.
      [BN Yth 2948].

   La Petite glaneuse (drame).
      Plancy: Société de S. Victor, 1852.
      [BN 8° Yth 26200].

   Qui vivra verra et Point de feu sans la fumée (proverbs).
      Lille: L. Lefort, 1852.
      [BN Yf 10744].

Un Bienfait n'est jamais perdu (proverb).
    Lille: L. Lefort, 1852.
    [BN Yf 8405, RON Rf. 76690, ARS GD 8° 31220].

Une Antipathie, ou En toutes choses il faut considérer la fin (proverb, 3 acts).
    Plancy: Société de Saint-Victor, 1853.
    [BN 8° Yth 18274].

Un Travers du siècle, ou Courts plaisirs, longs repentirs (drame).
    Paris: Société de Saint-Victor, 1857.
    [BN 8° Yth 18244].

L'Anneau de paille (drame).
    Paris: Putois-Cretté, 1860.
    [BN 8° Yth 967, ARS GD 8° 29186].

Trois proverbes: "L'Humour" (2 acts), "Tout vient à point à qui sait attendre" (3 acts), "Chacun son métier" (3 acts).
    Lille: L. Lefort, 1861.
    [BN Yf 8400, ARS GD 8° 24898].

La Vierge d'Alexandrie (drame, 3 acts).
    Lille, Paris: L. Lefort, 1871.
    [BN 8° Yth 26167].

La Rosière, ou Trop parler nuit (proverb).
    Lille: L. Lefort, 1878.
    [BN 8° Yth 24743, ARS GD 8° 35419].

La Machine à coudre (2 acts).
    Lille: L. Lefort, 1878.
    [BN 8° Yth 24684].

Les Mères réconciliées par leurs enfants (drame).
    Paris: Sagnier et Bray, 1882.
    [BN 8° Yth 11665].

BOVET (Marie-Anne de) (Mme de BOIS-HEBERT).
　　Pseudonym: MAB.
　　Metz, 1860 (or 1855) - ?
　　Journalist, novelist; author of travel literature and translations from
　　English.

　　Les Bécasses de Théodore (comedy, 1 act).
　　　　Private performance, 3-2-97; Salle des Agriculteurs, 26-2-99.

　　Le Mannequin (scène).
　　　　Private performance, 1-2-98.

　　Le Baiser du prince (comedy, 1 act).
　　　　Private performance, 17-6-98.

　　Petites Rosseries (1 act).
　　　　Paris: Lemerre, 1898.
　　　　Théâtre de l'Application (Bodinière), 25-2-99.
　　　　[BN 8° Y^2 51213].

　　Imberbe, Nos danseurs (monologues).
　　　　N.p. 1898.
　　　　[RON Rf. 53.669].

　　Bien gardée (1 act, verse).
　　　　Paris: A. Lemerre, 1906.
　　　　La Bodinière, 17-01-97.
　　　　[RON Rf. 53.668, BHVP 608 111].

BRADI (see EPINAY).

BREHIER (see DELAFAYE-BREHIER).

BROHAN (Joséphine-Félicité-*Augustine*) (Mme Ed. David DE GHEEST).
Paris, 1824 - *id.* 1893.
Actress.

Compter sans son hôte (proverb, 1 act, prose). Co-authored by Henry
de Pène.
>Paris: Perrotin, 1849.
>Paris, Hôtel Forbin-Janson, 13-3-49 (benefit performance for
>"les Enfants pauvres de la ville de Paris"); Théâtre Français,
>1-5-49.
>[BN 8° Yth 3838, RON Rf. 84.011, ARS GD 8° 7873, BHVP
>118 680, TF 1 COM Bro].

Les Métamorphoses de l'amour (comedy, 1 act, prose). Co-authored by
Henry de Pène.
>Paris: Lévy fr., 1851.
>Hôtel Castellane, 25-1-51.
>[BN 8° Yth 11723, RON Rf. 84.011, ARS GD 8° 21297, TF 1
>MET Bro].

L'Ile des Pierrots (pantomime).
>Spectacle Debaru, 31-8-58.

Qui femme a, guerre a (comedy, 1 act). Co-authored by Henry de
Pène.
>Paris: Librairie nouvelle, 1859.
>Théâtre Français, 13-12-59.
>[BN 8° Yth 15065, RON Rf. 84.017, ARS GD 8° 26223,
>BHVP 607 629 (5), SACD PC 511, TF 1 QUI Bro].

Quitte ou double (proverb). Co-authored by Henry de Pène.
>Performed at l'hôtel de Castellane.
>[RON Rf. 84.011].

Il faut toujours en venir là (proverb). Co-authored by Henry de Pène.
>Paris: Impr. Panckoucke, 1859.
>[BN 8° Yth 20327, RON Rf. 84.011, ARS GD 8° 798].

Piècettes. Contains: "Compter sans son hôte", "Les Métamorphoses de
l'amour", "Quitte ou double", "Il faut toujours en venir là", "Qui
femme a, guerre a", "Tintamarre et Fanfarinette".
>Versailles: impr. de Cerf et fils, 1888.
>[BN 8° Yf 357, RON Rf. 84.011].

BRUCHEZ (baronne de) (see EPINAY)

BRUN (Mlle Elisabeth).
School teacher; author of novels for girls and educational books.

Ernestine, ou Pour bien commander il faut savoir obéir (2 acts) and
Jacqueline (drame, 1 act).
   Paris and Lille: L. Lefort, 1859.
   [BN 8° Yth 6154, ARS GD 8° 3229].

BRUNET (Alice).
Actress at the Théâtre de l'Odéon (1876-78), then director of a drama
school.

  Charade (3 parts).
   Paris: Dupont, 1879.
   [BN 8° Yth 26175, ARS GD 8° 31626].

  Contentement passe richesse (proverb, 2 acts).
   Paris: Dupont, 1879.
   [BN 8° Yth 26176, ARS GD 8° 31895].

BRUNET (Pauline) (see JULIEN).

BRUN(N)E (Mme Claire).
Pseudonym of Mme MARBOUTY.
Author of novels, poetry and political essays.

  La Protectrice (comedy, 1 act, prose). Co-authored by E. Souvestre.
   Paris: Marchant, 1841.
   Théâtre Français, 22-5-41.
   [BHVP 611 116 (21), AN F^{18}674, TF ms. 744].

BRUNO (Camille).
Pseudonym of Mme de la TOMBELLE.
Author of poetry, novels and short stories; founder and director of Les
Saisons.

  Les Charités de Lucienne (comedy, 1 act, verse). Signed Mme la
  Baronne F. de la Tombelle.
   Paris: Imp. de la Société de Typographie, 1883.
   Théâtre du Marivaudage, 7-3-83.
   [RON Rf. 84.256, ARS GD 31619].

Piècettes (lectures et représentations de salon).
Paris: Dentu, 1889.
[BN 8° Yf 440, ARS GD 8° 3477].

Louise (drame, 1 act).
Théâtre de l'Application, 29-5-92.

La Rivale (comedy, 4 acts).
Théâtre de l'Application, 22-10-92.

L'Entrave (comedy, 3 acts).
Théâtre de l'Application, 22-2-93.

Supercherie (comedy, 1 act, verse). Co-authored by Elie Brachot and P.
de Montredun.
Théâtre Litt., 28-2-94.

L'Horloger de Strasbourg (drame, 4 acts and 6 tableaux, verse).
Paris: Ollendorff, 1894.
[BN Yth 26572, RON Rf. 53.974, ARS GD 8° 38872].

L'Enquète or La Petite enquète (saynète, 1 act, prose).
Paris: M. Bauche, 1908.
Nice, Capucines, 6-3-1907; Paris, Five o'clock du Figaro, 04-
03-1908.
[BN 8° Yth 32798, ARS GD 8° 29468, BHVP 608 531].

Les Trois clefs (2 acts). Co-authored by Gyp.
In Les Saisons 3 (1916).
Paris, Cercle Artistique, 09-06-1906.
[RON Rf. 53.977].

Les Voisins (1 act, prose).
In La Chanson 6 (June 1909).
[RON Rf. 53.975].

Pauvrette ! (comedy, 1 act, prose).
In Les Saisons, 2e année, n.1 (March 1914).
[RON Rf. 53.976].

L'Auteur avait raison.
In Les Saisons, 7e année, n.4 (December 1919).
[RON Rf. 53.978].

BUISSON (Mme Angèle).
　　Pseudonym: DUBUISSON.

　　Un Mari en loterie (vaudeville, 1 act).
　　　　Théâtre Beaumarchais, 31-1-64.

BUJAC (Madame).

　　Les Persans à Paris (comédie nationale, 2 acts, prose).
　　　　Bordeaux: Labothière, 1791.
　　　　Bordeaux, Théâtre de la Nation, 22-6-1791.
　　　　[ARS GD 8° 15859].

BURSAY (Aurore Domergue, Mme).
French actress in Rouen, Brussels, Brunswick, Moscow; director of the
French theater in Brunswick.

　　L'Ogre ou Aladin et Lisia (opera, 1 act), 17??.
　　　　[SACD ms. 153].

　　Pertharide (opera, 3 acts, verse).
　　　　Théâtre de Reinsberg, 17??.
　　　　[SACD ms. 153].

　　Sophie de Brabant (opéra héroï-comique, 2 acts). Music by
　　Kalkbrenner.
　　　　Brunswick: Pluchart, 1803.
　　　　Brunswick, Théâtre de Brunswick (preface says it was also
　　　　accepted by Théâtre Feydeau but not yet performed).
　　　　[ARS GD 8° 22197].

　　Longino tout seul (comedy-monologue, prose).
　　　　Brunswick: imp. français de Pluchart, n.d.
　　　　Brunswick, Théâtre de Brunswick, 1-8-1805.
　　　　[ARS GD 8° 21077, BHVP 611 136 (26)].

　　Un Quart d'heure du calife Haroun le Grand, empereur des Croyans
　　[sic].
　　　　Paris: J. Gratiot, 1813.
　　　　Brunswick, Théâtre de Brunswick, 2-12-1806.
　　　　[BN 8° Yth 18185, ARS GD 8° 16769, BHVP 611 722 (9).

C. L. B. (Mlle).

Ce que femme veut, Dieu veut (proverb, 3 acts). Written for her mother's saint's day, 23-10-1831.
[ARS ms. Douay 2249].

CADART (Mlle M.).
Author of educational books on the French language.

Théâtre de la jeunesse. Includes "Miranda", "Juliette ou la Jeune orpheline", "L'Amour filial", "L'Innocence calomniée".
London: Dulau, 1866.
[BHVP in-16 617 762].

CALONNE (see GALERON DE CALONNE).

CAMPAN (Jeanne-Louise-Henriette GENET ou GENEST, Mme).
Paris, 1752 - Mantes, 1822.
Reader for the King's daughters (1768-1774); lady in waiting for Marie-Antoinette; founder of a very fashionable boarding school for girls at St-Germain in 1794; director of the Maison de la légion d'honneur d'Ecouen in 1807; educational treatise and memoirs.

Théâtre d'éducation. Received an award from the Académie française.
"Les Deux éducations" (proverbe moral), "La Famille Dawenport" (comedy, 3 acts), "Cécilia, ou la Pension de Londres" (comedy, 2 acts), "Le Perroquet" (comic opera, 2 acts), "La Vieille de la cabane, ou la Piété filiale" (comedy, 2 acts), "Arabella" (comedy, 2 acts), "La Nouvelle Lucile" (comedy, 2 acts).
Paris: Baudouin fr., 1826.
[BN Yf 8494].

CANDEILLE (Amélie-Julie) (see Eighteenth Century).

CARISSAN (Mme de).

La Jeunesse d'Hayden (comic opera, 2 acts).
Salle Duprez, 27-3-89.

Ballade du plongeur (drame lyrique, 1 act). Co-authored by Mme de Courpon.
Théâtre de l'Application, 2-4-95.

La Novia (pantomime, 1 act).
　　Théâtre de l'Application, 31-5-96.

CAROLINA (Mme).

Mes débuts dans ma chambre (vaudeville, 1 act).
　　Théâtre des Funambules, 14-9-49.

CARON (Mme Thérèse).

Changer de nourrice (vaudeville, 1 act).
　　Alhambra, 8-3-90.

C'est la faute du petit journal (comedy, 3 acts).
　　Alhambra, 22-3-90.

Un Duel en partie double (vaudeville, 1 act). Co-authored by E. Hugot.
　　Alhambra, 17-4-90.

Le Rouge et la noire (vaudeville, 1 act). Co-authored by E. Hugot.
　　Alhambra, 24-1-91.

Les Fausses joies de la paternité (vaudeville, 1 act). Co-authored by
Pajol.
　　Alhambra, 14-4-91.

Le Neveu d'Elodie (vaudeville, 1 act).
　　Alhambra, 2-5-91.

CASAMAJOR or **CASAMAYOR** (Mme de).

Le Noeud gordien (comedy or drame, 5 acts, prose).
　　Paris: Lacrampe fils, 1846; Brussels: Lelong, 1847.
　　Théâtre Français, 5-11-1846.
　　[ARS GD 8° 14922, SACD PC 437, BHVP 118 592, TF 1
　　NOE Cas, TF ms. 830].

CASTELBAJAC (comtesse J. de) (see SÉMÉAC).

CASTIN (Mme).

La Veuve Mathurin (comedy, 1 act).
　　Théâtre St. Marcel, 8-3-60.
　　[AN F^{18}1140].

CÉRÉ-BARBÉ (see BARBÉ).

CHABRILLAN (Elisabeth-Céleste VENARD, comtesse Lionel de MORETON de).
>Stage name: Céleste MOGADOR.
>Paris, 1824 - 1909.
>Actress, dancer and theater director; author of novels and memoirs.

La Chasse aux baisers ou les Fileuses (vaudeville, 2 acts). Co-authored by Claunet.
>Théâtre de Luxembourg, 9-2-57.
>[AN F^{18}1080].

Bonheur au vaincu or Bonheur aux vaincus (comedy, 1 act).
>Paris: impr. Cosson, 1862.
>Théâtre des Champs-Elysées, 19-4-62.
>[BN 8° Yth 2155, RON Rf. 39.091, ARS GD 8° 299, BHVP 119 213, SACD PC 79, AN F^{18}1017].

En Australie (vaudeville, 1 act).
>Paris: impr. Cosson, 1862.
>Théâtre des Champs-Elysées, 19-7-62.
>[BN m. 18395, RON Rf. 39.092, ARS GD 8° 299, BHVP 611 818 (2), SACD, AN F^{18}1017].

Nedel (operetta, 1 act). Music by Marius Boullard.
>Paris: Le Bailly, 1863.
>Théâtre des Champs-Elysées, 23-5-63.
>[ARS GD 8° 48138, AN F^{18}1018].

Militairement (operetta, 1 act). Music by Marius Boullard.
>Paris: Librairie des Deux Mondes, 1864.
>Théâtre des Champs-Elysées, 28-10-63.
>[BN m. 18398, RON Rf. 39.093, ARS GD 8° 309, BHVP 611 818 (4), SACD PC 412].

Querelle d'Alleman [sic] (proverb, 1 act).
>Paris: Librairie des Deux Mondes, 1864.
>Théâtre des Champs-Elysées, 28-10-63.
>[BN 8° Yth 15044, RON Rf. 39.094, ARS GD 8° 309, BHVP 611 818 (3), SACD PC 510F^{18}1018].

En garde ! (operetta, 1 act). Music by Ventéjoux.
Paris: Librairie des Deux Mondes, 1864.
Théâtre des Champs-Elysées, 14-1-64.
[BN m. 18396, RON Rf. 39.095, ARS GD 8° 364, SACD].

Les Voleurs d'or (drame, 5 acts, preceded by a prologue).
Paris: Michel Lévy, 1864.
Théâtre de Belleville, 28-5-64.
[BN Yf 37 (2), RON Rf. 39.096, ARS GD 8° 39791, BHVP 615 572, AN F^{18}1306].

L'Amour de l'art or Les Martyrs de l'art (vaudeville, 1 act).
Paris: Alcan-Lévy, 1865.
Folies-Marigny, 4-6-65.
[BN 8° Yth 713, ARS GD 8° 321, SACD, AN F^{18}1019].

Un Homme compromis (vaudeville, 1 act).
Paris: Alcan-Lévy, 1865.
Folies-Marigny, 4-9-65.
[BN m. 18397, RON Rf. 39.097, ARS GD 8° 321, BHVP 611 818 (5), SACD, AN F^{18}1019].

Pierrots en cage (operetta, 1 act). Music by Kriezel.
Paris: Morris, n.d.
Folies-Marigny, 8-9-65.
[BN 4° Yth 3347, RON Rf. 39.098, ARS GD 8° 48220].

Chambre à louer (vaudeville, 1 act).
Folies-Marigny, 2-10-65.
[AN F^{18}1019].

A la bretonne (operetta, 1 act). Music by Oray.
Paris: impr. de Morris père et fils, 1868.
Folies-Marigny, 10-9-68.
[BN 4° Yth 12, ARS GD 8° 47424, AN F^{18}1020].

Les Crimes de la mer (drame, 5 acts).
Paris: impr. Morris, 1869.
Théâtre de Belleville, 8-5-69.
[BN microfiche 4° Yth 989, ARS GD 8° 48948, AN F^{18} 1 307].

L'Amour de la patrie (vaudeville, 1 act).
Paris: Dentu, 1869.
Théâtre de Cluny, 15-8-69.
[RON Rf. 39.099, AN F^{18}1027].

Les Revers de l'amour (comedy, 5 acts).
Paris: chez l'auteur, 1870.
Théâtre des Nouveautés, 28-1-70.
[BN 8° Yth 15472, RON Rf. 39.100, ARS GD 8° 35280].

L'Américaine (comedy, 5 acts).
Paris: Estienne, 1870.
Théâtre des Nouveautés, 3-4-70.
[BN 8° Yth 627, RON Rf. 39.101, ARS GD 8° 345, SACD, AN F^{18}1233].

Le Forgeron d'Ardente (drame, 1 act).
Théâtre de Cluny, 14-12-73.
[AN F^{18}1029].

La Plaideuse (comedy or monologue, 1 act).
Paris: Barbré, 1889.
Théâtre de L'Ambigu-Comique, 20-12-74; Théâtre du Château d'eau, November 1885.
[ARS GD 8° 37338].

L'Ambition fatale (drame, 5 acts).
Théâtre Beaumarchais, 15-4-75.
[AN F^{18}1131].

Le Trente et un de Victoire (monologue or vaudeville, 1 act). Also attributed de H. Chabrillat.
Théâtre de Cluny, 3-12-76.

Le Bonnet d'âne (comedy-vaudeville).
Théâtre de Cluny, 10 (or 26)-12-76.
[AN F^{18}1031].

La Dame des Louviers (drame, 5 acts). Also listed as Le Drame de Louvières, La Dame de Louvières, and Le Drame de Louviers.
Théâtre de l'Ambigu-Comique, 25-3-77.
[AN F^{18}962].

Entre deux balcons (monologue, 1 act).
    Paris: Barbré, 1883.
    Fantaisies parisiennes, 7-3-80.
    [RON Rf. 39.102, ARS GD 8° 36501].

L'Amour et la rose (comedy, 1 act).
    Théâtre des Arts, 10-7-80.

Au rideau (causerie).
    Galerie Vivienne, 18-11-94.

M'am Nicol (comedy, 3 acts).
    Paris: Barbré, 1880.
    Folies-dramatiques, 4-7-80.
    [BN 8° Yth 24685, RON Rf. 39.103, ARS 8° 34108, BHVP
    607 908 (1), SACD PC 378, AN F^{18}1011].

Pierre Pascal (drame, 5 acts, music).
    Paris: Chaix, 1885.
    Ambigu-Comique, 4-8-85.
    [BN microfiche 4° Yth 5147, RON Rf. 39.104, ARS GD 8°
    47216, BHVP 402 822 (19), AN F^{18}964].

Cordon, s.v.p. (revue). Also attributed to Bémond.
    Pépinière, 26-12-86.

Les Petites (comedy, 1 or 4 acts).
    Galerie Vivienne, 17-4-91.

Les Petites de Beaufort (comedy, 1 act).
    Select Théâtre, 14-6-92.

Marie-Margotte (monologue, 1 act, with songs).
    Paris: Barbré, 1893.
    Galerie Vivienne, 26-11-92.
    [RON Rf. 39.105, ARS GD 8° 28409].

Le Dernier rendez-vous (comedy, 3 acts).
    Galerie Vivienne, 26-11-92.

La Haine des femmes (drame, 5 acts).
    Théâtre de Belleville, 10-12-93.

Conversion (melodrama, 1 act).
>   Galerie Vivienne, 14-11-94.

Les Débutantes (comedy, 1 act).
>   Galerie Vivienne, 14-11-94.

Regain d'amour (comedy, 1 act).
>   Galerie Vivienne, 18-11-94.

Bastienne (monologue).

La Tirelire d'Yvonne (operetta, 1 act). Music by Georges Rose.

CHAMBRUN (comtesse Marie-*Jeanne* de) (née GODARD-DESMAREST).
Baccarat (Meurthe-et-Moselle), 1827 - Paris, 1891.
Poet.

Il ne faut pas courir deux lièvres à la fois (proverb).
>   Paris: Camerot, n.d. (handwritten note at end: "Jeanne, C^esse
>   de Chambrun, 1865-82").
>   [ARS GD 8° 38859bis].

CHAMPEIN (R. Jeanne) (Mme Jeanne LAVERPILLIÈRE).

Antigone (tragedy, 3 acts).
>   In Etudes poétiques.
>   Paris: Ladvocat, 1803.
>   [BN 8° Ye 11313].

CHANTAL (Mme de).

Une Anglaise à Paris (1 act). Co-authored by Mme Trécourt.
>   Théâtre des Capucines, 30-4-89.

La Retraite (drame, 1 act). Co-authored by Mme Trécourt.
>   Théâtre des Capucines, 30-4-89.

CHAPELLE (Ida).

Les Amours de Marinette (vaudeville, 1 act).
>   Angoulême: impr. Lugeol, 1875.
>   [BN 8° Yth 26086, RON Rf. 80850].

CHARTOULE DE MONTIFAUD (see Marc de MONTIFAUD).

CHELIGA (Marya) (CHELIGA-LOEVY) (née MIRECKA).
Jasienic (Poland), 1859 - Vélizy, 1927.
Feminist; founder of the Théâtre Féministe.

L'Ornière (3 acts).
Paris: Société nouvelle d'édition, 1896.
Théâtre Mondain, 24-1-96.
[RON Rf. 54.756, ARS GD 8° 34674, BHVP 933 457, AN F^{18}1358].

Les Déblayeurs (drame, 4 acts).
Nouveau Théâtre, 19-12-1908.

CHERVET (see NAVERY).

CHEVALIER (Pauline) (see GRANDPRÉ)

CHRISTIAN (Mme L.).

La Piscine. Co-authored by Yvos and Petit.
Eldorado, 25-2-88.
[AN F^{18}14 16].

Cocambo (vaudeville, 1 act). Co-authored by R. de St. Prest and H. Raymond.
Eldorado, 21-4-88.

Les Naïades de Chatou (1 act). Co-authored by Yvos and Petit.
Eldorado, 19-11-88.
[AN F^{18}1418].

On demande un modèle (vaudeville, 1 act). Co-authored by R. de St. Prest.
Trianon, 22-6-94.

Ka-ma-ki (vaudeville, 1 act).
Trianon, 6-7-94.
[AN F^{18}1 435].

CISTERNE de COURTIRAS (see DASH).

CLADEL (*Judith* -Jeanne).
>Paris, 1873 - *id.*, 1958.
>Novelist, historian, journalist; member of the Fémina committee, chevalier de la Légion d'honneur.

>Le Volant (3 acts, prose).
>>Paris: A. Lemerre, 1895.
>>Théâtre de l'Oeuvre, 28-5-95.
>>[BN 8° Yth 27247, RON Rf. 54.845, ARS GD 8° 36152, BHVP in-8° 609 454].

>Les Auryentys (idyll, 1 act).
>>Paris: A. Lemerre, 1904.
>>Théâtre de parc, 15-12-1904.
>>[RON Rf. 54.846].

CLIQUET (Mary).
>Author of a biography of Rouget de Lisle.

>Jeune et vieux (comedy, 1 act).
>>Paris: impr. Morris, 1870.
>>[BN 8° Yth 9549, ARS GD 8° 38936].

>Les Nuits de Boulevard (drame, 5 acts). Co-authored by P. Zaccone and T. Henry.
>>Paris: Dentu, 1881.
>>Théâtre des Nations, 28-8-80.
>>[ARS GD 8° 34559, BHVP 609 244, SACD PC 442, AN F^{18}740].

>C'est la loi (drame, 5 acts).
>>Théâtre de Cluny, 2-6-82.
>>[AN F^{18}1033].

COCHEVAL (see DUPRAT).

COLET (Louise REVOIL, Mme).
>Aix-en-Provence, 1810 - Paris, 1876.
>Poet, journalist, novelist, travel writer.

>L'Abencérage (opera, 2 acts). Music by Hippolyte Colet.
>>Sceaux: impr. de E. Déprée, 1837.
>>Paris, Théâtre de l'hôtel du Cte Jules de Castellane, 13-4-37.
>>[RON Rf.23.483, ARS GD 8° 40330, BHVP 611 102 (21)].

La Jeunesse de Goethe (comedy, 1 act, verse). Other title on censorship manuscript: Goethe ou l'Eldorado de Francfort.
>   Paris: Marchant, 1839.
>   Renaissance, 20-6-39.
>   [BN 4° Yth 2193, RON Rf. 23.484, ARS GD 8° 42512, BHVP 610 065 (42), SACD C.Gr.F.21BL, AN F^{18}1261].

Les Dernières heures de Mme Roland (1 act, verse).
>   Paris: impr. de H. Fournier,. [1841].
>   [RON Rf. 23.485].

Charlotte Corday et Madame Roland (tableaux dramatiques).
>   Paris: Berquet et Pétion, 1842.
>   [BN Yf 8654, RON Rf. 223.486, ARS 8° B.L. 14.665].

Une Famille en 1793 (drame, 5 acts, verse).
>   In La Presse, 10-16 Sept. 1850.
>   [BN Fol. Lc.^{2} 1416, RON Rf. 23.487, ARS GD 8° 20331].

L'Armée d'Italie (cantata).
>   Théâtre Lyrique National, 27-6-59.

COLOMB (Joséphine-Blanche BOUCHET, Mme Louis-Casimir).
Author of children's books and novels.

Les Béatitudes. Music by César Franck.
>   Paris: C. Joubert, n.d.
>   Châtelet, March 1893; Temps, 16-4-94.
>   [BN 4° Yf pièce 25, RON Ro. 3150, ARS GD 8° 24338bis, BHVP 949 722].

Inspiration. Co-authored by Walder.
>   Théâtre de l'Application, 4-7-94.

COMTE (Aglaé de BOUCAUVILLE, widow of M. LAYA, Mme Achille).
Author of books on natural history and *éloges* of Mme de Sévigné and Mme Salm-Dyck.

Le Veuvage (comedy, 2 acts, prose).
>   Paris: Breteau et Pichery, 1842.
>   Odéon, 19-2-42.
>   [BN 8° Yth 19015, RON Rf. 23,584, ARS GD 8° 22589, AN F^{18}706].

<u>Lucile ou l'Honneur d'une fille</u> (drame, 3 acts and 2 "époques", prose).
    Paris: impr. de Béthune et Plon, n.d.
    Odéon, 28-2-44.
    [RON Rf. 23.585, ARS GD 8° 42660, BHVP 610055, AN
    F^{18}707].

<u>Madame de Lucenne, ou une Idée de belle-mère</u> (comedy, 3 acts,
prose). Title on manuscript: <u>Madame de Lucenne ou Mère et belle-
fille.</u>
    Paris: Tresse, 1845.
    Théâtre Français, 11-4-45.
    [BN 4° Yth 2450, RON Rf. 23.586, ARS GD 8° 42630, BHVP
    610056, TF ms. 796].

<u>Le Luxe et la charité</u> (comedy).
    Nantes: impr. de W. Busseuil, 1859.
    Nantes, Grand-Théâtre, 17-6-45.
    [BN 8° Yth 10412, ARS GD 8° 23508].

<u>L'Amant de sa femme</u> (comedy, 1 act, verse).
    Versailles: impr. de Beau jeune, 1850.
    Odéon, 1830.
    [BN 4° Yth 101, RON Rf. 23.588, ARS GD 8° 40245].

<u>Mon ami Babolin</u> (comedy-vaudeville, 1 act). Co-authored by Louis
Monrose.
    Paris: Beck, 1851.
    Gymnase dramatique, 13-5-51.
    [BN 8° Yth 2830, RON Rf. 23.589, ARS GD 8° 39715, BHVP
    607772, AN F^{18}829].

<u>Vaut mieux tard que jamais</u> (comedy-proverb, 1 act, prose).
    Versailles: Beau jeune, 1852.
    [ARS GD 8° 44464].

<u>Madame Berthe</u> (comedy, 2 acts, prose).
    Versailles: Beau jeune, 1853.
    [ARS GD 8° 42637].

CONINCK (Mathilde COURANT, Mme William de).
  Pseudonym: "Une mère de famille".
  Paris, 1824 - ?
  Author of children's novels and educational works.

  La Conquête d'un grand papa.
    Paris: Picad-Bernheim, 1885.
    [BN 8° Yth 21514, ARS GD 30088].

  Cousin-cousine (comedy, 2 acts).
    Paris: Picard et Kaan, 1898.
    [ARS GD 8° 30097].

  Saynètes et monologues pour les écoles et les familles. Includes:
  "Cousin-cousine", "La Graphologie" (1 act), "Lequel des deux"
  (vaudeville, 1 act), "Les Mauvaises farces" (saynète), "Le Moulin de
  Mathurine" (comedy, 2 acts), "Tout ce qui brille n'est pas de l'or", "Un
  Nouveau".
    Paris: Picard et Kaan, 1898.
    [BN 8° Yf. 632].

  Tout ce qui brille n'est pas de l'or (proverb, 1 act).
    Paris: Picard et Kaan, 1899.
    [BN 8° Yth 28982].

  Un Nouveau (saynète pour enfants).
    Paris: Picard et Kaan, 1899.
    [BN 8° Yth 28983, ARS GD 8° 30261].

COPIN-ALBANCELLI (Mme Anne) (see Simone ARNAUD).

COUEFFIN (Mme Lucie) (née PIGACHE).
  Poet.

  Repentir et Miséricorde, ou le Retour du prodigue (drame, 3 acts).
    Bayeaux: Léon Nicolle, 1847.
    [BN 8° Yth 15316].

  Agar (scènes dramatiques).
    N.p., n.d.
    [BN 8° Yth 4487].

Débora (esquisse dramatique, 4 acts, vers).
    Bayeaux: Léon Nicolle, 1848.
    [BN 8° Yth 4487, ARS GD 8° 8450].

COURPON (Mme S. B. de).

Ballade du plongeur (drame lyrique, 1 act). Co-authored by Mme
Carissan.
    Théâtre de l'Application, 2-4-95.

L'Habit ne fait pas le moine (comedy, 1 act). Co-authored by Mme Alq.
    In Comédies et monologues by Mme Alq.
    Paris: au bureau des "Causeries familières", 1898.
    Théâtre Mondain, 24-6-96.
    [BN 8° Yf 118, AN F^{18}1 398].

Hier et demain (à propos, 1 act).
    Théâtre de la République, 4-4-97.

La Légende du roi de Sicilie (1 act).
    Trocadéro, 23-5-97.

Sous la lampe (1 act, prose).
    Salle de l'Institut Charras, 1902.
    [AN F^{18}1367].

CRAON (princesse de).
    Author of biographies and historical essays; wrote for Souvenirs du
    vieux Paris and Journal des jeunes personnes.

Deux drames: "Jacobed, mère de Moïse" (drame saint, 5 tableaux) and
"Les Fils de Clodomis" (drame historique, 5 acts).
    Paris: H.-L. Delloye, 1836.
    [BN Yf 8812, RON Rf. 23.815, ARS GD 8° 4589, SACD].

CURO (Mlle Marie).
    Novelist and author of religious and educational essays.

Théâtre moral de la jeunesse. Three one-act comedies: "La Petite
femme de ménage", "Le Prodige", "La Nouvelle connaissance".
    Paris: Bernadin-Béchet, n.d.
    [RON Rf. 85433].

Théâtre moral de la jeunesse: "Malice et bonté ou les Deux pensionnaires (comedy, 2 acts), "La Petite cousine ou le Mardi gras" (comedy, 2 acts), "Stéphanie et Jeannette ou les Soeurs de lait" (comedy-vaudeville, 2 acts), "Léonie ou les Vieilles" (comedy, 2 acts), "Le Bal ou la Vengeance" (vaudeville, 1 act), "Les Conjectures" (vaudeville, 3 acts), "Léonore ou la Jeune égoïste" (comedy, 2 acts), "Les Deux régentes" (comedy, 3 acts).
>   Paris: Bernadin-Béchet, 1869.
>   [BN Yf 8839, RON Rf. 85434].

Nouveau théâtre des jeunes filles: "La Jeune savante ou le Premier jour de pension" (2 acts), "Le Jour de congé ou la Liberté absolue", "Le Testament" (2 acts), "Les Fausses amies" (3 acts), "L'Idée fixe ou un Pélérinage à Sainte-Anne" (2 acts), "Le Vieux château ou la Fausse bravoure" (2 acts), "Adèle ou la Susceptibilité" (2 acts), "Une Mouche sur le nez ou la Folie de la grande dame" (2 acts).
>   Paris: Sarlit, 1866.
>   [BN Yf 8834, RON Rf. 85436].

DAILLENS (Mme Marie de).

La Robe (bluette, 1 act, with music).
>   Poitiers: impr. de A. Dupré, 1878.
>   [BN 8° Yth 24890, RON Rf. 79742].

La Pâtée à Toto (saynète, 1 act).
>   Poitiers: A. Dupré, 1878.
>   Private performance, 1-3-93.
>   [BN 8° Yth 26145].

Les Exploits de Drogonette (operetta, 1 act). Co-authored by A. Mellerino. Music by Pierraccini.
>   Paris: A. Zuinzard, 1892.
>   Salle Duprez, 8-6-89.
>   [BN 8° Yth 25697, RON Rf. 55.960].

DAMINOIS (Angélique-Adèle HUVEY, dame) (Mme SOISSONS, then Mme Charles-Antoine-Guy DU FRENAY).
Clermont (Oise), 1785 - Paris, 1876.
Feminist lecturer at l'Athénée des Arts and novelist.

La Servante Marie (proverb, 1 act).
    In Une mosaïque,
    Paris: Charles Mary, 1832.
    [BN Y^2 2507, RON Rf. 23.894].

La Chasse au renard (vaudeville, 1 act). Co-authored by M. de Saint-Hilaire.
    Paris: Quoy, 1823.
    Théâtre du Vaudeville, 10-9-23.
    [BN 8° Yth 3110, AN F^{18}646].

DANGEVILLE (Henriette) (Jean SERY) (see Twentieth Century volume).

DANGLARS (Mme Renée).

Comédies enfantines: "La Fête d'une institutrice", "Les Vacances", "Un Jour de congé", "Une Heure de paresse", "L'Action la meilleure", "Les Etrennes", "La Veille de la Sainte Catherine".
    Paris: P. Leloup, 1869.
    [BN 8° Yth 3739].

Le Théâtre en famille. Contains 9 comedies: "Deux amies" (2 acts), "La Révolte des grandes", "Un Bouquet de roses" (1 act), "Une Institutrice", "Les Emigrantes" (2 acts), "Une Rivalité", "La Maîtresse d'études" (2 acts), "Une Belle-mère" (3 acts), "Une Réconciliation" (2 acts).
    Paris: Firmin Didot, 1873.
    [BN Yf 8879, RON Rf. 85438].

La Révolte des grandes and Les Emigrantes.
    Paris: Firmin-Didot, 1889.
    [BN 8° Yf. 404].

DANIEL (Mme).
Boarding school teacher.

Albertine ou l'Envie (drame, 1 act).
    Paris, Lyons: Périsse, n.d.
    [ARS GD 8° 4888].

Gourmandise et mensonge (drame, 1 act).
>   Lyons: Périsse, n.d.
>   [RON Rf. 85439].

Nouveau théâtre d'éducation à l'usage des jeunes personnes. Includes: "Egoïsme et sensibilité", "Le Triomphe de l'amitié", "Ruth et Noémi", "La Jeune fille colère", "L'Enfant gâté", "Evélina, ou la Veill de l'an", "Petite pièce pour l'ouverture d'une distribution de prix".
>   Lyons: Guyot; Paris: P. Mellier, 1845.
>   [BN Yf 8880].

DARC (Daniel) (see REGNIER).

DARFEUIL or **D'ARFUEIL** (Mlle Fanny).

Double héroïsme (1 act, verse).
>   Meulan: Impr. Auguste Rety, 1897.
>   Société Philotechnique, 20-12-96.
>   [RON Rf. 83.924].

Par contradiction (comedy, 1 act).
>   Salle de géographie, 12-12-97.

DASH (comtesse).
Pseudonym of the vicomtesse Gabrielle-Anne de POILLOÜE de SAINT-MARS, née CISTERNE de COURTIRAS.
Poitiers, 1805 - Paris, 1872
Novelist.

Les Comédies des gens du monde. 5 comedies and proverbs.
>   Paris: Michel Lévy fr., 1868.
>   [RON Rf. 84.088, BHVP 615 233].

Le Mari de ma soeur (proverb).
>   Paris: Michel Lévy, n.d. (1874).
>   Performed at the Théâtre de Bade.
>   [RON Rf. 84.091, ARS GD 8° 39791].

DAVID (Marie) (see Raoul de NAVERY).

DEBIERNE-REY (Mme Lisbeth).

Cendrillon (opéra-bouffe).
>   Auteuil-Paris: l'auteur, 1873.
>   [BN 8° Yth 2882, RON Rf. 85448].

Fleurs et serpents (opéra-bouffe).
Paris: l'auteur, 1873.
[BN 8° Yth 7330].

Jeanne Darc [*sic*] (dialogue, 3 acts).
Paris: l'auteur, 1875.
[BN 8° Yth 9437].

Le Nouveau seigneur du village (opéra-bouffe).
Auteuil-Paris: l'auteur, 1877.
[BN 8° Yth 26010].

Ruth (opéra sacré).
Paris: l'auteur, 1881.
[BN 8° Yth 20493].

Les Savoyards (opéra-bouffe).
Paris: l'auteur, 1881.
[BN 8° Yth 20486].

La Pie voleuse (opéra-comique).
Paris: l'auteur, 1882.
[BN 8° Yth 20493, RON Rf. 85450].

DEFERRIERE (see LEBLANC DE FERRIERE).

DEGOTTY (Mlle Augustine) (or DEGOTTI).
c. 1785 - ?
Actress, novelist.

Matilde (drame, 3 acts, prose). Adaptation of a novel by Mme Cottin.
Odéon, 8-9-14.
[AN F^{18}597A].

DEJAZET (Virginie)
Pseudonym: Mlle D...
Paris, 1797 or 1798 - Paris, 1875.
Actress.

Le Sommeil de la Marquise (operetta, 1 act). Co-authored by Théod.
Barrière (A.B.C.).
Théâtre des Menus Plaisirs, 20-10-72.
[AN F^{18}1226].

DELAFAYE-BREHIER (Mme Julie) (Mme de la FOYE).
Author of novels and short stories for children.

Théâtre de l'enfance. (4 volumes).
I. "Le Polichinelle" (comedy, 1 act), "Le Jeune précepteur, ou les Avantages de l'éducation" (comedy, 2 acts), "La Lettre et la chanson" (comedy, 1 act).

II. "L'Echange" (comedy, 1 act), "Le Petit Joueur, ou la Partie de Vingt-et-Un" (comedy, 2 acts), "Les Vendanges" (comedy, 1 act).

III. "Les Petites saturnales" (comedy, 2 acts), "La Petite médisante" (comedy, 1 act), "Les Petits héritiers" (comedy, 2 acts).

IV. "La Soeur jalouse" (comedy, 2 acts), "Le Petit glorieux" (comedy, 2 acts), "La Fontaine du sphinx" (comédie-féerie, 1 act).
Paris: Eymery, Fruger et Cie, 1828.
[BN Yf 9693-9695, SACD 21 P9].

DELAVIGNE (Mlle Juie) (see MOLE-LEGER).

DELCAMBRE (baronne).

Un Mauvais quart d'heure en chemin de fer (saynète).
Paris: A. Picard et Kaan, 1893.
[BN 8° Yf 632, RON Rf. 85471].

DELISLE (Léone) (L. LISLE, Léone de LISLE).
Pseudonyms of Mme Céline ENOUF.
Paris, 1853 - ?.

Mes châteaux en Espagne (comedy, 1 act).
Paris: Barbré, 1890.
Théâtre Beaumarchais, 9-5-90.
[RON Rf. 44.854, AN F^{18}1135].

La Journée orageuse (comedy, 1 act).
Théâtre Artistique, 1-2-92.

DELORME (Marie).
Pseudonym of Marie HARDOUIN, Mme Léon VESCO.
Author of novels and an essay on family hygiene and good housekeeping.

Le Théâtre chez grand-mère. 10 *pièces de salon* (saynètes, comedies, charades), 5 proverbs and 8 monologues.
Paris: Armand Colin, 1895.
[BN 8° Yf. 721, RON Rf. 85473].

DELYSLE (voir LYSLE).

DERAINS (Mme Camille).
Author of children's novels.

Nouveau théâtre des familles. Includes "Les Etrennes" (comedy, 1 act, prose), "L'Eclipse" (comedy, 1 act, prose), "L'Etourderie" (comedy, 1 act, prose), "Les Deux chats" (drame tragi-comique, 1 act), "Le Maître de l'écriture" (comedy, 1 act), "La Tirelire" (comedy, 1 act), "L'Enfant de la providence" (comedy, 1 act).
Paris: Libr. des auteurs et de l'académie des bibliophiles, 1858.
[BN 8° Yf 8932, RON Rf. 85485, ARS GD 8° 2135, SACD].

DERAISMES (Maria)
Paris, 1828 - *id.*, 1894.
Journalist, feminist orator, director of Le Républicain de Seine-et-Oise.

A bon chat bon rat (comedy proverb, 1 act).
Paris: Amyot, 1861.
Théâtre de l'Application (Bodinière), 3-2-98.
[BN 8° Yth 6, RON Rf. 40.746, ARS GD 8° 30714, BHVP 619 416, AN F^{18}1300].

Retour de ma femme (comedy, 1 act).
Paris: Amyot, 1862.
[BN 8° Yth 15355, RON Rf. 40.747, ARS GD 8° 37998].

Le Père coupable (comedy, 4 acts).
Paris: Amyot, 1862.
[BN 8° Yth 13758, RON Rf. 40.748, ARS GD 8° 39365].

Un Neveu s'il vous plaît (comedy, 3 acts, prose).
>> Paris: Amyot, 1862.
>> [BN 8° Yth 18114].

Théâtre chez soi.
>> Paris: Michel Lévy, 1864.
>> [RON Rf. 40.745, BHVP in-8° 616 677, SACD P27].

DEROSNE (Judith).
>> Pseudonym of Judith BERNARD.
>> Paris, 1827 - ?
>> Actress at the Théâtre Français under the stage name of Mlle Judith;
>> author of novels and translations from English.

Quand la mariée est trop belle (operetta, 1 act). Co-authored by
Rouland and Wanier.
>> Scala, 1-8-80.

DES ARMOISES (Olivier).
>> Pseudonym of Mme des Armoises.
>> Novelist.

Monsieur Jean (comedy, 1 act, verse). Co-authored by Truffier.
>> Odéon, 15-12-90.
>> [AN F^{18}725].

DES ATOURS (Mlle Jeanne-Iris).

La Femme de chambre, ou le Chansonnier des toilettes.
>> Paris: Delaunay, Mongie, Janet, 1826.
>> [ARS GD 8° 4511, BHVP 26315].

DESBORDES-VALMORE (Marceline DESBORDES, Mme Prosper
VALMORE, called Marceline).
>> Douai, 1786 - Paris, 1859.
>> Actress (1803-1823); poet and novelist.

Arlequin (pièce à tiroirs). Co-authored by Elise Moreau (Mme Gagne)
and M. de Jussieu.
>> Paris: A. Boyer, n.d.
>> [BN 8° Yth 32432].

DESLOGES (Mme Adèle).
Author of one novel and a collection of poetry.

Une Loge grillée (proverb).
N.p., n.d.
[ARS GD 8° 23501].

DESPREAUX (Mlle Stéphanie-Aline)
c. 1791 - ?

Le Retour de Trajan ou Rome triomphante (intermède, 2 acts, verse).
Music by M. Charles Boscha fils.
Bordeaux: P. Beaume, 1807.
[BN 8° Yth 15391, RON Rf. 77666, ARS GD 8° 17079,
SACD PC 520].

DESPRES (Marie) (also called DEP).
Pseudonym of Mme Ph.-B.-G. RAYNAL de TISSONIERE.
Novels.

La Grève des femmes (adaptation of Lysistrada).
Paris: Savine, 1895.
[BN 8° Yth 27384, RON Rf. 56.682, ARS GD 8° 32972,
BHVP 615 786].

Autour de l'héritage (comedy, 5 acts, 11 tableaux, verse).
Paris: Société d'éditions littéraires, 1900.
[BN 8° Yth 29387, RON Rf. 56.525].

L'Or Dieu (comedy, 6 acts).
Paris: Société d'édition littéraire, 1901.
[BN 8° Yth 29708, RON Rf. 56.526].

DEUTZ (Marguerite).

A propos.
Versailles: Cerf et fils, n.d. [1889].
Théâtre de Saint-Gratien.
[ARS GD 8° 38296].

DIDOT (Mme).

La Bourse trouvée (vaudeville, 3 acts).
Paris: Didot, 1825.
[ARS GD 8° 6594].

L'Amour filial (vaudeville, 3 acts).
    Paris: Didot jeune, 1834.
    [ARS GD 8° 19539].

Quelques traits de l'enfance d'un auteur du dix huitième siècle
(comedy, 3 acts, prose).
    Paris: Didot, 1834.
    [ARS GD 8° 16817].

Le Double engagement volontaire (3 acts).
    Paris: Didot jeune, 1825 or 1835.
    [ARS GD 8° 9291, SACD PC 191].

Le Bon enfant (drame, 5 tableaux).
    Paris: Didot, 1835.
    [ARS GD 8° 6424].

Le Droit d'aînesse (comedy, 1 act).
    Paris: Didot, 1835.
    [ARS GD 8° 1858 (4)].

Linval ou On ne peut plaire à tout le monde (comedy, 3 acts, prose).
    Paris: Didot, 1835.
    [ARS GD 8° 1858 (1)].

L'Honnête cocher (vaudeville, 2 acts).
    Paris: Didot, 1836.
    [ARS GD 8° 1858 (3)].

l'Innocence justifiée (vaudeville, 3 acts).
    Paris: Surcey et Cie, 1839.
    [SACD PC 309].

La Chaumière changée de place (vaudeville, 3 acts). Signed Mme
D***.
    Paris: Vrayet de Surcey, 1843.
    [BN 8° Yth 3201].

L'Artiste de Noyan (vaudeville, 3 acts).
    Paris: Vrayet de Surcey, 1844.
    [ARS GD 8° 5614].

DINAUX (Madame).

Le Panache blanc, ou la Fête de la reconnaissance (vaudeville, 1 act, prose). Written in honor of the victory of the French army in Spain.
Valenciennes: Lemaître, 1824.
Théâtre de Valenciennes, 18-2-1824.
[BN 8° Yth 13339, ARS GD 8° 15477].

DOIN (Sophie MAMY, Mme).
Paris, 1800 - ?
Novelist, poet.

Théâtre. 2 volumes.
I: "La Fortune et l'amour" (comedy, 1 act), "Encore une revanche" (comedy, 2 acts), "L'Amour d'une femme" (comedy, 3 acts), "Le Frère" (comedy, 1 act).

II: "La Muette" (comedy, 3 acts), "La Petite châtelaine ou la Cour d'amour" (comedy, 3 acts).
Paris: impr. de Ducessois, 1833.
[BN Yf 9033-4, RON Rf. 24.947, ARS GD 8° 1669, SACD P27].

DORIAN (Mme Tola) (see Twentieth Century volume).

DORSAN (Claire).

L'Education des femmes (comedy, 2 acts).
Moutiers; Brides les Bains: F. Duclos, 1889.
[BN 8° Yth 23579, RON Rf. 80888].

Mademoiselle Sans-Peur (saynète, 1 act).
Paris: Librairie théâtrale, 1890.
[BN 8° Yth 23915].

Une Gageure (comedy).
Paris: Librairie théâtrale, 1891.
[BN 8° Yth 24150].

DOSSIN (Mlle Elise).

La Femme du franc-tireur (monologue).
St-Valéry-en-Caux: Pillore, 1882.
[BN 8° Yth 20839].

DOUILLON (Mme C.).

Le Roman d'un prince, ou le Crime du Prado (drame, 5 acts).
Théâtre Beaumarchais, 5-2-87.
[AN F^{18}1134].

Le Secret de Marianne (vaudeville, 1 act).
Théâtre Beaumarchais, 26-3-87.
[AN F^{18}1134].

Une Héroïne (drame, 1 act).
Galerie Vivienne, 31-5-91.

DOZE (Léocadie-Aimée, dame Roger de BEAUVOIR).
Château de Pontkallec (near Hennebout), 1822 - 1859.
Actress and novelist.

Dos à dos (comedy-proverb, 1 act, prose).
Paris: J. Claye, 1856.
Salle Herz, February 1852; Odéon, 2-4-52.
[BN 8° Yth 5385, RON Rf. 47.382, AN F^{18}1530].

L'Un et l'autre (comedy, 1 act, prose).
Comédie Française, 5-4-52.
[TF ms. 913].

L'Amour à la Maréchale (comedy, 2 acts, prose).
Paris: Tresse, 1852.
Théâtre de la Montansier (Palais Royal), 14-8-52.
[BN 4° Yth 120, RON Rf. 47.381].

Au coin du feu (comedy, 1 act).
Paris: Librairie nouvelle, 1855.
Théâtre des Variétés, 27-1-55.
[BN 8° Yth 1376, RON Rf. 47.382, SACD D.C. 50].

A deux pas du bonheur (proverbe lyrique, 1 act).
Salle Herz, 1856.

Drelin ! Drelin ! (vaudeville, 1 act). Co-authored by Varin.
Paris: Lévy fr., 1858.
Folies-Dramatiques, 26-5-58.
[BN Yf 25(2), RON Rf. 47.386, AN F^{18}999].

Un Coup de fouet (comedy, 1 act, prose).
    In Théâtre des salons. Ed. E. Rasetti.
    N.p.: Impr. Jouast, 1859.
    Private performance by the actors of the Comédie Française at
    the residence of Madame la Princesse Vogoridès.
    [BN Yf 11919, RON Rf. 84.454].

DROHOJOWSKA (Antoinette-Joséphine-Françoise-Anne SYMON DE
LATREICHE, comtesse Félix).
    Pseudonyms: C. d'AULNOY and A.S. de DONCOURT.
    Saint-Chély (Lozère), 1822 - 1893.
    Author in a variety of genres: history, biography, studies of famous
    women, travel narratives, pedagogy, novels.

    Proverbes et charades à l'usage des maisons d'éducation.
        Paris: Tolra et Haton, 1864.
        [BN Yf 9065].

    La Grande cantate. Music by Gambini.
        Pré-Catalan, 15-8-66.

    Charades et proverbes en action (nouvelles scènes dialoguées pour
    servir aux récréations des pensionnats de jeunes filles). 13 plays.
        Paris: Sarlit, 1867.
        [BN Yf 9063, RON Rf. 85533].

    Mieux vaut tard que jamais (proverb, 3 acts).
        Limoges: Barbou frères, 1880.
        [BN 8° Yth 24871].

    Le Prix Monthyon (2 acts).
        Limoges: Barbou frères, 1880.
        [BN 8° Yth 24888].

DUBARRY (Eugénie) (see Twentieth Century volume).

DUBUISSON (see BUISSON).

DUCROS (Mme Adèle, called Aline) (née MOREL).

    Le Choix d'un nom (comedy, 1 act).
        Paris: A. Gautherin, 1896.
        Théâtre Montmartre, 9-9-74.
        [BN 8° Yth 27650].

DUDEVANT (see George SAND).

DUFRESNOY (Mme).

Alfred (comedy, 3 acts), 1848.
[SACD ms.].

DUMONT (Mme Mélanie).
Children's books.

L'Atelier de David (vaudeville, 1 act). Co-authored by Eugénie Niboyet.
Théâtre du Gymnase Enfantin, 1-8-40.
[AN F^{18}1184].

DUPERRÉ DE LYSLE (see Fernande de LYSLE).

DUPIN (Aurore) (see George SAND).

DUPUIS (*Charlotte*-Catherine BORDES, Mme).
Pseudonym: Antoine de NANTES.
Paris, 1813 - *id.*, 1879.
Actress.

La Croix à la cheminée (comedy-vaudeville, 1 act). Co-authored by Najac.
Théâtre du Vaudeville, 28-10-55.
[AN F^{18}758].

Deux veuves pour rire (vaudeville, 1 act).
Paris: Michel Lévy, 1856.
Folies dramatiques, 22-1-56 (performed under the pseudonym Antoine de Nantes).
[BN 8° Yth 5075].

Les Confitures de ma tante (vaudeville, 1 act). Co-authored by E. Goby.
Théâtre Beaumarchais, 11-7-63.
[AN F^{18}1120].

Les Démons de l'argent (drame, 5 acts). Co-authored by E. Goby.
Théâtre Beaumarchais, 19-9-63.
[ARS Th.N 14766].

Autant de tués que de blessés (comedy-vaudeville, 1 act).
Délassements comiques, 23-9-63.

Où l'on va (comedy, 3 acts).
Paris: Lévy fr., 1869.
Théâtre du Vaudeville, 16-10-68.
[BN 8° Yth 13255, RON Rf. 41.661, ARS GD 8° 235, BHVP in-18 607713, AN F^{18}765].

Le Petit frère (*sic vos non vobis*) (vaudeville, 1 act).
Paris: Lévy fr., 1870.
Folies Marigny, 2-2-70.
[BN 8° Yth 13883, RON Rf. 41.662, ARS GD 8° 344, SACD].

Le Loup muselé (comedy, 2 acts).
Théâtre de Cluny, 23-12-71.
[AN F^{18}1028].

DUPUIS (Eudoxie).

Comédies enfantines.
Paris: Delagrave, 1878.
[ARS GD 8° B.L. 15.189].

DURAND (Mlle).

Fille de marbre (ballet-pantomime). Parody of La Fille de Marbre by C. Pugni and A. de St. Léon. Co-authored by Levassor.
Palais-Royal, 15-3-1851.

DURAND (Mlle). Possibly same as above.

Mariage et divorce (1 act).
Théâtre Lazary, 18??.
[SACD ms. 88].

DURAND-GRÉVILLE (Mme Emile) (see Henry GRÉVILLE).

DUSAUTOY (Mme J).

Vénus au bois (comedy, 1 act, verse). Co-authored by d'Harchies.
Comédie Parisienne, 1895; Théâtre d'Appel, 17-12-97.

DUVAL (Mlle).

>Le Rêveur éveillé (comic opera, 1 act). Music by Leprévost.
>>Opéra-Comique, 21-3-48.

ELSSLER (Thérèse).
>Vienna, 1808 - Meran (Tyrol), 1878.
>Sister of ballet dancer, Fanny Elsser.

>La Volière, ou les Oiseaux de Boccace (ballet-pantomime). Music by C. Gide.
>>Paris: impr. de A. Everat, 1838.
>>Académie Royale de Musique, 5-5-1838.
>>[BN 4° Yth 4718].

EMERY (Marie).
>Pseudonym of Mme VAN DEN BUSSCHE.
>Dunkerque, 1816 - ?
>Children's books.

>Nouveau théâtre des maisons d'éducation pour les jeunes gens: "L'Aîné de la famille", "La Main invisible", "Le Testament", "Bruno", "Deux écueils".
>>Lille: J. Lefort, 1848.
>>[BN Yf 10504].

>Nouveau théâtre des maisons d'éducation pour les jeunes gens: "La Gouvernante", "L'Epreuve", "La Femme du monde", "Les Dangers de l'indiscrétion", "Marie la savoyarde".
>>Lille: J. Lefort, 1848.
>>[BN Yf 10596].

>On récolte ce qu'on a semé and Vertu passe richesse (proverbs).
>>Lille: J. Lefort, 1853.
>>[BN Yf 12232].

>Les Dubourg, Sourd-muet and A quelque chose malheur est bon.
>>Lille: J. Lefort, 1855.
>>[BN 8° Yth 5489, ARS GD 8° 4075].

>Cécile, ou le Devoir (drame, 2 acts).
>>In Le Magasin de Familles, November (1st act) and December (2nd act), 1859.
>>[BN 4° Z. 144 (IIe volume, 1859)].

La Maîtresse du logis (drame, 2 acts).
   Lille: L. Lefort, 1859.
   [BN Yth 10719, ARS GD 8° 34102].

Deux écueils (comedy, 2 acts).
   Lille-Paris: J. Lefort, 1862.
   [BN 8° Yth 21678].

Ce que coûte un caprice, Un Coup de foudre sous un ciel serein and La Rosée de mai.
   Lille: J. Lefort, 1862.
   [BN 8° Yf 9194, ARS GD 8° 31552].

Le Testament (proverb, 1 act).
   Lille-Paris: J. Lefort, 1865.
   [BN 8° Yth 21698].

Bruno (drame, 3 acts).
   Lille-Paris: J. Lefort, 1884.
   [BN 8° Yth 21543].

L'Aîné de la famille (2 acts).
   Lille-Paris: J. Lefort, 1885.
   [BN 8° Yth 21667].

La Main invisible (drame, 3 acts).
   Lille-Paris: J. Lefort, 1885.
   [BN 8° Yth 21845].

ENOUF (see DELISLE).

EPINAY (Marie de L').
   Pseudonym of Eve-Olivia-Angela de BRADI, baronne de BRUCHEZ.
   Near Orléans, 1805 -1864.

Le Dîner du bûcheron (comedy, prose).
      In Les Jours de congé ou Les matinées du grand oncle.
      Paris: chez Postel fils, 1838.
      [BN R. 39688, ARS GD 8° 15912, SACD PC 474].

L'Ecole d'un fat (comedy, 1 act). Co-authored by Numa Jautard.
> Paris: Tresse, 1844.
> Odéon, 16-6-44.
> [BN 4° Yth 1325, RON Rf. 29.998, ARS GD 8° 41541, SACD PC 201].

Un Amour d'eau douce (proverb). Subtitle added handwritten: "ou Il n'y a que les montagnes qui ne se rencontrent pas" (proverb).
> In La Patrie, 17/18-9-185?.
> [SACD PC 25].

Comment l'amour vient en causant (scène intime, 3 parts).
> [SACD PC 135].

FALLET (Céline).
> Pseudonym: Alexandre MÜLLER.
> Bar-le-Duc, 1829 - ?
> Children's books and novels.

Théâtre de jeunesse (scènes morales for boarding school girls). Includes six one-act comedies: "L'Orgueilleuse", "Le Testament de l'oncle", "L'Amour filial", "La Double épreuve", "Une Bonne action porte bonheur", "Le Tableau".
> Paris, Lyons: Périsse frères, 1852.
> [BN Yf 9278].

Récréations des pensionnats (for boarding school children). Includes: "La Réconciliation" (comedy, 1 act, prose), "La Curiosité" (comedy, 1 act, prose), "Deux soeurs de lait" (comedy, 1 act, prose), "La Flatterie" (comedy, 1 act, prose), "Claire et Marie" (comedy, 1 act, prose), "Le Pieux mensonge" (comedy, 1 act, prose), "L'Ecrin" (comedy, 1 act, prose).
> Paris, Lyons: Périsse, 1854.
> [BN Yf 9277].

La Curiosité (comedy, 1 act, prose).
> Paris: Bourget-Calas, 1878.
> [BN 8° Yth 24810].

L'Héritage de la baronne (comedy, 1 act).
> Paris: A. Maugars, 1867.
> [BN 8° Yth 8417, RON Rf. 41.936].

La Croix d'or (comedy, 1 act).
Paris: Maugars, 1867.
[BN 8° Yth 4272].

Donner et pardonner (comedy, 1 act).
Paris: Maugars, 1867.
[BN 8° Yth 5371, RON Rf. 85636].

L'Hôtel de la Pomme de Pin (comedy, 1 act).
Paris: Maugars, 1867.
[BN 8° Yth 8758, RON Rf. 85638, ARS GD 8° 37369].

L'Oiseau de paradis (comedy, 1 act).
Paris: Maugars, 1867.
[BN 8° Yth 12968].

La Paix et la guerre (comedy, 1 act).
Paris: Maugars, 1867.
[BN 8° Yth 13309, RON Rf. 85639].

FARRENC (Césaire GENSOLLEN, dame).
Draguignan (Var), 1802 - 1875.
School teacher, author of children's books and poetry.

L'Homme du peuple et la grande dame or L'Expiation (drame, 3 acts).
Paris: Gallet, Tresse, Vert, 1840; Nice: Veranie et Cie, 1874.
Théâtre du Panthéon, 10-10-40.
[BN 4° Yth 2005, RON Rf. 80684, ARS GD 8° 10053, AN F^{18}1254].

La Fille du matelot (drame, 3 acts).
Paris: Tresse, 1848.
Théâtre Beaumarchais, 20-2-48.
[BN 4° Yth 1654, ARS GD 8° 41972, AN F^{18}1115].

Drames à l'usage des collèges et des pensionnats. Includes: "Jean, ou l'Orphelin reconnaissant", "Ernest, ou le Repentir d'un bon coeur", "Julien, ou le Mensonge", "Henri, ou le Jeune instituteur", "Bastien, ou l'Enfant dissipé", "Charles, ou l'Enfant jaloux", "L'Epée", "Adolphe, ou l'Arrogant puni", "Le Prix de la sagesse".
Lille: L. Lefort, 1842.
[BN Yf 9052].

Petit théâtre pour les jeunes filles. Contains: "Amélie ou la Jeune institutrice" (1 act), "Une Fête" (1 act), "Martha, ou la Jeune fille reconnaissante" (1 act), "Emma, ou les Etrennes" (1 act), "Junia, ou la Jeune fille charitable" (1 act), "La Paresseuse" (petit drame, 1 act), "Adèle, ou l'Orgueil puni" (drame, 1 act), "Caroline" (2 acts).
>   Lille: L. Lefort, 1842.
>   [BN Yf 9288, RON Rf. 85644].

FAURE (Mme Hermance).

Au café (comedy, 1 act).
>   Bordeaux: Duverdier, 1872.
>   [BN 8° Yth 1372, RON Rf. 77780, ARS GD 8° 36359].

FERRAND (Mme G.).

Dernier amour (comic opera, 1 act). Co-authored by P. Barbier.
>   Théâtre Mondain, 12-6-95.
>   [AN F^{18}1357].

FIGUIER (Juliette BOUSCARET, Mme Louis).
Montpellier, 1829 - Paris, 1879.
Author of short stories.

Gutenberg (drame historique, 5 acts). Later published under her husband's name: Louis Figuier.
>   Paris: Librairie internationale, 1869.
>   [BN 8° Yth 13726, RON Rf. 42.286, ARS GD 8° 33026, BHVP 16° 948 926, SACD PC 279].

Les Peletons de Clairette (comedy, 1 act).
>   Nice: Visconti, 1871; Paris: Michel Lévy, 1872.
>   Paris, Théâtre du Vaudeville, 1-11-71.
>   [BN 8° Yth 14646, RON Rf. 42.285, ARS GD 8° 34825, BHVP in-18 611570 (6), SACD PC 469].

Le Presbytère (drame, 3 acts).
>   Paris: Tresse, Stock, 1888.
>   Paris, Théâtre Cluny, 11-5-72; Déjazet, 26-4-88.
>   [BN 8° Yth 14646, RON Rf. 42.290, ARS GD 8° 255, BHVP in-18 607895 (4), SACD PC 497].

La Vie brûlée (comedy, 2 acts).
Paris: Michel Lévy, 1873.
Paris, Folies-Marigny, 12-11-72.
[BN 8° Yth 19074, RON Rf. 42.285, ARS GD 8° 353, BHVP
in-18 607897 (1)].

La Parisienne (comedy, 1 act).
Paris: Michel Lévy, 1873.
Paris, Renaissance, 30-5-73.
[BN 8° Yth 12460, RON Rf. 42.292, ARS GD 8° 262, SACD
PC 461, AN F^{18}1263].

Pied-à-terre (comedy, 1 act).
Paris: Michel Lévy, 1874.
Paris, Cluny, 7-12-73.
[BN 8° Yth 14202, RON Rf. 42.285, ARS GD 8° 262, SACD
PC 483, AN F^{18}1029].

Les Pilules de Brancolar (comedy, 1 act).
Paris: Michel Lévy, 1874.
Paris, Folies-Marigny, 10-12-73.
[BN 8° Yth 14280, RON Rf. 42.293, ARS GD 8° 359, SACD
PC 486].

L'Enfant (drame, 4 acts).
Paris: Michel Lévy, 1874.
Paris, Cluny, 7-7-74.
[RON Rf. 42.294, SACD PC 209, SACD ms. 46, BHVP in-8°
607897 (5), AN F^{18}1030].

La Fraise (comedy, 1 act).
Paris: Michel Lévy, 1874.
Théâtre de Cluny, 7-7-74.
[BN 8° Yth 7520, RON Rf. 42.295, ARS GD 8° 266, BHVP
in-8° 119548, SACD PC 259, AN F^{18}1030].

La Dame aux lilas blancs (comedy, 2 acts).
Paris: Michel Lévy, 1875.
Paris, Théâtre du Vaudeville, 24-7-75.
[BN 8° Yth 4350, RON Rf. 42.296, ARS GD 8° 32265, BHVP
in-12 607722 (1), AN F^{18}769].

Barbe d'or (drame historique, 5 acts).
    Paris: Calmann Lévy, 1876.
    Paris, Théâtre Beaumarchais, 22-4-76.
    [BN 8° Yth 19565, RON Rf. 42.285, ARS GD 8° 30995,
    SACD PC 60, AN F^{18}1131].

Les Deux carnets (comedy, 3 acts).
    Paris: Calmann Lévy, 1877.
    Paris, Cluny, 30-7-77.
    [BN 8° Yth 19647, RON Rf. 42.299, ARS GD 8° 32018,
    SACD PC 172, AN F^{18}1032].

FLAGEL (Mme L. Ch. V.).

Tirza et les deux soeurs (drame, 3 acts, prose) and L'Ecolière maîtresse
(comedy, prose).
    Clermont-Ferrand: Landriot, 1808.

FLAGY (Aymar de) (see MIRABEAU).

FLAMANVILLE (Madame de) (née Princesse de MENSCHIKOFF).
Tutor of Princesse de Schacowsky's daughter.

Le Masque de fer, ou la Vengeance du roi de Castille (melodrama, 3
acts with dancing, combats and pantomime).
    In Le Naufrage d'Azema.
    Paris: Dujardin, 1805.
    [ARS GD 8° 1854].

FLAVIGNY (Marie de) (see Daniel STERN).

FLEURIOT (Mlle Zenaïde).

Le Théâtre chez soi. Contains: "Un Rêveur" (comedy, 3 acts, verse),
"Le Doigt mouillé" (comedy, 1 act, prose), "Païenne et chrétienne" (1
act), "Sous le même toit" (comedy, 3 acts, prose), "Fais ce que dois,
advienne que pourra" (1 act), "Mystère".
    Paris: C. Dillet, 1873; Paris: Librairie Hachette, 1888.
    [RON Rf. 84.136, ARS GD 8° 3512].

FOULD (Mme G.-E.) (see Gustave HALLER).

FRANCE (Jeanne) (see Twentieth Century volume).

FRANEL (Mme Marie S.).
Bavais (Switzerland), 1847 - ?
Director of a boarding school for girls.

Le Théâtre en famille. Proverbes et comédies. (dedicated to Caroline
Berton, née Samson). Contains: "Fais ce que dois, advienne que
pourra !" (proverb), "Le Secret du bonheur" (féerie, 2 acts), "Quand les
chats sont loin les souris dansent" (proverb), "Tout est bien qui finit
bien" (proverb), "Etre et paraître" (4 acts), "Qui trop embrasse, mal
étreint" (proverbe de société, 2 acts).
      Paris: Sandoz et Thuiller; Geneva: Desrogis; Neuchâtel:
      Sandoz, 1883.
      [RON Rf. 84.170, ARS GD 8° 3630].

FRANK (Mme Elisa) (née REGNAULT).
Lyons, 1814 -1899 (or 1900).
Author of numerous novels and short stories for children

Les Sabots d'Yvonnette (comedy, 2 tableaux).
      Paris: Ducrocq, 1875.
      [ARS GD 8° 35390].

FRANTZ (Mme).

La Boule merveilleuse ou Arlequin protégé par Pierrot (pantomime, 2
acts).
      Théâtre des Funambules, before 1830.
      [SACD ms.].

FRANTZIA (Marie).

Le Donjon du Maure (drame, 5 acts, 9 tableaux). Music by M. Laurent.
      Paris: Mifliez, 1860.
      Théâtre de Belleville, 26-5-60.
      [BN 4° Yth 1284, RON Rec. 133, ARS GD 8° 46136, SACD
      G.C. supp., AN F[18]1305].

FRED (Mme).

Les Nouvelles couches (1 act).
      Théâtre de l'Application, 7-6-94.

FRIAS-DESJARDINS (Louise-*Jenny*).
Amiens, 1811-1896.
Founder and director of a school at Guéret.

Philippe II, roi d'Espagne (tragedy, 5 acts).
Guéret: Amiault, 1900 (published posthumously by her students).
[BN 8° Yth 29372, ARS GD 8° 38004].

FRIEDELLE (Mme Alexandre).
Pseudonym: Mme ALEXANDRE.

Amélie ou le Protecteur mystérieux (melodrama, 3 acts). Music by M. Taix.
Paris: Hénée et Dumas, 1807.
Théâtre de la Gaîté, 11-6-07; Cirque Olympique 27-5-17.
[BN 8° Yth 621, ARS GD 8° 5104].

Barbe-bleue ou les Enchantements d'Alcine (melodrama). Preceded by La Grotte d'Alcine (prologue). Both co-authored by Hapdé.
Paris: Barba, 1811.
Jeux Gymnastique, 16-12-11.
[RON Rf. 26.914, BHVP in-12 609987 (9)].

La Lévite d'Ephraïm ou la Destruction des Benjamites (pantomime, 3 acts). Music by Propiac.
Paris: Barba, 1813.
Théâtre de la Gaîté, 29-7-13.
[BN 8° Yth 10173, RON Rf. 26.915, SACD PC 356].

Les Empiriques d'autrefois (comedy-vaudeville). Co-authored by Scribe.
Paris: Pollet, 1825.
Théâtre Du Gymnase Dramatique, 11-6-25.
[BN 8° Yth 5877, RON Rf. 26.916, BHVP in-12 611338 (6)].

FROMENT (Mme Blanche).

Les Malins (comedy, 1 act).
Théâtre Montmartre, 30-6-87.

Le Sapho (vaudeville, 1 act).
Folies Voltaire, 19-5-88.

Demande en mariage (comedy, 1 act).
    Théâtre Montmartre, 12-4-89.

Le Divorce au village (comedy, 1 act).
    Folies Voltaire, 2-11-89.

J'arrivons à l'exposition (vaudeville, 1 act).
    Folies Voltaire, 23-11-89.

L'Avocat de mon ancien (vaudeville, 1 act). Co-authored by Touzé.
    Théâtre des Batignolles, 26-4-90.

FROMENT (Mme Marguerite) (see Twentieth Century volume).

GABRIELLE (Jeanne) (Mme Paul THÉROND).
    St. Petersburg, 1867 - ?
    French parents.

Cerise ! naïveté (verse).
    Paris: Westhauser, 1887.
    [BN 8° Yth 22739].

Quelle heure est-il ? (saynète enfantine).
    Paris: Westhauser, 1887.
    [BN 8° Yth 22583, RON Rf. 85663, ARS GD 8° 26456].

GAGNE (Elise MOREAU (DU RUS), Mme Paulin).
    Rochefort-sur-mer, 1813 - ?
    Author of poetry, children's novels, tales and a biography of Mme de
    Bawr; co-founder of a literary revue entitled Le Théâtre du monde
    (1854-1857).

Arlequin (pièce à tiroirs). Co-authored by Mme Desbordes-Valmore
and M. de Jussieu.
    Paris: A. Boyer, n.d.
    [BN 8° Yth 32432].

Omégar, ou le Dernier homme (proso-poésie dramatique de la fin des
temps en 12 chants).
    Paris: Didier, 1859.
    [BN Yf 9419, ARS GD 8° 34625, BHVP in-18 919403].

GALERON DE CALONNE (Berthe de CALONNE, Mme GALERON).
   1859 - ?
   Poet.

Chez la Champenesle (comedy (à propos), 1 act, verse). Co-authored
by E. de Calonne (her father).
      Paris: A. Lemerre, 1886.
      Petit Odéon, 21-12-86.
      [BN Yth 22321, RON Rf. 3.840(8), ARS GD 8° 31690, BHVP
      in-16 608 003 (8), AN F^{18}724].

Ambroise Paré (drame, 1 act).
      Union Nationale, rue de Lancry, 22-4-99.
      [AN F^{18}1465].

GALLOIS (Mme).

La Religieuse malgré elle (comedy, 3 acts, prose).
      Théâtre des Variétés, 28-3-1791.

GAUTIER (Louise-Charlotte-Ernestine, called *Judith*).
      Paris, 1845 (other sources have 1846 and 1850) - S. Énogat (or
      Dinard), 1917.
      Novelist; author of translations of Wagner, adaptations of Chinese
      poetry, and memoirs; first woman elected to the Académie Goncourt;
      daughter of Théophile Gautier, briefly married to Catulle Mendès.

La Marchande des sourires (Japanese play, 5 acts, 2 parts). Music by
Benedictus.
      Paris: G. Charpentier, 1888.
      Odéon, 21-4-88.
      [BN 8° Yth 23059, RON Rf. 59.953, ARS GD 8° 33310,
      BHVP in-12 608006 (2), SACD, AN F^{18}725].

Le Camargo (ballet-pantomime, 2 acts, 3 tableaux). Co-authored by
Armand Tonnery.
      Paris: A. Colin, 1893.
      [BN 8° Yth 26329].

La Barynia (comedy, 3 acts). Co-authored by J. Gayda.
      Odéon, 20-9-94.
      [AN F^{18}727].

La Sonate de clair de lune (opera, 1 act). Music by Benedictus.
>   Paris: Armand Colin, 1894.
>   [BN m. 23876, RON Rf. 59.955].

La Larme du diable (mystery play, 2 acts). Co-authored by Th. Gautier.
Music by Benedictus.
>   Petit Théâtre, 7-5-95; Salle Charras, May 1898.

La Tunique merveilleuse (Chinese comedy, 1 act, prose).
>   Odéon, 1899.
>   [AN F^{18}729].

La Geisha et le chevalier (Japanese drama, 1 act).
>   In Les Parfums de la pagode.
>   Paris: Fasquelle, 1919.
>   Mathurins, 15-12-1900.
>   [RON Rf. 59.956, AN F^{18}1337].

L'Avare chinois. Adaptation of unknown Chinese comedy.
>   In Les Parfums de la pagode.
>   Paris: Fasquelle, 1919.
>   Odéon, 30-1-1908.
>   [RON Rf.59.956].

Princesse d'amour (4 acts and 7 tableaux).
>   Théâtre du Vaudeville, 24-1-1907.

L'Embûche fleurie (1 act).
>   Théâtre Michel, 20-02-1911.

La Fille du ciel (Chinese drama). Co-authored by P. Loti.
>   Paris: Calmann Lévy, 1911.
>   New York, Century Theater, October 1912.
>   [BN 8° Yth 34095, RON Rf. 59.960].

Les Portes rouges (Chinese drama, 5 acts).
>   [RON ms. 1633].

Le Petit chien de la marquise (comedy, 3 tableaux). Adaptation of
novel by Th. Gautier.
>   [RON Rf. 59.965, RON ms. 1632].

L'Apsara (pièce hindoue, 4 acts).
>   [RON Re. m. 38].

GAY (Cécile).

> Qui ne risque rien, n'a rien (proverb).
> > Paris: Librairie G. Fischbacker, 1882.
> > [RON Rf. 84.179, ARS GD 8° 26511].

GAY (Marie-Françoise-*Sophie* NICHAULT DE LA VALETTE, Mme Gaspard LIOTTIER, then Mme Jean-Sigismond).
> Paris, 1776 - *id.*, 1852.
> Novelist and musician; also known for her literary salon.

> La Sérénade (comic opera, 1 act). Music by Mme Gail and Garcia. Adaptation of Regnard.
> > Paris: Barba, 1818.
> > Opéra-Comique, 2-4-18.
> > [BN 8° Yth 16359, RON Rf. 27.097, SACD P5, AN F^{18}611].

> Le Marquis de Pomenars (comedy, 1 act, prose).
> > Paris: Ladvocat, 1820.
> > Théâtre Français, 18-12-19.
> > [BN 8° Yth 11265, RON Rf. 27.098, ARS GD 8° 13690, BHVP in-12 610922, TF 1 MAR Gay, TF ms. 538, AN F^{18}587].

> Le Maître de chapelle ou le Souper imprévu (comedy, 1 act). Music by Paër. Adaptation of M. Alex. Duval.
> > Paris: Stock, 1830.
> > Opéra-Comique, 29-3-21.
> > [BN 8° Yth 10696, RON Rf. 27.103, ARS GD 8° 42945, BHVP in-4° 118104, SACD PC 375, AN F^{18}592].

> Une Aventure du Chevalier de Grammont (comedy, 3 acts, verse).
> > Paris: Tardieu, Barba, 1822.
> > Théâtre Français, 5-3-22.
> > [BN 8° Yth 18289, RON Rf. 27.104, ARS GD 8° 5847, SACD PC 52, TF 1 AVE Gay, AN F^{18}589].

> Marie ou la Pauvre fille (drame, 3 acts, prose).
> > Paris: Ponthieu & Barba, 1824.
> > Théâtre Français, 9-11-24.
> > [BN 8° Yth 7898, RON Rf. 27.105, ARS GD 8° 23539, BHVP in-8° 118133, TF 1 MAR Gay, AN F^{18}592].

Le Chevalier de Canolle (comic opera, 3 acts). Music by Fontmichel.
Paris: impr. de Vve Dondey-Dupré, 1836.
Opéra-Comique, 6-8-36.
[BN 8° Yth 3253, ARS GD 8° 19831, AN F^{18}690].

Les Mines de blagues (revue fantastique à spectacle).
Ambigu-Comique, 31-12-38.

La Duchesse de Châteauroux (drame, 4 acts).
Paris: Marchant, 1844.
Second Théâtre Français, 25-12-43.
[BN 8° Yth 1306, RON Rf. 27.106, ARS GD 8° 41582].

GEFFROY (Marie).

Maman Gâteau (drame, 6 acts). Co-authored by F. Meynet.
Paris: Barbré, 1896.
Théâtre de la République, 28-8-96.
[BN 8° Yth 27732, ARS GD 8° 34112, BHVP in-18 129884,
AN F^{18}1178^A].

Le P'tit gars (drame, 5 acts). Co-authored by F. Meynet.
Théâtre de la République, 25-11-97.
[AN F^{18}1178^B].

L'Auvergnate (drame, 5 acts). Co-authored by F. Meynet.
Théâtre de la République, 27-9-99.
[AN F^{18} 1179].

GELLEE (Claire).

L'Expiation ou une Nuit en Lorraine (drame). Co-authored by Alph.
Buisselle.
Théâtre de la Banlieue, 1851.
[AN F^{18}1354].

GEVRIE (Mme M. de).

Comédies de salon: "A l'abordage !" (proverb), "Le Flacon d'or"
(comedy), "Un Mauvais jour qui finit bien" (proverb), "Tous
diplomates" (comedy), "Ni cousin ni cousine" (proverb).
Paris: E. Lachaud, 1872.
[RON Rf. 84.188, ARS GD 8° B.L. 15.201].

GIRARD (Mlle).
Boarding school teacher.

Nouveau théâtre dédié à la jeunesse chrétienne. "Le Choix d'une
mère", "Une Journée de Marie Stuart", "La Petite savante",
"L'Etourdie", "La Petite paresseuse", "Le Coeur et l'esprit".
Lyons: E.-B. Labaume, 1853.
[BN Yf 9480].

Nouveau théâtre dédié à la jeunesse chrétienne. "La Fille de Jephté",
"La Répétition d'Athalie, ou l'Epreuve", "La Jalousie", "Les
Bohémiennes".
Paris: Ch. Guyot, 1855.
[BN Yf 9481, ARS GD 8° 2487].

La Fille de Jephté (drame, 3 acts).
Paris: Sarlit, 1876.
[BN 8° Yth 24840, RON Rf. 85699].

Les Bohémiennes, ou la Reconnaissance (comedy, 3 acts).
Paris: Sarlit, 1886.
[BN 8° Yth 22244].

La Répétition d'Athalie (comedy, 2 acts).
Paris: Bricon, 1893.
[BN 8° Yth 26338].

GIRARDIN (Delphine GAY, Mme Emile de).
Pseudonyms: Vicomte de LAUNAY, Léon LESPES.
Aix-la-Chapelle, 1804 - Paris, 1855.
Poet, journalist, novelist.

L'Achille de Normandie (vaudeville, 1 act). Co-authored by J. Adler.
Théâtre St. Antoine, 11-8-38.
[AN F^{18}1276].

L'Ecole des journalistes (comedy, 5 acts, verse).
Paris: Dumont, Desrez, 1839.
Accepted by the Comédie Française on 21-12-39 but banned
by the censorship committee.
[BN 8° Yth 5651, RON Rf. 42.886, ARS GD 8° 9447, BHVP
in-18 920190, SACD PC 199, TF 2 GIR Eco 1839].

Judith (tragedy, 3 acts).
Paris: Tresse, 1843.
Théâtre Français, 24-4-43.
[BN 4° Yth 2239, RON Rf. 42.892, ARS GD 8° 42462, BHVP in-16 118467, TF 1 JUD Gir, AN F^{18}675, TF ms 765].

Cléopâtre (tragedy, 5 acts).
Paris: Michel Lévy, 1847.
Théâtre Français, 13-11-47.
[BN 8° Yth 3516, RON Rf. 42.896, ARS GD 8° 7589, BHVP fol. 402983, SACD NS C, TF 1 CLE Gir, TF ms. 845].

C'est la faute du mari, ou les Bons maris font les bonnes femmes, ou l'Amour après le mariage (proverb, 1 act, verse).
Paris: Lévy fr., 1851.
Comédie Française, 1-5-51.
[BN 8° Yth 2413, RON Rf. 42.899, ARS GD 8° 7137, BHVP in-18 607618 (3), AN F^{18}676, TF ms. 895].

Lady Tartuffe (comedy, 5 acts). Original title: La Prude ou Lady Tartuffe.
Paris: Michel Lévy, 1853.
Comédie Française, 10-2-53.
[BN 8° Yth 9963, RON Rf. 42.902, ARS GD 8° 12701, BHVP in-18 607621, TF 1 LAD Gir, AN F^{18}677, TF ms 926].

La Joie fait peur (comedy, 1 act).
Paris: Michel Lévy, 1854.
Théâtre Français, 25-2-54; Odéon, 10-12-1941.
[BN 8° Yth 9715, RON Rf. 42.905, ARS GD 8° 12523, BHVP 607 622 (2), TF 1 JOI Gir, TF ms. 942, AN F^{18}677].

Le Chapeau de l'horloger (comedy, 1 act).
Paris: Michel Lévy, 1855.
Gymnase-dramatique, 16-12-54.
[BN 8° Yth 3004, RON Rf. 42.908, ARS GD 8° 7208, TF 2 GIR Cha 1864, BHVP in-12 610030 (9), AN F^{18}831].

Une Femme qui déteste son mari (comedy, 1 act).
Paris: Michel Lévy, 1856.
Gymnase-dramatique, 10-10-56.
[BN 8° Yth 1390, RON Rf. 42.911, ARS GD 8° 20402, BHVP in-18 607785 (8), SACD NS F, TF 2 GIR Fem 1856, AN F^{18}832].

Oeuvres complètes. Volume VI, "théâtre", includes: "L'Ecole des journalistes", "Judith", "Cléopâtre", "C'est la faute du mari", "Lady Tartuffe", "La Joie fait peur", "Le Chapeau de l'horloger", "Une Femme qui déteste son mari".
> Paris: Plon, 1860.
> [BN Z 30413, RON Rf. 42.885, ARS 8° B.L. 34.674, SACD P29, TF 2 GIR O 1860-1861].

GOMIEN (see FRANCE).

GOURAUD (Mlle Julie).
Pseudonym of Louise d'AULNAY.
Tours, 1810 - Paris, 1891.
Prolific novelist, primarily for children; founded Journal des jeunes personnes (1836) and La Femme et la famille (1867).

La Comédie au salon (scènes et proverbes pour la jeunesse): "Une Etourderie" (2 acts), "Alix et Suzanne" (2 acts), "Le Premier pas à l'étranger" (3 acts), "Rien de trop" (3 acts), "Une Jeune femme" (3 tableaux), "Un Bienfait n'est jamais perdu" (2 acts).
> Paris: Maillet, 1864.
> [BN Yf 9499, BHVP in-8° 702 754].

Madame Ledoux (comedy, 3 acts).
> Paris: Périsse, n.d.
> [ARS GD 8° 26386].

Les Petites marchandes (2 acts).
> Paris: Périsse, 1875.
> [BN 8° Yth 26127].

Un Poisson d'avril.
> Paris: Bourget-Calas, 1881.
> [BN 8° Yf 12646].

Une Nouvelle connaissance.
> Paris: Bourget-Calas, 1881.
> [BN 8° Yf 12647].

Scènes et proverbes pour la jeunesse: "Frère et soeur", "La Sainte-Catherine", "La Sellette", "Un Poisson d'avril", "Les Petites marchandises", "La Journée d'une petite fille", "Les Souliers de Gaspard", "La Potichomanie", "Une Nouvelle connaissance".
Paris: Julien, Lanier et Cie., 1885.
[BN Yf 9500, RON Rf. 85704].

Mieux vaut douceur que violence (comedy, 3 acts, prose).
Paris: P. Delarue, 1894.
[BN 8° Yth 26736].

La Sainte-Catherine (comedy, 1 act, prose).
Paris: P. Delarue, 1896.
[BN 8° Yth 27578].

GRAND (Mlle G.).

Le Secret d'une reine (drame, 5 acts).
Folies Voltaire, 4-7-91.

GRANDPRÉ (Mlle de).
Pseudonym of Pauline CHEVALIER.
Novelist.

Le Marquis de Valbert (comédie de salon).
Paris: E. Dentu, 1863.
[BN Yf 9506, RON Rf. 84.195, ARS GD 8° 3218].

GRE(E)CH (Jehan) (Mme LERAY) (see Twentieth Century volume).

GRÉVILLE (Henry).
Pseudonym of Alice-Marie-Céleste HENRY, Mme Emile DURAND-GRÉVILLE.
Paris, 1842 - Boulogne-sur-Mer, 1902.
Journalist, novelist, lecturer.

Denise (comedy, 3 acts).
In Théâtre des Inconnus 11 (1-9-73).
[BN Yf 1345 (12), RON Rf. 43.879, ARS GD 8° 46091].

A Soukham Kaleb (comédie russo-circassienne). Co-authored by R... and A. Bertran. 1876.

Pierrot ermite (comedy, 1 act).
    Paris: Plon, 1877.
    Troisième Théâtre Français, 2-4-77.
    [RON Rf. 43.380, ARS GD 8° 35027].

La Brouille (proverb, 1 act).
    Cercle Saint-Simon.

Saveli (drame, 6 tableaux).
    Théâtre de Lille, 1888.

Comédies de paravent. Contains: "Cassandre pendu" (opéra-bouffe, 1 act), "Ma tante" (comedy, 1 act), "Annette" (1 act);
"A la campagne" (vaudeville, 1 act),
    Jeux Artistiques, 2-9-74;
"L'Oiseau" (proverb, 1 act),
    Théâtre du Vaudeville, 1875;
"Les Cloches cassées" (comedy, 1 act),
    Odéon, 30-11-77 [AN F^{18}721];
"Etourdie" (monologue).
    Paris: Plon, 1888.
    [ARS GD 8° 3046].

Louk-Loukrich (drame, 4 acts).
    Galerie Vivienne, 20-3-90.

Cléopâtre (5 acts).
    [RON Rf. 61.240 (plot summary only)].

GRIMON (Mme Cornélie).

Le Tyran domestique ou les Trois bouquets (vaudeville).
    Théâtre de Mme Saqui (Délassements Comiques), 16-4-44.
    [AN F^{18}1050].

J'ai perdu mon père.
    Théâtre de Mme Saqui (Délassements Comiques), 12-8-45.

L'Ecole des braves (vaudeville, 1 act).
    Théâtre de Mme Saqui (Délassements Comiques), 18-1-46.
    [AN F^{18}1052].

GROSJEAN (see MELIN).

GUÉNARD (Mme BROSSIN DE MERÉ, baronne de MÉRÉ, née Elisabeth).
Paris, 1751 - *id.*, 1829.
Very prolific novelist.

Deux agneaux (pastorale, 1 act, prose).
    In Contes à nos enfants.
    Paris: Locard et Davi, 1825.
    [ARS GD 8° 942].

GUÉNOT-MORVANCHER (Mme).
School teacher.

Nouveau théâtre des jeunes personnes. Contains: "La Veille d'une
distribution de prix", "Le Prix d'honneur", "Une Bonne journée",
"Zéïla la créole, ou la Nouvelle élève", "Les Pensionnaires d'Ecouen"
(petit drame historique, 3 acts), "Le Petit dîner, ou les Amies de
pension" (comedy, 2 acts), "Louise et Marie, ou Ange et démon"
(comedy, 1 act), "Les Vocations" (petit drame, 3 acts).
    Paris: Guiller, 1858.
    [BN Yf 9533].

Louise et Marie, ou l'Ange de démon (comedy, 1 act).
    Paris: A. Maugars, 1864.
    [BN 8° Yth 10338].

Les Pensionnaires d'Ecouen (drame historique, 3 acts). Adaptation of a
short story by Eugénie Foa.
    Paris: Maugars, 1864.
    [BN 8° Yth 13750].

Le Prix d'honneur (1 act).
    Paris: Maugars, 1864.
    [BN 8° Yth 14790].

Une Bonne journée (comedy, 1 act). Co-authored by Quenot.
    Paris: Maugars, 1864.
    [BN 8° Yth 18298, SACD].

La Veille d'une distribution de prix (1 act).
    Paris: Maugars, 1864.
    [BN 8° Yth 18792].

Les Vocations (petit drame, 3 acts).
>Paris: Maugars, 1864.
>[BN 8° Yth 19281].

Zeïla la créole, ou la Nouvelle élève (1 act).
>Paris: Maugars, 1864.
>[BN 8° Yth 19461].

GUERRIER DE HAUPT (Marie).
Novelist and translator from English.

Les Petites merveilleuses (comedy-vaudeville, 2 acts).
>Paris: Aug. Boyer, 1878.
>[BN 8° Yth 26053, RON Rf. 85718].

La Comédie au pensionnat Contains 2 vaudevilles: "Fête d'une mère"
and "La Fin des vacances".
>Tours: Mame et fils, 1891.
>[BN 8° Yf. 540].

Le Chemin de l'école (saynète).
>Paris: Bricon, 1894.
>[BN 8° Yth 26835, RON Rf. 85717].

Les Enfants de la France (saynète).
>Paris: Bricon, 1894.
>[BN 8° Yth 6834].

La Leçon à la poupée (saynète).
>Paris: Bricon, 1894.
>[BN 8° Yth 26836].

Jean Bonhomme et la Tour Eiffel (monologue).
>Paris: Bricon, 1895.
>[BN 8° Yth 27333].

Un Diable à quatre (monologue, verse).
>Paris: O. Bornemann, 1896.
>[BN 8° Yth 28019].

Un Vrai malheur (monologue).
>Paris: O. Bornemann, 1896.
>[BN 8° Yth 27999].

Les Petits souliers (monologue).
>Paris: Picard et Kaan, 1898.
>[BN 8° Yf. 632].

La Revanche des belles-mères (monologue villageois).
>Paris: Picard et Kaan, 1900.
>[BN 8° Yf 632].

Moqueuse (monologue, verse).
>Paris: Lib. d'éducation nationale, 1901.
>[BN 8° Yth 29636].

GUIBERT (Henriette).

Les Deux amis (1 act).
>Bordeaux: impr. Laborie, 1895.
>[RON Rf. 77791].

GUICHARD (see GUITTY).

GUILBERT (Yvette) (Mme SCHILLER).
Paris, 1867 - Aix-en-Provence, 1944.
Actress, cabaret singer and song writer, novelist.

Comment on devient étoile (monologue).
>P. Dupont, 1893.
>[BN 4° Yth 5973].

Madame Chiffon (comedy), 1933.

Les Amants légitimes (comedy-vaudeville, 3 acts).
>[RON ms. 1698].

GUITTY (Madeleine) (Madeleine Marguerite GUICHARD).
Corbeil, 1871 - Paris, 1936.
Actress.

Paris à l'ombre (revue, 1 act). Co-authored by de Collens.
>Eden Concert, 3-4-91.
>[AN F^{18}1425].

Conte blanc (pantomime, 1 act). Co-authored by Arnould and Ch. Lancelin.
>Cercle Pigalle, 20-2-94; Eden Concert, 3-8-94.

Il n'y a plus d'enfants (operetta, 1 act). Co-authored by Dumat and R. Casa.
>Carillon, 13-11-97.
>[AN F^{18}14 52].

Passez muscade (operetta, 1 act). Co-authored by Dumat and R. Casa.
>Théâtre de l'Application, 22-11-97.
>[AN F^{18}1299].

Pages intimes (pantomime, 1 act). Co-authored by Jean Sery and R. Casa.
>Théâtre de L'Application, 1898.
>[AN F^{18}1300].

Qu'a-t-on fait de Victorine ? (vaudeville, 1 act). Co-authored by Paul Bonhomme.
>Paris: C. Joubert, 1911.
>Performed at the Chansonia.
>[BN 8° Yth 34325, ARS GD 8° 36955, BHVP in-18 610 659].

Le Macaroni (comedy, 1 act). Co-authored by Paul Bonhomme.
>Paris: C. Joubert, 1912.
>Performed at the Chansonia.
>[BN 8° Yth 34618, ARS GD 8° 36897, BHVP in-18 610 662].

Tableau à vendre (vaudeville, 1 act). Co-authored by Paul Bonhomme.
>Paris: Joubert, 1912.
>Performed at the Chansonia.
>[BN 8° Yth 34619, ARS GD 8° 36937].

Madame Bou-dou-ba-da-boum ! (operetta, 2 acts).
>Concert Mayol, December 1915.

Vingt-deux, rue des Vertus (2 acts).
>Grand-Guignol, 2-6-1922.

Cette pauvre Elisa (comedy, 1 act).
>Grand-Guignol, 1-7-1927 and 21-7-31.

GYP   Pseudonym of Sibylle-Gabrielle-Marie-Antoinette de RIQUETTI de MIRABEAU, comtesse de MARTEL de JANVILLE.
Château de Coëstal (Morbihan), 1849 - Neuilly-sur-Seine, 1932.
Novelist, journalist; active in politics; memoirs.

Autour du mariage (comedy, 5 acts). Co-authored by H. Crémieux.
    Paris: C. Lévy, 1883.
    Gymnase dramatique, 19-10-83.
    [BN 8° Yth 21204, RON Rf. 61.769, ARS GD 8° 31007, BHVP in-18 607835 (1), SACD m. 3090, AN F^{18}846].

Mademoiselle Eve (comedy, 3 acts).
    Paris: C. Lévy, 1889.
    St. Petersburg, Théâtre Michel, 6-1-1885; Comédie-Parisienne, 4-3-95.
    [RON Rf. 61.768, ARS GD 8° 44684 (1), SACD m. 2933].

Tout à l'égout ! (revue, 3 acts).
    Paris: C. Lévy, 1889.
    Paris, Salons du Helder, 10-1-89.
    [BN 8° Yth 23360, RON Rf. 61.768, ARS GD 8° 35858, BHVP in-12 610284, SACD].

Sauvetage (comedy, 1 act).
    Théâtre de l'Application, 2-5-90.

Le Dernier sentiment de Loulou (comedy, 1 act).
    Paris: Revue d'art dramatique, 1892.
    Cercle Artistique et Littéraire, 11-5-1892; Cercle Volney, 14-5-1892.
    [ARS GD 8° 44684 (2)].

Scène d'intérieur (comedy, 1 act).
    Salle Lancry, 10-2-95.

Rencontre (comedy, 1 act).
    Institution dramatique, 4-10-95.
    [AN F^{18}1357].

Flirtage (saynète, 1 act).
    Théâtre de l'Application, 7-3-98.

L'Idéal (1 act).
>   Salle des Agriculteurs, 13-5-98.

Miquette (comedy, 1 act). Co-authored by Drault.
>   Théâtre Pompadour, 1-12-98.
>   [AN F^{18}1360].

Bob chez lui (comedy, 1 act).
>   Théâtre de l'Application, 23-3-99.
>   [AN F^{18}1301].

L'Ange gardien (comedy, 1 act).
>   Théâtre de l'Application, 22-6-99.
>   [AN F^{18}1370^{A}].

Premier nuage (saynète, 1 act).
>   Grenoble, 14-05-1900.

Une Nuit agitée (comedy, 1 act).
>   Grenoble, Cas., 14-05-1900.

Le Premier flirt de Loulou (comedy, 1 act).
>   Mathurins, 29-1-1903.
>   [AN F^{18}1339].

Les Trois clefs (2 acts). Co-authored by Camille Bruno.
>   In Les Saisons 3 (Aug. 1916).
>   Cercle artistique et littéraire, 9-6-1906.
>   [RON Rf. 61.774].

Toutoune (comedy, 1 act).
>   In Lectures pour tous, December 1910.
>   [BN 8° Z. 14580, RON Rf. 61.775, ARS 4° Jo. 11975].

La Pintade bleue. Contains 14 short dialogues, including:
"La Pintade bleue" (comedy, 1 act),
>   Performed in Bordeaux, 27-4-1913.
>   Paris: Calmann Lévy, 1914.
>   [BHVP in-16 935591].

H. (Mme).

> Le Bonnet à poil (pantomime, 1 act). Co-authored by Mélandri.
> Concert des Décadents, December 1894.
> [AN F^{18}1437].

HADOT (see BATHELEMY-HABOT).

HALLER (Gustave).
Pseudonym of Wilhelmine-Joséphine SIMONIN, Mme Gustave-Eugène FOULD, then princesse Georges B. STIRBEY.
Paris, 1836 - Pontaillac, 1919.
Actress at the Théâtre Français (stage name, Mme Valérie), artist, novelist, art critic.

> Le Médecin des dames (comedy).
> Paris: La Croix, Verboeckhoven et Cie, 1870.
> Théâtre Cluny, 16-1-70.
> [BN 8° Yth 11455, RON Rf. 43.483, AN F^{18}1027].

> La Comtesse Romani (comedy). Co-authored by Dumas fils.
> Paris: C. Lévy, 1877.
> Gymnase, 16-11-1876.
> [RON Rf. 41.447, AN F^{18}843].

> Le Duel de Pierrot (5 acts).
> Paris: impr. Menetière, 1881.
> Gymnase, 22-7-1881.
> [RON Rf. 43.484, AN F^{18}846].

> Les Elections (translation of English comedy by Robertson).
> Gymnase-dramatique, 17-8-1881.
> [AN F^{18}846].

HAMEAU (Mlle Louise).
La Roche-sur-Yon (Vendée), 1837 - ?
Children's novels.

> La Mort de Chatterton (scène dramatique, verse).
> Paris: Clavel, 1885.
> [ARS GD 8° 26469].

Une Bonne action récompensée (saynète-proverbe, 1 act). Music by
Georges Meugé.
>   Paris: Haton, 1896.
>   [BN 4° Yth 6575].

Une Confidence (monologue).
>   Paris: Vve Benoit, 1897.
>   [BN 4° Yth 6399].

Les Plaisirs de la campagne (monologue).
>   Paris: Vve benoit, 1897.
>   [BN 4° Yth 6402].

Histoire d'une soupe à l'oignon (monologue).
>   Paris: Sulzbach, 1898.
>   [BN 4° Yth 6641].

Peroquette [*sic*] (monologue).
>   Paris: Sulzbach, 1898.
>   [BN 4° Yth 6647].

Les Violettes (monologue).
>   Paris: Lesot, 1911.
>   [BN 8° Yth 34245].

HART (Maria).

Fumée (saynète).
>   Private performance, February 1894.

Minerve and Ne jouez pas avec le feu (bluettes, 1 act).
>   Private performance, June 1894.

HATTON (Mme Emilie).

Les Six sous du petit barbiste (1 act).
>   Paris: V. Goupy, 1867.
>   [BN 8° Yth 16569, RON Rf. 85730, ARS GD 8° 35622].

L'Arbre de Noël (1 act).
>   Paris: V. Goupy, 1869.
>   [BN 8° Yth 26048].

HAUTPOUL (see BEAUFORT DE HAUTPOUL).

HENRI (Félicie).
Pseudonym of Mlle Félicie SERPH, Mme BELLOT.
Poitiers, 1847 - ?

Mariana (drame, 5 acts, 9 tableaux).
Paris: Dentu, 1884.
Théâtre Beaumarchais, 7-6-84.
[BN 8° Yth 21681, RON Rf. 43.529, BHVP in-8° 609582, AN F^{18} 1133^A].

HENRY (Alice-Marie-Céleste) (see Henry GRÉVILLE).

HENRY (Mme).

Barnabé fabricant d'allumettes chimiques allemandes (mistification [*sic*], 1 act).
Manuscript belonging to the Théâtre Lazari but possibly never performed.
[SACD ms.].

HERBELOT (Mme Jenny SABATIER).

Famille et Patrie (comedy).
Théâtre Corneille, November 1877.

Une Méprise et Dindonneau.
Théâtre parisien, 1877.
[AN F^{18}1260].

HERBLAY (Mme).

Les Apparences (comedy, 1 act). Co-authored by Sainvictor.
Théâtre du Nouveau Tivoli, 11-4-96.

HOLMÈS (*Augusta*-Mary-Anne).
Pseudonym: Hermann ZENTA.
Paris, 1847 - *id.* 1903.
Poet, pianist, singer and composer of Irish parentage.

Héro et Léandre (opera).
Théâtre du Châtelet, 1874?.
[VER ms.].

La Montagne noire (drame lyrique, 4 acts).
    Paris: Maguet, 1895.
    Académie Royale de Musique (Opéra), 8-2-95.
    [BN 8° Yth 27053, ARS GD 8° 32742, BHVP in-8° 609374,
    AN F^{18}672].

Astarté (opera).
    [VER ms.].

Lancelot du Lac (opera).
    [VER ms.].

HOMSY-MASSABO (Mathilde).

Trois actes en vers. Includes:
"Le Page du Trouvère" (comedy, 1 act, verse), 1898;
"Le Voeu d'Estelle" (drame, 1 act, verse), 1899;
"La Maison de verre", 1908.
    Villeneuve-la-Garenne: Ed. du Luth français, n.d.
    [BN 8° Yf 2023, RON Rf. 62.615].

HORDE (Mme Adélaïde).
    ? - 1812.
    Author of historical novels; actress.

La Cause célèbre, ou l'Épouse enterrée vivante (melodrama, 4 acts, prose).
    Théâtre de la Porte St. Martin, 16-7-07.

HOUDETOT (Elisabeth-Louise-Joséphine GALOS, comtesse de).
    Author of children's novels.

Nouveau théâtre d'éducation: "Pour la patrie" (drame patriotique, 4 tableaux), "L'Oncle d'Amérique" (comedy, 1 act), "Le Retour d'une mère" (comedy, 2 acts).
    Paris: Hachette, 1885.
    [BN 8° Yf 179, RON Rf. 85740].

Le Théâtre de la famille: "Sainte Népomucette" (comedy, 4 acts), "Le Procès de Jeanneton" (comedy, 1 act), "Le Coq et la perle" (comedy, 1 act), "La Sous-maîtresse" (comedy, 3 acts), "Le Bouquet" (monologue), "C'est le chat" (comedy, 1 act).
    Paris: H. Gautier, 1888.
    [BN m. 8° Yf 368].

HUARD (Mme Ferdinand).

> Les Suites d'une indiscrétion (comedy).
> > Paris: Duverger, 1843.
> > [BN 8° Yth 3956, ARS GD 8° 44369].

HUBERT (Florence).

> Un Voyage à Metz (pièce patriotique, 1 act).
> > Paris: George Robert, 1886.
> > [RON Rf. 43.636].

ISOLE (Louise d') (see RIOM).

JOLY (Mad.).

> L'Illustre toréador and Le Petit chaperon rouge.
> > Ba-ta-clan, 1869.
> > [AN F^{18}1347].

JOURDAIN (Mme Laure).
Author of one novel.

> L'Anneau de la marquise (comic opera, 1 act). Co-authored by Chapelle and Cormon. Probably a musical adaptation of the comedy-vaudeville by the same title by Chapelle and Cormon (1842).
> > Salle Bonne-Nouvelle, 20-12-48.

JULIA (Æmilia).
Pseudonym of Miss Emily BLACKE.

> Le Prince du Liban (tragedy, 5 acts).
> > Paris: A. Bourdillicit, 1861.
> > [RON Rf. 43.917, BHVP in-12 610008 (6)].

JULIEN (Mme).
Pseudonym of Pauline BRUNET.
Author of translations from English.

> Une Famille du peuple (drame vaudeville, 3 acts).
> > Paris: chez l'auteur, 1850.
> > Théâtre Montparnasse, 8-2-50.
> > [BN 8° Yth 18361, RON Rf. 43.923, SACD ms 52].

KERHALVÉ (Sylvane de).
Pseudonym of Laure LE BORGNE.

Deux monologues: "Vieille femme", "Les Hiboux".
Paris: A. Lemerre, 1893.
[BN 8° Yf. pièce 195].

Saynètes: "Rêve d'artiste", "Partie carrée", "Avant la demande",
"Maman".
Paris: A. Lemerre, 1897.
[RON Rf. 84.238].

Trop tard.
Vannes: imp. de Lafolye, 1899.
[BN 8° Yth 29145].

KRYSINSKA (Marie).
Poet.

La Nuit de Cléopâtre (scène lyrique). Music by Laramolat.
Théâtre Moderne, 9-5-94.

Anniversaire (comedy, 1 act).
Théâtre Mondain, 4-3-97; Théâtre des Capucines, 1-2-1902.

Les Trois amours (pantomime, 1 act). Co-authored by Séry and
Colomb.
Théâtre Mondain, 4-3-97.

Kaïn (mystery play). Music by G. Street.
Théâtre de l'Application, 11-12-99.

Baba Yaga. Translated from Russian. Co-authored by Princesse
Amathouny.
[RON ms. 1838].

Un Homme raisonnable (1 act, prose). Other title: Les Gens
raisonnables.
[RON ms. 1841].

Pardonnée (2 acts, prose).
[RON ms. 1842].

Ménage moderne (comedy, 1 act).
Trocadero, 24-11-1901.

Le Mariage de Chloé (opérette-bouffe, 1 act).
Théâtre Grévin, 1902.
[AN F^{18}1364].

L. (Mme Georges) (or Madame GEORGE?).

Demoiselle et grisette (vaudeville, 1 act).
Théâtre de Montparnasse, 17-8-72.
[AN F^{18}1317].

Madeleine, ou le Paria de village (drame, 2 acts).
Théâtre de Montparnasse, 10-8-72.
[AN F^{18}1317].

L'Ami de Madame (vaudeville, 1 act).
Théâtre de Montparnasse, 14-9-72.
[AN F^{18}1317].

Les Jeunes gens du temps passé (comedy, 1 act).
Théâtre des Gobelins, 5-11-72.

Le Souper du diable (vaudeville, 1 act).
Théâtre de Montparnasse, 19-1-73.
[AN F^{18}1317].

Une Nuit d'orage or Une Soirée d'orage (drame, 1 act).
Théâtre de Montparnasse, 25-3-73.
[AN F^{18}1317].

LABOUREAU (Mlle Adèle).

Le Mariage par quiproquo (operetta). Music by Mlle Sabatier-Blot.
Salle Herz, 25-2-62.

LACOUR (Mme Léopold).

Don Juan aux enfers (ballet-pantomime, 1 act). Music by José.
Casino de Paris, 29-11-97.
[AN F^{18}14 51, RON Rf. 32.867 (plot summary only)].

Un Pauvre bûcheron (1 act).
    Odéon, 20-12-1923.

LAGE (Mlle de) (see Simone ARNAUD).

LALIRE (Mme Clémence).
Wrote for the Journal des connaissances utiles and the Journal des jeunes personnes.

Loin du nid, proche du péril (proverb, 1 act).
    In Magasin des demoiselles, 25-12-1851.
    Paris, 1856.
    [BN Z. 4215, ARS GD 8° 42690].

LAMARQUE de la GARRIGUE (see TRAMAR).

LAMBER (see ADAM).

LANCRY (Mme P. de) (ou LANY?).

Faute de grives (comedy, 1 act).
    Salle Duprez, 1-6-94.

LANDRIEUX (Mme Vve).

Le Diable amoureux, "composé à l'âge de vingt ans" (vaudeville, 1 act).
    Paris: impr. Bailly, Divry et Cie, 1857.
    [BN Yf 9750, ARS GD 8° 8911].

LANGLOIS (Mlle E.).

Le Dévouement récompensé (drame, 2 acts) and Rominagrobis (comedy, 1 act).
    Paris: E. Belin, 1875.
    [BN 8° Yth 25029, ARS GD 8° 29176].

Le Prix de la vertu, ou les Deux amies (drame, 2 acts).
    Paris: E. Belin, 1875.
    [BN 8° Yth 25155, ARS GD 8° 29643].

Octavie, ou la Petite sauteuse (drame, 4 acts with songs).
    Paris: E. Belin, 1880.
    [BN 8° Yth 20294, ARS GD 8° 29216].

La Correction maternelle, ou le Vase mystérieux (drame, 3 acts).
Paris: E. Belin, n.d.
[ARS GD 8° 29678].

Remède contre la paresse (dialogue), Elan de coeur d'élèves reconnaissantes pour la meilleure des maîtresses (1 act), Le Compliment (drame, 1 act).
Paris: E. Belin, n.d.
[ARS GD 8° 29206].

LANNER (Mlle).

Claribella (ballet d'enfants, 4 tableaux).
Paris: Librairie du Pré-Catalan, 1858.
Paris, Pré-Catalan (Théâtre des Fleurs), 17-6-1858.
[BN 4° Yth 832, ARS GD 8° 40900, BHVP in-8° 131578].

LAPAUZE (see LESUEUR).

LAUNAY (vicomte de) (see GIRARDIN).

LA VAUDERE (Jane de) (see Twentieth Century volume).

LAVERPILLIÈRE (Mme Jeanne) (see CHAMPEIN).

LE BARILLIER (see BERTHEROY).

LEBLANC DE FERRIERE (Mme) (Madame DEFERRIERE).

Les Etouffeurs (drame, 2 acts, prose). Co-authored by Ch. Foliquet.
Paris: Gallet, 1839.
Théâtre de Mme Saqui (Théâtre du Temple), 27-11-38.
[BN 8° Yth 1478, AN F^{18}1246].

LEFEVRE-DEUMIER (Marie-Louise ROULEUX-DUGAGE, dame).
Argentan (Orne), 1816 - 1877.
Artist-sculptor.

La Comtesse est marquise (comedy, 1 act).
In Théâtre des salons. Ed. E. Rasetti.
N.p.: Impr. Jouast, 1859.
[BN Yf 11919, RON Rf. 84.454].

LÉGER (Mme) (see MOLE-LEGER).

LELOGEAIS (Madame).

    Isabella (drame, 2 acts).
        Théâtre Lazari, 1843.
        [ARS ms. Douay 606].

LEMAIGNIEN (Mme).

    Richard III (tragedy, 5 acts, verse). Signed Mme Lem...
        Paris: Egron, 1818.
        [BN 8° Yth 15539, ARS GD 8° 21914, SACD PC 523].

LEMARIE (Mme H.).

    La Momie (pantomime, 1 act).
        Cercle Funambules, 2-2-94.

LE MOULLE (Mme).

    L'Oublié (comedy, 1 act).
        Galerie Vivienne, 25-4-93.

LEONTINE (Mme).

    Bon mari fait mauvais auteur ! (historical proverb, 1 act).
        In Almanach des coulisses (Annuaire des théâtres), 1843.
        [RON Rf. 82.863].

LÉPINE (Madeleine).
    Born in Cherbourg.
    Poet.

    Azraël (scène dramatique).
        Paris: Bibliothèque de l'association, 1896.
        [BN 8° Yf pièce 262, RON Rf. 64.585, ARS GD 8° 38396].

    Le Jour prédit (drame, 4 tableaux, verse).
        Paris: Bibliothèque de l'association, 1897.
        [BN 8° Yth 27830, RON Rf. 64.587, ARS GD 8° 38928].

    Rosemonde (drame historique, 3 acts, verse).
        Paris: Bibliothèque de l'association, 1897.
        [BN 8° Yth 28073, RON Rf. 64.588, ARS GD 8° 36736,
        SACD PC 532].

Gilbert (drame, 3 acts, verse).
Paris: Bibliothèque de l'association, 1903.
[RON Rf. 64.589].

Abélard (drame, 3 acts, verse).
Paris: Bibliothèque de l'association, 1904.
[RON Rf. 64.590].

Jeanne d'Arc (drame, 5 acts, verse).
In Revue littéraie de Paris et Champagne, 1906.
[BN 8° Yth 31956, RON Rf. 87.675].

Philumena (drame, 3 acts, verse).
Vanves: éd. du Monde nouveau, 1917.
[RON Rf. 64.591, BHVP in-12 939756].

LE PRIEUR DE BLAINVILLIERS (Anne-Charlotte-Honorée BELLOT, dame).
1764 - Paris, 1820.
Author of romances and articles for the Journal littéraire and the Courrier des spectacles.

Le Port de Morlaix (pantomime-dialogue, prose). Signed Mme L...
[BN ms. fr. 9254].

Le Thé, ou l'Usage à la mode (comedy, 1 act, prose).
Unpublished.
Théâtre de la Gaîté, c. 1800.

L'Heureuse rencontre, ou le Pouvoir d'un bon exemple (comedy, 2 acts, prose). Signed Mme B. L. P***.
Paris: Maldan, 1806.
Paris, Théâtre des jeunes élèves, 1-9-1806.
[BN 8° Yth 8507, BHVP in-8° 611650 (1), SACD PC 291].

LERAY (see GREECH).

LE RICHE (Mlle) (Mlle L. R***).

Caroline et Storm, ou Frédéric digne du trône (melodrama, 3 acts). Co-authored by Labenette. Music by M. Quaisain; ballets by M. Richard.
Paris: Fages, 1804.
Théâtre de l'Ambigu-Comique, 20-9-04.
[BN 8° Yth 2715, RON Rf. 30.022, ARS GD 8° 7003, BHVP in-8° 608970, SACD PC 101].

La Bataille de Neurode (mélodrame à grand spectacle, 3 acts). Music by M. Leblanc. Ballets by M. Hus.
Paris: l'auteur, 1805.
Théâtre de la Gaîté, 28-3-05.
[BN 8° Yth 1779, RON Rf. 30.022, ARS GD 8° 6153, SACD PC 63].

L'Ermite de la Sierre-Morena (melodrama, 3 acts). Music by M. Quaisan.
Paris: Maradan, 1806.
Théâtre de l'Ambigu-Comique, 5-4-06.
[BN 8° Yth 8447, RON Rf. 30.022, ARS GD 8° 11534, BHVP in-8° 609984 (2), SACD PC 288].

LESCUYER (comtesse de).

Blanche (comedy, 3 acts). Signed Comtesse de L***
Montargis: impr. Chrétien, 1852.
[ARS GD 8° 49729].

LESGUILLON (Hermance SANDRIN, Mme Jean).
Paris, 1812 - id., 1882.
Poet and novelist.

Le Prisonnier d'Allemagne (scène).
Paris: Dentu, 1871.
[BN 8° Yth 14773, ARS GD 8° 36548].

Ninette et Ninon (comic opera, 1 act). Music by Penavaire.
Théâtre de la Gaîté, 25-4-73.

LESUEUR (Daniel).
Pseudonym of Jeanne LOISEAU, Mme Henri LAPAUZE.
Paris, 1860 - *id.* 1920.
Feminist novelist and poet.

Hors du mariage.
Théâtre féministe International, 26-6-92; Théâtre des Menus
Plaisirs, 25-6-97.

Fiancée (drame, 4 acts).
Odéon, 20-10-94.
[SACD m. 2897, AN F^{18}727].

Le Masque d'amour (drame, 5 acts and 9 tableaux).
In L'Illustration théâtrale, 04-11-1905.
Théâtre Sarah Bernhardt, 10-10-1905.
[BN 8° Yth 31453, RON Rf. 64.682, ARS GD 8° 46785,
BHVP in-8° 400599].

LETORIÈRE (see PERONNY).

LINANGE (Mme M. de).

Ça passe à 16 ans (comedy, 1 act).
Théâtre de Belleville, 1864.
[AN F^{18}1306].

LISLE (L. de) (see DELISLE).

LOISEAU (see LESUEUR).

LOISSE (Mme de).

Françoise aimable (drame, 1 act).
[SACD PC 260].

LORTAL (Mlle Louise Lavermoadie de).

Ambition trompée (comedy, 2 acts, prose).
Paris, Lyons: Librairie d'Education de Périsse, 1854.
[ARS GD 8° 5096].

Les Aventures de Robert de Non-savoir (tableaux dramatiques).
Paris, Lyons: Périsse, 1854.
[ARS GD 8° 5861].

Le Marquis de Sarus (comedy, 3 acts, verse).
          Paris, Lyons: Périsse, 1854.
          [ARS GD 8° 13691].

Médiocrité et grandeur (comedy, 5 acts, prose).
          Paris, Lyons: Périsse, 1854.
          [ARS GD 8° 13943].

Philaminte ou la Malade imaginaire (comedy, 4 acts, verse).
          Paris, Lyons: Périsse, 1854.
          [ARS GD 8° 16011].

Les Romantiques (comedy, 3 acts, prose)
          Paris: Périsse, 1854.
          [RON Rf. 85889].

Récréations du château de Grenelle (théâtre nouveau pour les distributions de prix et les récréations littéraires dans les pensionnats de demoiselles): "Médiocrité et grandeur", "Les Romantiques", "Philaminte ou la Malade imaginaire", "Ambition trompée", "Les Aventures de Robert de Nonsavoir", "Le Marquis de Sarus".
          Paris, Lyons: Périsse, 1854.
          [BN Yf 9970].

Filiola, ou la Bru de Mme Furius Contradictor (tableaux dramatiques destinés aux récréations littéraires des jeunes filles).
          Paris: Librairie d'éducation de Périsse frères, 1855.
          [RON Rf. 85888].

Les Fêtes du pensionnat de Florigny: "Le Revers de la médaille", "Filiola", "Le Château de la Bouillère", "La Fée des roses", "La Marquise de Grauçot".
          Paris, Lyons: Périsse, 1855.
          [BN Yf 9969].

Le Martyre de Sainte Philomène (drame religieux).
          Paris: Ruffet et Cie., 1872.
          [BN 8° Yth 11330].

Le Revers de la médaille (proverb).
          Paris: Bourguet-Calas, 1875.
          [BN 8° Yth 25340, ARS GD 8° 17165].

La Marquise de Grauçot (tableaux dramatiques).
Paris: Bourguet-Calas, 1877.
[BN 8° Yth 25316].

Julie (drame, 3 acts).
Paris: Bourguet-Calas, 1878.
[BN 8° Yth 25097].

Le Château de la Bouillère, ou Deux jours chez une grande tante (comedy).
Paris: Bourguet-Calas, 1885.
[BN 8° Yth 21745].

LOUIN-MURCIE (Mme).

La Vie manquée (comedy, 4 acts).
Bouffes du Nord, 10-11-92.

LYSLE (Fernand or Fernande de).
Pseudonym of Fernande DUPERRÉ DE LYSLE, Mme VAN DER TAELEN.

Les Sept femmes de Barbe-bleue (verse).
Palais Royal, 1-5-52.
[ARS 4° B.L. 3835].

Un Voisin de campagne (comedy-vaudeville, 2 acts). Co-authored by Edmond de Manne.
Paris: Mifliez, 1852.
Délassements-comiques, 27-3-52.
[BN 8° Yth 4421, ARS GD 8° 45205, BHVP in-8° 611111 (11), AN F^{18}1055^A].

Après l'orage le beau temps (proverb or vaudeville, 1 act). Possibly co-authored by E. de Manne.
Paris: D. Giraud, 1853.
Folies-dramatiques, 15-2-53.
[BN 8° Yth 1058, RON Rf. 44.915, ARS GD 8° 5402, AN F^{18}994].

J'ai perdu ma vicomtesse (folie-vaudeville, 1 act).
Paris: Michel Lévy, 1875.
Folies-Marigny, 10-4-75.
[BN 8° Yth 9220, RON Rf. 44.918, ARS GD 8° 33233].

MAB (see Marie-Anne de BOVET).

MAGUERA (Mme).

  La Leçon d'amour (pantomime, 1 act). Co-authored by P. Franck.
  Batignoles, 14-10-92.

MALGAT (Madeleine).

  Les Barbets (comic opera, 2 acts).
  In Revue Monégasque, 1-3-1894.
  [BN 8° Yth 29906, RON Rf. 80628, ARS GD 8° 38386].

MALLAC (see Jenny SABATIER).

MALLET (Joséphine).
  Author of studies of the Bible and of women in prison.

  Jeanne d'Arc (drame, 5 acts, 15 tableaux, prose).
  Paris: Librairie générale des auteurs, 1867.
  [BN 8° Yth 9433, RON Rf. 87.687, ARS GD 8° 24413, BHVP
  in-18 610006 (5)].

MANCEAU (Adélaïde-Victoire-Antoinette de LUSSAULT, Mme).
  Near Lagny, 1788 - ?
  Boarding school teacher; author of children's novels.

  Théâtre des jeunes filles: "Les Vacances", "La Fausse sous-maîtresse,
  ou la Bonté gagne tous les coeurs", "Le Retour désiré", "L'Inspectrice
  du pensionnat", "Les Deux filles adoptives", "Les Petites institutrices
  ambulantes".
  Paris: Périsse, 1851.
  [BN Yf 10006].

  Le Portefeuille perdu (vaudeville, 1 act, prose).
  Paris: Périsse, 1857.
  [RON Rf. 85919].

  Théâtre destiné aux récréations littéraire dans les pensionnats de
  jeunes filles: "Un Page sous Charles-Quint", "La Jalousie",
  "Dévouement de Régulus", "Le Portefeuille perdu", "Le Roi de la
  Saint-Nicolas", "Mauvaise tête et bon coeur", "Frédéric et Colas".
  Paris: Périsse, 1857.
  [RON Rf. 85920].

Nouveau théâtre de la jeunesse (scènes et dialogues pour les fêtes des pensionnats de jeunes filles): "Le Prix de la vertu", "La Belle-mère et la belle-fille", "La Sainte-Catherine", "La Fille inconnue", "Les Jeunes filles corrigées", "La Tante inconnue".
  Paris: Sarlit, 1870.
  [BN 8° Yf 146, RON Rf. 85918].

MANCEL (Sabine) (Mme Ed. Mancel).
  Pseudonym: Jacques SABINE.

La Leçon de Reowa (scène). Music by Lemaire.
  Private performance, 4-3-95.

En tandem (saynète, 1 act). Co-authored by B. Rey (d'Ulmès).
  Grand Guignol, 5-11-98.
  [AN F^{18}1217].

La Fille du roi René (comédie lyrique, 1 act, verse). Music by P. Jumel, R. Lapara and C. Spirelli.
  Grenoble: impr. Allier fr., 1900.
  Mathurins, 12-6-99.
  [BN 8° Yth 29204, RON Rf. Rés. 18.721, BHVP in-16 121363].

MANÉGLIER (Mlle Sophie).
  Poet.

Comédies en prose et en vers: "Charles ou le Jeune avocat" (3 acts, prose), "Amour, honneur, patrie" (4 acts, prose), "Il ne faut jurer de rien" (3 acts, verse), "Une Vieille fille" (4 acts, verse), "Qui choisit prend le pire" (3 acts, prose), "Rage de noblesse" (5 acts, prose).
  Reims: impr. Coopérative, 1879.
  [BN Yf 10010, RON Rf. 77411].

MANUELA (Mme).
Pseudonym of Marie-Adrienne-Anne-Victorienne-Clémentine de ROCHECHOUART-MONTEMERT, duchesse d'UZES.
1847 - 1933.
Member of the Union des femmes peintres et sculpteurs; author of novels, poetry, travel narratives and an essay on women and the vote.

Le Coeur et le sang (drame, 3 acts).
> Paris: impr. S. Merlandier, 1890.
> Théâtre de L'Application, 23-5-91.
> [BN 16° Yth 1710, RON Rf. 44.981].

Germaine (opera). Music by F. Thorné.
> Private performance, 12-4-95.

Au Soleil d'or (operetta, 1 act).
> Folies Parisiennes, 1899.

Une Saint-Hubert sous Louis XV (saynète, 1 act, verse).
> Paris: A. Lemerre, 1909.
> Pré-Catalan, 27-6-1920.
> [RON Rf. 73.616].

Nord-Sud (comedy, 2 acts).
> Le Lycéum, 29-3-1922.

MARBOUTY (Mme) (see Claire BRUNNE).

MARC (Mlle).

La Dame au bois dormant (comic opera, 1 act). Co-authored by Delorme. Music by Leroy.
> Galerie Vivienne, 11-2-95.
> [AN F^{18}135 7].

MARC (Rose-*Emilie*).

Sous un parapluie (comedy, 1 act).
> Rouen: impr. de D. Brière et fils, 1867.
> Rouen, Centre dramatique, 24-11-67.
> [BN 8° Yth 16778].

Les Suites d'un coup de vent (comedy, 1 act).
Rouen: impr. H. Boissel, 1867.
Rouen, Centre dramatique, 24-11-67.
[BN 8° Yth 16883].

Un Préjugé (comedy, 1 act).
Rouen: impr. de D. Brière et fils, 1872.
Rouen, Théâtre Français, 1-6-72.
[BN 8° Yth 18165, RON Rf. 79492].

MARCELLI (Mme Anaïs).
Pseudonym of Mme la comtesse A. PERRIERE-PILTÉ.
Poetry.

La Contagion (comedy, 1 act, prose).
Théâtre Beaumarchais, 25-5-59.

A Beyrouth (vaudeville, 1 act).
Théâtre Beaumarchais, 25-1-61.

Le Sorcier (comic opera, 1 act).
Paris: Michel Lévy, 1866.
Théâtre-Lyrique Impérial, 13-6-66.
[BN 8° Yth 16705, RON Rf. 45.021, ARS GD 8° 368, AN
$F^{18}738$].

Jaloux de soi (comic opera, 1 act).
Théâtre de la Gaîté, 6-6-73.

Le Talon d'Achille, ou la Raison et l'amour (dramatic comedy, 3 acts,
verse).
N.p.: Impr. Claye, 1865.
Porte St. Martin, 25-4-75.
[ARS GD 8° 35699, BHVP in-18 610037 (1)].

Jeu de dominos ou une Nuit sous Louis Quinze (comedy, 1 act, verse).
[AN $F^{18}1535$].

MARIETTI (Mme).

Patoura au Dahomey (pantomime, 1 act). Co-authored by Boucart.
Théâtre des Nouveautés, 24-12-95.

MARILLY (Mme Octave).

> Dire et faire (proverb, 1 act).
> > Paris: chez tous les libraires (Répertoire des salons), 1857.
> > [BN 8° Yth 5230, ARS GD 8° 23100].

MARNI (Jeanne) (see Twentieth Century volume).

MARSAY (Mme Févrie de).

> L'Anniversaire (comedy, 1 act).
> > Théâtre de l'Application, 10-5-99.

MARTEL de JANVILLE (comtesse de) (see GYP).

MARTIN DE VERM[AREN] (Marie) (Marie Martir de Verm..., marquise de ***).

> La Clef du masque ou Flora (drame historique).
> > Paris: impr. de Cosse et G. Laguionic, 1838.
> > [RON Rf. 30.803, ARS GD 8° 7564, SACD].

MARTY (Dorothée Rose TIBAUT-LAVEAUX, Mme Jean-Baptiste).
Stuttgart, 1786 - Charenton, 1861.

> La Malédiction paternelle (melodrama).
> > Unpublished.
> > Staged at Bordeaux.

> La Peste de Marseille (historical melodrama, 3 acts). Co-authored by Guilbert de Pixérécourt and Pellissier.
> > Paris: Duvernois, 1828.
> > Théâtre de la Gaîté, 2-8-28.
> > [BN 8° Yth 13852, ARS GD 8° 15891, AN F^{18}606^B].

MASTERS (Julia).

> Les Scellés (comedy, 3 acts).
> > Paris: impr. Alcan-Lévy, 1882.
> > [RON Rf. 45.138, ARS GD 8° 26214].

MATHIEU (Mlle Emilie).

> L'Orpheline (comedy, 1 act).
> > In La Poupée modèle, 15-11-1890.
> > [BN 4° R. 82, ARS GD 8° 46396].

La Babillarde (comedy, 1 act). Also attributed to Emile Mathieu
Lille: Desclé, de Brower et Cie, 1896.
[BN 8° Yth 27509].

La Somnambule (comedy, 1 act). Also attributed to Emile Mathieu
Lille: Desclé, de Brower et Cie, 1896.
[BN 8° Yth 27518].

Les Bijoux de la marquise (comedy, 1 act).
Lille: Desclé, de Brower et Cie, 1903.
[BN 8° Yth 30415].

Le Jeune fanfaron (comedy, 1 act).
Lille: Desclé, de Brower et Cie, 1903.
[BN 8° Yth 30417].

Trop heureuse (comedy, 1 act).
Lille: Desclé, de Brower et Cie, 1903.
[BN 8° Yth 30418].

Un Catalogue du Louvre (comedy, 1 act).
Lille: Desclé, de Brower et Cie, 1903.
[BN 8° Yth 30416].

MAUCS (Mlle).

Le Félon (drame historique, 3 acts, prose). Co-authored by Merville
(P.-F. Camus). Music by Amédée.
Paris: Malaisie, 1830.
Ambigu-Comique, 2-2-30.
[BN 8° Yth 6759, AN F^{18}937].

MAUGIRARD (Victorine).

Les Soirées de sociétés ou Nouveaux proverbes dramatiques, 2 tomes.
Paris: Thuiller, 1813.
[RON Rf. 82.833 (1-2), ARS GD 8° 2215, SACD P29].

MAX (Mme Lucie).

Oreste et Pylade (monologue bouffe).
Périgueux: impr. de Dupont, 1883.
[BN 8° Yth 20925].

L'Amour maternel (dramatic monologue).
    Périgueux: impr. de Dupont, 1883.
    [BN 8° Yth 21015].

Oeuvres complètes. Contains:
"Le Truc ou le Traquenard du Colonel" (comedy, 1 act),
    Concert des Ternes, 23-4-87;
"Un Sous-préfet en détresse" (dialogue, verse), "Il ne faut pas se fier aux apparences" (dialogue, verse), "Sarah, ou le Sorcier l'avait dit" (dialogue, verse), "A chacun selon ses oeuvres" (petite pièce pour pensionnats), "Une Leçon inutile" (petite pièce pour pensionnats), "La Méprise de Barnabé" (intermède comique), "Un Brevet supérieur" (vaudeville, 1 act), "Le Hanneton de M. Malarmé" (vaudeville, 1 act), "Un Million de dot" (vaudeville, 1 act), "Un Arrêté municipal ou le Mariage de Rosette" (vaudeville, 1 act), "Les Deux billets ou Tout est bien qui finit bien" (vaudeville, 1 act), "Oreste et Pylade ou les Tribulations de l'amitié" (monologue-bouffe), "Satanée Mandarine !" (opérette, 1 act), "Un Mariage à la porte" (opérette, 1 act).
    Paris: Dentu, 1890-1891.
    [BN 8° Z. 12023, ARS GD 3476].

MAYNARD (Caroline).
Author of one novel and a collection of poetry.

Nos petits monologues et dialogues (11 monologues, 3 dialogues).
    Paris: Fischbacher, 1894.
    [BN 8° Yf. 664, RON Rf. 85963].

MECHTCHERSKI (see DORIAN).

MELIN (see MILNE).

MENESTRIER (see MINETTE).

MERCKEL (Mme Emile).

Le Bonheur en trois mots (comedy, 1 act, prose).
    Brest: imp. Lefournier, 1865.
    Paris, Théâtre des Variétés, 8-8-1865.
    [ARS GD 8° 31269].

MERCOEUR (Elisa).
Nantes, 1809 - Paris, 1835.
Poet and novelist.

Abencerrages ou Boabit, roi de Grenade (tragedy, 5 acts, verse).
[RON ms. 606].

MÉRÉ(E) (la baronne de) (see GUÉNARD).

METZ (Mlle M. de).

Dévouement filial (comedy, 1 act).
Paris: Larousse, 1887.
[BN 8° Yth 22485].

Les Idées de Rosalie (comedy, 2 acts and 3 tableaux).
Paris: Larousse, 1888.
[BN 8° Yth 22896, RON Rf. 86027].

Bianca ou la Vengeance du bandit (drame, 2 acts).
Paris: Larousse, 1891.
[BN 8° Yth 24345].

Un Conte de Perrault (comedy for young girls, 3 acts).
Paris: Larousse, 1894.
[BN 8° Yth 30974].

Un Héritage (comedy, 1 act).
Paris: Larousse, 1903.
[BN 8° Yth 30269].

MEUNIER (Mme Stanislas).

Théâtre de salon. Contains six one-act comedies: "Belle-mère !",
"Avant le suicide", "Le Séminariste", "Le Rendez-vous", "Les Silex",
"Le Nihiliste".
Paris: A. Lemerre, 1894.
Private performance.
[BN 8° Yf 703, RON Rf. 84.325, ARS GD 8° 3275].

MEYERHEIM (Jane).

L'Enfant du mari. Co-authored by Serge Rello.
Nouveau Théâtre (Théâtre Féministe), 1898.
[AN F^{18}1243].

MICHEL (Louise).

Vroncourt (Haute Marne), 1830 - Marseilles, 1905.

School teacher affiliated with the International; deported for her activities in the Commune of Paris (1871); militant anarchist after the amnesty (1881).

Nadine (drame, 5 acts).
Bouffes du Nord, 29-4-82.
[AN F^{18}116 7^A].

Le Coq rouge (drame, 6 acts and 8 tableaux).
Paris: Edinger, 1888.
Théâtre des Batignoles, 19-5-88.
[RON Rf. 45.555, ARS GD 8° 32251, BHVP in-16 615 181].

La Grève (drame, 5 acts).
La Villette, 6-12-90.
[AN F^{18}1321].

MILNE (Mme) (also Pauline de MÉLIN).

Pseudonyms of Apolline GROSJEAN.

Actress.

Vient de paraître de la Profanation de l'art or de La Prostitution de l'art (satire, 1 act). Co-authored by N***.
Paris: Dentu, 1864.
[BN 8° Yth 19133, RON Rf. 45.358, ARS GD 8° 36121,
BHVP in-16 5305].

MINETTE

Pseudonym of Mlle Jeanne Marie Françoise MÉNESTRIER.

Besançon, 1789 - Neuilly-sur-Seine, 1853.

Actress.

Piron chez Procope (vaudeville, 1 act). Co-authored by Th. Pelicier.
Paris: Mason, 1810.
Théâtre du Vaudeville, 25-7-10.
[BN 8° Yth 14300, RON Rf. 31.484].

MINETTI (Mme Paule).

Le Pain de la honte et Qui l'emportera ?
Maison du Peuple, 24-5-94.

MIRABEAU (Marie le HARIVEL de GONNEVILLE, la comtesse de).
Pseudonym: Aymar de FLAGY.
Cossesseville (Calvados), 1829 - ?
Historical and religious novels; mother of Gyp.

Châteaufort (comedy, 3 acts).
Gymnase dramatique, 13-7-76.
[AN F^{18}843].

MIRABEAU (S.-M.-G.-A. de RIQUETTI de) (see GYP).

MOGADOR (see CHABRILLAN).

MOISSONNIER (Mme Amélie).
Winner of the *Concours à Victor Hugo*.

Les Légionnaires du Rhône, épisode de 1870-1871 (comedy-melodrama, 5 acts).
Lyons: imp. Générale, 1883.
[BN 8° Yth 21088].

Le Vieux mineur (scène dramatique, 1 act, verse).
Vienna: L. Girard, 1887.
Théâtre de Vienne, 10-4-1887.
[ARS GD 8° 37295].

MOLÉ-LÉGER (Mme) (Mlle Julie DELAVIGNE, also called Mme MOLÉ aîné DALAINVILLE; later Mme LÉGER, also called MOLÉ-LÉGER; and finally Mme ALBITTE, also called la comtesse ALBITTE DE VALLIVON).
c. 1777 - 1832 (or 1845).
Actress.

Les Vainqueurs généreux, ou le Triomphe de la liberté (comedy, 1 act, prose). Signed la citoyenne Molé (actrice de Paris).
Amsterdam: C.N. Guérin, 1795.
[ARS GD 8° 1308].

Misanthropie et repentir (drame, 5 acts, prose).
Adaptation of German play by Kotzebue (Menschenhass und Rue, 1789) from a translation by Mme Bursay.
Paris: le Libraire au Théâtre du Vaudeville, an VII (1799).
Odéon, 28-12-1798; Comédie Française, 30-8-1800.
[BN Yf 11241, RON Rf. 18.934, ARS GD 8° 14188, SACD PC 413, TF 1 MIS Kot].

La Paix, ou l'Heureux retour (comedy).
   Théâtre des Nouveaux Troubadours, 28-7-07.

L'Orgueil puni (comedy, 1 act, prose).
   Paris: Mme Masson, 1809.
   Théâtre de l'Impératrice (Odéon), 27-3-09.
   [BN 8° Yth 13145, RON Rf. 18.938, ARS GD 8° 21460,
   OP LIV. 19/1371a, SACD PC 451, TF 2 MOL Org 1809].

Les Indiens (comedy, 4 acts).
   Théâtre de l'Impératrice (Odéon), 1810.

MON (Blanche-Denise) (D. Mon).
   Poet.

Graine de paradis (scène). Co-authored by Marque.
   Paris: A. Ghio, 1880.
   [BN 8° Yth 25084, ARS GD 8° 26416].

L'Etang (poème dramatique).
   Paris: Vanier, 1886.

Un Mari dans les branches (saynète).
   Paris: Tresse et Stock, 1890.
   [BN 8° Yth 24335].

L'Automobiliste écrasante (monologue).
   Paris: Stock, 1902.
   [BN 8° Yth 30074].

La Lessive de marraine (monologue).
   Paris: Stock, 1902.
   [BN 8° Yth 30089].

MONMERQUÉ (Mme de) (see SAINT-SURIN).

MONTANCLOS (dame de) (see Eighteenth Century).

MONTGOMERY (née Lucy DITTE, Madame G. de).
Saint-Rémy (Seine-et-Oise), 1861 - ?
Poet.

Aréthuse (idylle antique).
Moutiers-Tarentaise: Ducloz, 1894.
Théâtre de Monte-Carlo, 10-2-1894.
[ARS GD 8° 38293].

MONTIFAUD (Marc de) (also Paul Erasme, Ibo).
Pseudonyms of Mme Léon QUIVOGNE DE MONTIFAUD, née Marie
CHARTOULE DE MONTIFAUD.
Paris, 1850 - ?
Author of several works, notably the anticlerical book Les Vestales de
l'Eglise; journalist for La Fronde ; co-founder of L'Art Moderne.

Nos sous-officiers (drame, 5 acts). Co-authored by de Ricaudy.
Bouffes du Nord, 20-12-90.
[AN F^{18}116 8].

Le Petit Balandard (comedy, 1 act). Co-authored by E. Blédort.
Bataclan, 20-2-92.

A la frontière (drame, 5 acts).
Théâtre de Montparnasse, 8-10-92.

La Loi d'Aristote (1 act, verse).
Théâtre des Poètes, 23-5-93.

Un Crime héroïque (patriotic monologue).
Paris: A Repos, 1895.
[BN 4° Yth 6159].

Le Forçat (drame, 5 acts).
Grenelle, 22-8-96.

Alsace (1 act, verse).
Paris: A Michel, 1904.
[BN 8° Yth 30641].

MONTRESOR (Mme A. de).

> La Défense de Strasbourg (pièce historique et populaire à grand spectacle, 5 acts, 8 tableaux). Co-authored by Charles Prillard.
> > Lyons: impr. de J. Rossier, 1871.
> > [BN 8° Yth 4512].

> Pour la patrie (comedy, 1 act).
> > Besançon: Ch. Cahot, 1872.
> > [BN 8° Yth 14544, RON Rf. 77541, ARS GD 8° 33940, SACD PC 494].

> Le Cousin de ma femme (vaudeville, 1 act). Co-authored by Charles Prillard (mentioned in Pour la patrie).

MOREAU (Elise) (see GAGNE).

MORETON (comtesse Lionel de de) (see CHABRILLAN).

MORVANCHER (see GUÉNOT-MORVANCHER).

MOUSTELON (Mme Elisabeth).

> Un Mariage (drame, 1 act, verse).
> > N.p., n.d.
> > [ARS 8° 45391].

MOUZAY (Mme la comtesse Fanny de).
Author of children's books and religious novels.

> Le Portrait de la jardinière, ou la Fin justifie les moyens (comedy-proverb).
> > Paris: Dentu, 1863.
> > Salle Herz, 9-4-63.
> > [BN 8° Yth 14485, RON Rf. 84.365].

> Monsieur mon secrétaire (monologue).
> > Poitiers: impr. A Dupré, 1878.
> > [BN 8° Yth 25965].

MÜLLER (Alexandre) (see Céline FALLET).

MULLERAS (Mme Marie).

> Les Deux amours (comedy, 1 act).
> > Théâtre St. Marcel, 26-4-60.

NANTES (Antoine de) (see Mme DUPUIS).

NAVERY (Raoul de).
> Pseudonym of Marie SAFFRAY, Mme CHERVET.
> Pseudonym used for plays: Marie DAVID.
> Ploërmel, 1831 (or 1834) - La Ferté-sous-Jouarre (S.-et Marne), 1885.
> Novelist and poet.

> Nanita la bohémienne (comedy-vaudeville, 1 act).
> > Metz: Alcan, Léhuby, 1856.
> > Private performance at the residence of M. de Roeder.
> > [BN 8° Yth 12550].

> Souvenirs du Pensionnat (drames et mystères dédiés aux élèves des maisons du Sacré Coeur).
> "Marthe et Marie" (mystère, 1 act, verse),
> > Sacré-Coeur de Metz, 15-8-1856;
> "La Princesse Myosotis ou la Reine d'un jour" (comedy-vaudeville, 1 act),
> > Sacré-Coeur de Metz, 25-6-1856;
> "L'Enfant prodigue" (drame biblique, 3 acts, verse);
> "Bibiche et Musette" (vaudeville, 1 act),
> > Sacré-Coeur de Metz, 1-1-1857.
> > Paris: Douniol; Lyons: Girard et Josserand, 1857.
> > [ARS GD 8° 4553].

> Sabine (comedy, 1 act, prose).
> > In Théâtre des salons. Ed. E. Rasetti. Impr. Jouast, 1859.
> > Private performance at the residence of M. de Roeder.
> > [BN Yf 11919, RON Rf. 84.454].

> La Fête de famille (comedy, 1 act).
> > In La Ruche Parisienne, 12-4-62.
> > [BN Z. 10012, RON Rf. 46.169].

Les Fils aînés de la République (drame, 5 acts, 9 tableaux). Co-authored by M. Masson.
>   Paris: Maillet, 1873.
>   Grand Théâtre Parisien, 23-11-72.
>   [BN 8° Yth 7198, RON Rf. 46.170, ARS GD 8° 291, AN F^{18}12 59].

Comédies, drames et proverbes. Contains: "Marthe et Marie-Madeleine" (mystère, 1 act, verse), "A brebis tondue Dieu mesure le vent" (proverb), "La Laitière et le pot au lait" (comedy-vaudeville, 1 act), "Ruth et Noémi" (drame biblique), "Paquita" (vaudeville, 1 act), "La Fille du roi Yvetot" (vaudeville, 1 act), "La Fille de Jaïre" (mystère), "Nathalie" (drame, 3 acts, verse).
>   Paris: A Le Clerc et C. Dillet, n.d.
>   [ARS 8° B.L. 15.241].

NELLY or **NELLI** (Mme H. de G.).
Novelist.

Jour des prix dans un pensionnat (comedy, 3 acts). Signed Mme N.D.G. NELLI.
>   Paris: Delacombe, 1839.
>   [BN 8° Yth 9791, SACD PC 335].

NÉRON (Marie-Louise).
Novelist.

La Lune de miel parlementaire (comedy, 1 act).
>   Paris: Motteroz, 1900.
>   Bodinière, 4-5-99.
>   [BN 8° Yth 29285, RON Rf. 68.338, ARS GD 8° 24394, BHVP in-18 121343, AN F^{18}1301].

NESLE (Mme Roger de).
Poet.

L'Astronome et la muse (dialogue, verse).
>   Paris: A. Ghio, 1887.
>   [BN 8° Ye. Pièce 1626, ARS GD 8° 30100].

Le Soulier de Noël (monologue, verse).
>   Paris: A. Ghio, 1887.
>   [BN 8° Yth 22420].

NIBOYET (Eugénie MOUCHON, Mme).
Montpellier, 1797 - Paris, 1883.
Militant feminist, saint-simonnienne; founder of La Paix des deux mondes, Conseiller des femmes, Journal pour toutes and Société de la Voix des Femmes; novelist.

Le Protecteur (vaudeville, 1 act). Co-authored by Lurine.
Théâtre du Vaudeville, 10-5-37.
[AN F^{18}746^A].

La Justice au village (comedy).
Théâtre de M. Comte (Théâtre Choiseul), 23-12-37.
[AN F^{18}1186^B].

L'Atelier de David ou les Jeunes peintres (vaudeville, 1 act). Co-authored by Mélanie Dumont.
Théâtre du Gymnase Enfantin, 1-8-40.
[AN F^{18}118 4].

NINOUS (Pierre) (see ROUSSEN).

NIXARPA (Eiluj) (see BATTHYANY).

NOUR (Mlle).

La Petite correspondance (comedy, 1 act). Co-authored by Lescalier.
Also attributed to Michel Nour.
Théâtre Moncey, 11-5-95.
[AN F^{18}13 57].

OLAGNIER (Mme Marguerite).

Le Saïs (conte arabe, 4 acts, with music).
Paris: Tresse, 1882.
Renaissance, 18-12-81.
[BN 8° Yth 20506, RON Rf. 46.399, ARS GD 8° 35475].

OLIVETTI (Mme N.).

Le Revenant (drame, 5 acts, 11 tableaux).
Paris: Librairie théâtrale, 1862.
[BN 8° Yth 15460, ARS GD 8° 35300].

ORDRE (Sophie MOSER, baronne T.-J. du WICQUET d').
    Born in Switzerland.
    Author of fables, poems and short stories.

    Histoires dramatiques: "La Bataille de Sempach", "Le Retour de Marie
    Stuart en Ecosse", "Les Bannis à la bataille de Morgarten" (drames, 5
    acts).
        Paris: G.A. Dentre, 1839.
        [BN Yf 10533, RON Rf. 32.259, SACD P31].

OTTENFELS (Baronne d').

    Un Décret d'exil (comedy, 1 act). Signed Baronne ***.
        Paris: Librairie Théâtrale L. Michaud, 1883.
        Performed at the homes of Mmes du Terrail and de Castex.
        [RON Rf. 84.398, ARS GD 8° 28053].

OUTRELEAU (Mlle A. d').

    Charité (charade, 4 acts).
        Lyons: P.-N. Josserand, 1867.
        [BN Yf 10538 (1)].

    L'Etude et le plaisir (dialogue, 1 act).
        Lyons: P.-N. Josserand, 1867.
        [BN Yf 10538 (2), ARS GD 8° 32420].

    Courage (charade, 3 acts).
        Lyons: P.-N. Josserand, 1867.
        [BN Yf 10538 (3)].

    Orphée (charade, 3 acts).
        Lyons: P.-N. Josserand, 1867.
        [BN Yf 10538 (6), ARS GD 8° 34673].

    Roseaux (charade, 3 acts).
        Lyons: P.-N. Josserand, 1867.
        [BN Yf 10538 (5), ARS GD 8° 35431].

    Le Secret du bonheur (comedy, 3 acts).
        Lyons: P.-N. Josserand, 1867.
        [BN Yf 10538 (4), ARS GD 35531].

La Morale sous les fleurs. (collection of above plays).
Lyons: P.-N. Josserand, 1867.
[BN Yf 10538].

PACCAUD (Elisa).

Essais dramatiques et moraux. Signed Mlle E.-P. Co-authored by Juchereau ("l'auteur de FLORENCE").
Contains: "Félicie et Charlotte, ou l'Orgueil puni et la vertu récompensée" (5 acts, prose), "Geneviève, ou les Bienfaits de la providence et de la religion" (prose).
Lille: Lefort, 1833.
[BN Yf 9228].

PANNIER (Mme Sophie).

La Sortie du collège, ou le Choix d'un état (comedy, prose).
In Les Jours de congé, ou Les matinées du grand oncle.
Paris: Postel fils, 1838.
[BN R. 39688, ARS GD 8° 15912, SACD PC 474].

PATON (Mme Emilie-Thérèse, née PACINI).
Pseudonym: Jacques ROZIER.
? - 1887.
Novelist.

Le Divorce de Sarah Moore (drame, 3 acts).
Théâtre de la rue Louvois (Odéon), 16-4-85.
[AN F^{18}724].

PATUSSET (Mme).

Chadi (bouffe, 1 act). Co-authored by Valnod.
Eldorado, 13-2-94.

PEAN DE LA ROCHE-JAGU (see ROCHE-JAGU).

PENQUER (Léocadie HERSENT, Mme Auguste).
Château de Kerouartz (Finistère), 1827 - Brest, 1889.
Poet; honorary member of the Société Académique de Brest.

L'Œillet rose (comedy, 1 act, verse).
Paris: A. Lemerre, 1874.
Théâtre de Brest, 14-5-1874.
[BN 8° Yth 12944, RON Rf. 77163, ARS GD 8° 39211].

PÉRIÉ (see CANDEILLE).

PERRIERE-PILTÉ (see MARCELLI).

PERRONNET (Amélie) (Amélie Léopardine GOUSSAN).
Pseudonym: Léon BERNOUX.
? - 1903.
Composer, singing teacher.

La Saint-François (comedy, 1 act).
Paris: Librairie dramatique, 1868.
Odéon, 8-1-68.
[BN 8° Yth 29675, RON Rf. 46.632, ARS GD 8° 232, BHVP
in-16 607982 (2), SACD, AN F^{18}719].

Les Revenants (comedy).
Salle Herz, 1868.
[AN F^{18}1347].

Monsieur et Madame, épisode de guerre (monologue, verse).
Paris: Dentu, 1872.
Théâtre de Cluny, 13-3-71; Salle Herz (performed by Mlle
Magnier of the Théâtre du Gymnase).
[RON Rf. 46.627, ARS GD 8° 28412, SACD].

Chien et chat (1 act).
Théâtre Italien, 21-4-72.

Ce qui brouille les femmes (comedy, 1 act).
Salle Herz, 1874.
[AN F^{18}13 49^A].

John et Jean (comedy-vaudeville, 1 act).
Théâtre de Cluny, 28-2-75.
[AN F^{18}1031].

La Succession chamouillée (1 act).
Salle Herz, 14-5-76.
[AN F^{18}13 59^B].

La Chanson de l'Aubépin (comic opera, 1 act).
Théâtre Italien, 12-3-77; Galerie Vivienne, 8-4-95.

Gilles de Bretagne (opera, 4 acts, 5 tableaux). Music by H. Kowalsski.
Paris: Tresse: 1879.
Théâtre Lyrique, 24-12-78.
[BN 8° Yth 20084, ARS GD 8° 29875, BHVP in-16 619 872,
SACD PC 271].

Je reviens de Compiègne (comedy, 1 act).
Salle Erard 3-2-78; Porte St. Martin, 7-4-78.
[AN F^{18}1350^A].

Catiche et Gribiche (comedy for children, 1 act).
Paris: Librairie théâtrale, 1884.
Théâtre Déjazet, 25-11-83.
[BN 8° Yth 21456, RON Rf. 46.628].

Les Révoltes de Liline (1 act for children, prose).
Paris: Librairie théâtrale, 1885.
Théâtre du Châtelet, 18-4-84.
[BN 8° Yth 21764, RON Rf. 46.629, AN F^{18}1347].

Malechance [sic](monologue for children).
Paris: Librairie théâtrale, 1886.
[BN 8° Yth 22008, RON Rf. 83.708].

Le Ménage de Scapin (1 act, verse).
Paris: Librairie Molière, 1901.
Salle Herz, 13-5-66; Salle Beethoven, 21-3-87.
[BN 8° Yth 29675, RON Rf. 46.632, ARS GD 8° 33476,
SACD PC 406].

Un Coup de tête (comedy, 1 act).
Paris: Librairie théâtrale, 1885.
Salle Labourdney, 6-11-87.
[BN 8° Yth 21660, RON Rf. 46.630, ARS GD 8° 27135,
BHVP in-16 619 509].

Mozart enfant (comedy, 1 act).
Théâtre Indépendant, 22-3-88.

La Cigale madrilène (comic opera, 2 acts). Music by Joanni Perronnet.
Paris: Librairie théâtrale, 1889.
Opéra-Comique, 15-2-89.
[BN 8° Yth 23432, RON Rf. 46.631, ARS GD 8° 31763,
SACD, AN F^{18}700].

Entre serin et moineau (dialogue philosophique et humoristique).
Paris: Librairie théâtrale, 1899.
[BN 8° Yth 28923, BHVP in-16 619 932].

Capitulation (scène, 1 act).
Salle Lancry, 18-6-95.

Cascarette (opera, 1 act).
Théâtre de l'Application, 27-2-98.
[AN F^{18}1300].

Pauv' Zizi ! (comedy, 1 act).
Paris: Librairie Molière, 1901.
Théâtre de l'Application (Bodinière), 11-3-99.
[BN 8° Yth 29676, RON Rf. 46.633, ARS GD 8° 34848,
BHVP in-16 619 403, SACD PC 467, AN F^{18}1301].

Le Marchand de sable a passé.
Paris: Librairie théâtrale, 1900.
[BN 8° Yth 29231, BHVP in-16 619 874].

Le Petit billet (monologue, verse).
Paris: Librairie théâtrale, 1901.
[BN 8° Yth 29677].

Sermon à la poupée (monologue for children, verse).
Paris: Librairie Molière, 1901.
[BN 8° Yth 29678].

Le Songe d'un soir d'été (1 act, with songs).
Salle du Journal, 1902.
[AN F^{18}13 64].

PERRY BIAGIOLI (Mlle Antonine).
Born in Paris.

La Première leçon (saynète, verse).
Paris: Librairie générale, 1873.
[RON Rf. 46.642, ARS GD 8° 30335].

Les Héroïques (drame lyrique, 3 parts). Music by Henri Perry-Biagioli.
Paris: Calmann Lévy, 1876.
Opéra Comique, 4-5-76.
[BN 8° Yth 22606, RON Rf. 46.643, ARS GD 8° 32936].

PERT (Camille).
Pseudonym of Louise Hortense GRILLE, Mme H. ROUGEUL.
Lille, 1865 - 1952.
Novelist.

La Camarade (comedy, 3 acts, 4 tableaux).
Union Nationale, rue de Lancry, 28-1-99.
[AN F^{18}14 63].

PEYRONNY (Henriette d'ISLE, Mme la vicomtesse Jules de).
Pseudonym: Vicomte Georges de LETORIÈRE.
Novelist.

Une Provinciale (comedy, 4 acts).
In Théâtre des Inconnus 8 (15-7-1873); Paris: C. Lévy, 1877.
Troisième Théâtre Français, 8-5-77.
[BN 8° Yth 19906, ARS GD 8° 33401, BHVP in-8° 607901
(2)].

La Part du butin (comedy, 1 act).
Paris: Ollendorff, 1880.
Gymnase Dramatique, 11-3-80.
[BN 8° Yth 20297, ARS GD 8° 34820, BHVP in-8° 607830
(4), AN F^{18}845].

La Corbeille de mariage (comedy, 1 act).
Paris: Ollendorff, 1878.
Salle des Agriculteurs, 26-11-96.
[BHVP in-18° 17550 (5)].

PHILASTRE (Mme).

Le Tremblement de terre de Mendoce (drame, 5 acts). Co-authored by
Frantz Beauvallet.
Théâtre de l'Ambigu-Comique, 27-6-72.
[AN F^{18}960].

PIPELET DE LEURY (see SALM-DYCK).

PIRIOU (Marie).

La Boîte de Pandore (comédie mythologique, 1 act, verse).
N.p., [1875].
[ARS GD 8° 38359].

PLAGNIOL (see SAINTE-MARIE).

PLAINCHANT de LEVANGE (Mme H., née DELAIRE).

> La Ville et la campagne (comedy, 2 acts).
>> Paris: Tresse, 1854.
>> [BN 8° Yth 19197, RON Rf. 46.693, ARS GD 8° 19113].

> On ne prévoit jamais tout (comedy, 1 act, prose).
>> Paris: Tresse, 1855.
>> [BN 8° Yth 13041, ARS GD 8° 15261].

POILLOÜE de SAINT-MARS (see DASH).

POLI (Clémentine-Félicie-Hemery CHOISEUL-GOUFFIER, comtesse Jean-Philippe de).
> Pseudonym: Raymond de BELFEUIL.

> Cousin et cousine (comedy, 1 act).
>> Paris: Impr. des Apprentis orphelins d'Auteuil, 1884.
>> Salle Kriegelstein, 18-5-84.
>> [BN 8° Yth 21525].

> Corbeille de mariages (vaudeville, 1 act). Signed Raymond de Belfeuil.
>> Paris: Dentu, 1885.
>> Concert des Ternes, 12-12-85.
>> [SACD].

> Les Deux Charlotte (dialogue).
>> Paris: Dentu, 1885.
>> [BN 8° Yth 21881].

> L'Hospitalité ou la Mort (operetta, 1 act).
>> Concert des Ternes, 8-5-86.

PRIOU (Mme Louise).
> Author of poetry for children.

> Causerie avant la classe, un lundi matin (dialogue).
>> Paris: Maugars, 1867.
>> [BN Yf 12895, SACD PC 105].

Les Muguets (petites scènes et dialogues pour pensionnats de demoiselles).
>   Paris: Maugars, 1879.
>   [BN Yf 12895].

PRIVAT (Marie).

L'Homme du siècle (vaudeville, 1 act).
>   Théâtre des Batignoles, 16-8-90.
>   [AN F^{18}131 5].

Louise d'Albret (drame, 5 acts).
>   Théâtre des Batignoles, 18-8-90.
>   [AN F^{18}1315].

PRUDHOMME (Marguerite).

La Nuit de Noces de Beauflanchet (operetta, 1 act). Co-authored by Touzé. Music by Gramet.
>   Paris: Joubert, 1897.
>   Bijou-Concert, January 1897.
>   [BN 8° Yth 28055, ARS GD 8° 34569, AN F^{18}1447].

La Belle Camargo (opérette carnavalesque). Co-authored by George Touzé. Music by Louis Lust.
>   Bobino, 1897.
>   [AN F^{18}1447].

Leurs vengeances (comedy-vaudeville, 1 act). Co-authored by Touzé and L. Dargueil.
>   Paris: Patay, 1899.
>   Paris, Concert du XXe siècle, 26-11-98.
>   [BN 8° Yth 28845].

QUIVOGNE DE MONTIFAUD (see Marc de MONTIFAUD).

RACHILDE (see Twentieth Century volume).

RATTAZZI (Mme) (princesse Marie-Studolmine BONAPARTE-WYSE, Mme de SOLMS, then Mme Urbain RATTAZZI, and finally Mme Luis de RUTE).

Pseudonyms: vicomte d'Albens, vicomte de Tresserve, Camille Bernard, baron Stack, Louis Kelner.

Waterford (Ireland), between 1832 and 1835 - Paris, 1902.

Novelist and poet; in exile from 1853 to 1860 due to her opposition to the Empire; founder of several journals; wrote translations/adaptations.

Quand on n'aime plus trop, l'on n'aime plus assez (proverb, 2 acts, verse).

Genoa: imp. ligue-économique, 1858.

[BN 8° Yf. pièce 13, RON Rf. 80895].

L'Aventurière des colonies (drame, 5 acts).

Florence: Le Monnier, 1867; Paris, Jouast et Sigaux: 1885.

[BN 8° Yth 19561, RON Rf. 80901, ARS GD 8° 31071, BHVP in-16 615 682, SACD].

Théâtre complet. Contains: "Le Dernier jour d'une muse" (comédie-drame, 1 act, verse), "Aux pieds d'une femme" (parody of Caprice, marivaudage en quelques scènes), "L'Amour se change en haine aussitôt qu'il expire" (proverbe-idylle, 2 tableaux, verse), "L'Epreuve" (comedy-proverb, 1 act), "Quand on n'aime plus trop, on n'aime plus assez" (proverb, 2 tableaux, verse), "L'Auberge de la Madonne" (proverb, 1 act), "Les Suites d'un ménage de garçon" (essai-comédie, 1 act), "Madame de Staël à Coppet" (comédie inédite, 1 act, verse), "Une Livre de chair" (pochade, 1 tableau), "Molière à Vienne" (comedy, 2 acts, prose).

Chambéry: imp. de Gouvernement, 1860.

[RON Rf. 80893, ARS GD 8° 39769].

Les Soirées d'Aix-les-Bains. Collection of proverbs and bluettes: "Quand on n'aime plus trop, on n'aime plus assez", "Corinne", "L'Auberge de la Madonne", "Les Suites d'un ménage de garçon", "Une Livre de chair", "Aux pieds d'une femme"; "L'Amour se change en haine aussitôt qu'il expire"; "Madame de Staël à Coppet"; "L'Epreuve"; "Le Dernier jour d'une muse" (comedy, 1 act).

Paris: A. Faure, 1865.

[RON Rf. 80894, SACD P31].

Les Suites d'un ménage de garçon (comedy, 1 act).
Chambéry: imp. du Gouvernement, n.d.
[RON Rf. 80896, ARS GD 8° 47896].

Le Portrait de la comtesse (comedy, 1 act, verse).
Paris: Degorce-Cadot, n.d.
[RON Rf. 80900, ARS GD 8° 26227, SACD PC 492].

Corinne (essai dramatique).
In Nouvelle Revue internationale, Sept. 1900.
[BN 4° Z. 345, RON Rf. 80899].

REAL (Mme).

Le Clou aux maris (comedy-vaudeville, 1 act). Co-authored by Labiche
et Eugène Lemoine-Moreau.
Paris: M. Lévy, 1858.
Palais-Royal, 1-4-58.
[BN 8° Yth 3548, ARS GD 8° 7613].

REGNAULD DE PREBOIS (Mme Adèle).
Collective pseudonym with T. Barrière: F. OLLIVIER.

Trèfle à quatre feuilles.   Includes "Un Préjugé du grand monde"
(comedy, 1 act, prose), "Un Tournoi à Madrid" (comédie-drame, 2
acts, prose), "Un Amour de tête et un Amour de coeur " (comedy, 2
acts, prose), "Scène de la vie du monde, ou la Duchesse d'Argisse"
(nouvelle dialoguée, 5 acts, prose).
Paris: Desessart, 1839.
[ARS GD 8° 3151, SACD P31].

Une Femme charmante (comedy-vaudeville, 1 act). Co-authored by
Chapelle or Laurencin. Attribution uncertain.
Paris: Hanriot, Mifliez, Tresse, 1840.
Gymnase-dramatique, 11-4-40.
[BN Yf 1281(36), RON Rf. 47.084, ARS GD 8° 41679, AN
$F^{18}822$].

L'Art de ne pas donner d'étrennes (vaudeville, 1 act). Co-authored by
Labiche and Lefranc. Attribution uncertain.
Gymnase-dramatique, 29-12-47.
[AN $F^{18}828$].

Evelyne (drame, 2 acts, prose).
Paris: Tresse, 1849.
Odéon, 5-10-49.
[BN 4° Yth 1493, RON Rf. 47.085, ARS GD 8° 41764].

Les Infidélités conjugales (comedy, 1 act).
Paris: Tresse, 1850.
Délassements Comiques, 26-10-50.
[BN 4° Yth 2090, RON Rf. 47.086, ARS 4° B.L. 3867, SACD PC 308].

Marion (comedy-vaudeville, 2 acts).
Paris: Tresse, 1851.
Délassements Comiques, 22-3-51.
[BN 4° Yth 2666, RON Rf. 47.087, ARS 4° B.L. 3867].

Chien et chat (comedy-vaudeville, 1 act).
Paris: Mifliez, 1853.
Délassements Comiques, 20-11-52.
[BN 4° Yth 809, RON Rf. 47.088, ARS 8° B.L. 3868, AN F^{18}1055].

Le Moulin de l'Ermitage (drame, 5 acts).
Paris: Lévy fr., 1856.
Théâtre de l'Ambigu-Comique, 22-11-55.
[BN Yf 16 (21), RON Rf. 47.089, ARS GD 8° 39783, AN F^{18}950].

Ben-Salem (drame, 5 acts). Co-authored by François Arnault.
Cirque National, 1-5-58.

Une Pécheresse (drame, 5 acts). Co-authored by Th. Barrière.
Paris: M. Lévy, n.d.
Théâtre de la Gaîté, 25-5-60.
[BN 8° Yth 18561, RON Rf. 37.921, ARS GD 8° 155].

Le Tattersall brûlé (comedy, 1 act). Co-authored by Th. Barrière.
Paris: M. Lévy, 1865.
Gymnase Dramatique, 11-10-65.
[RON Rf. 46.401, AN F^{18}837].

Le Roman d'une honnête femme (comedy, 3 acts). Co-authored by Th. Barrière.
>   Paris: Lévy, 1868.
>   Gymnase Dramatique, 4-11-67.
>   [BN 8° Yth 15755, RON Rf. 37.959, ARS GD 8° 230, SACD, AN F^{18}838].

La Comtesse de Somerive (comedy, 4 acts). Co-authored by Th. Barrière.
>   Paris: Calmann Lévy, 1878.
>   Gymnase Dramatique, 20-4-72; Vaudeville, 23-3-73.
>   [BN 4° Yth 919, RON Rf. 37.972, ARS GD 8° 256, AN F^{18}768].

REGNIER (Marie SERRURE, Mme R.-E.).
Pseudonym: Daniel DARC.
Paris, 1840 - ?
Novelist.

Les Rieuses (comedy, 1 act).
>   Paris: Charpentier, 1879.
>   Théâtre du Vaudeville, 27-9-78.
>   [BN 8° Yth 19963, BHVP in-18° 607724 (6), AN F^{18}770].

Les Folies de Valentine (comedy, 1 act).
>   Paris: Charpentier, 1880.
>   Gymnase Dramatique, 13-4-80.
>   [BN 8° Yth 20177, BHVP in-8° 607830, AN F^{18}845].

REICHARD (Méa).

La Coquette (comedy, 4 acts) and A cinq heures (comedy-vaudeville, 1 act).
>   Brussels: G. Balot, 1899.
>   [ARS GD 8° 31873].

REICHENBERG (Suzanne) (baronne Pierre de BOURGOING).
Paris, 1854 - ?
Actress at the Comédie Française (1872-1898).

Steeple chase (scène de la vie mondaine, 1 act). Co-authored by H. Lecomte du Nouy.
>   Paris: C. Levy, 1896.
>   [BN 8° Yth 27351, ARS GD 8° 35645].

RENNEVILLE (Sophie de SENNETERRE, Mme de).
Author of children's books; biographies of saints and other famous
women.

Le Petit charbonnier (drame, 1 act, prose). Signed Mad. D. R***.
In Le Livre des enfants laborieux.
Paris: Alexis Eymery, 1815.
[BN R. 42072].

REY (Berthe) (see ULMES).

REYNERY (Mme).

Les Conscrits, ou le Triomphe de la vertu (vaudeville, 1 act, prose).
Lyons: Thomassin et Chambet, an XI (dedicated to the
Ministre de l'Intérieur).
[BN 8° Yth 3923, ARS GD 8° 7995, BHVP in-8° 611163 (1),
SACD PC 142].

REYNOLD (Berthe) (see Twentieth Century volume).

RICHARD-MEYNIS (Gabrielle).

Oeuvres poétiques. Contains: "Saint-François Xavier" (drame
religieux) and "Sainte-Germaine Cousin" (pastorale).
Lyons: Impr. Catholique, 1884.
[BN 8° Ye. 820, RON Rf. 86246].

RIOM (Mme Eugène) (née Adine BROBAND).
Pseudonyms: Louise d'ISOLE and le comte de SAINT-JEAN.
Pellerin (Loire-Atlantique), 1818 - 1899.
Poet and novelist; held a literary salon in Nantes.

Les Oiseaux des Tournelles (comedy, 1 act, prose).
Troisième Théâtre Français, 19-5-77.

ROBERT (Mme Antoinette-Henriette-*Clémence).*
Mâcon, 1797 - Paris, 1872.
Novelist.

L'Héritage du château (drame-vaudeville, 2 acts).
Paris: Bibliothèque Théâtrale (impr. de Bry aîné), n.d.
Théâtre Beaumarchais, 1-5-61.
[RON Rf. 47.320, ARS GD 8° 47796].

La Chambre de feu (drame, 5 acts, prose). Possible co-author.
Théâtre Beaumarchais, 13-12-61.

ROCHE-JAGU (Mme Jean de la) (also Mlle E. PEAN DE LA ROCHE-JAGU).

La Jeunesse de Lully (comic opera, 1 act).
Théâtre Montmartre, 17-12-46; Théâtre de M. Comte (Th. Choiseul), 1-2-51.
[AN F^{18}1190, 1312].

ROCHEBLAVE (Mme) (see ADAM-BOISGONTIER).

ROCHEMONT (la baronne Antoinine L. de).
Author of children's books.

La Tante Angélique (comedy).
Paris: Stock, 1892.
[BN 4° Yth 5972, RON Rf. 47.361, ARS GD 8° 46746].

Ruse de valets (comedy, 1 act, verse).
Paris: Stock, 1897.
[BN 8° Yth 27809].

ROGER de BEAUVOIR (see DOZE).

ROGER DE NESLES (see NESLE).

ROSTOPTCHINA (Mme la comtesse Lydiia (Lydie) ANDREEVNA).
Novelist of Russian origin.

Le Dévouement or Le Dévoument de Gontran (comedy, 1 act).
Paris: Librairie théâtrale, 1898.
Théâtre de l'Application or Théâtre Pompadour, 27-6-98.
[BN 8° Yth 28610, ARS GD 8° 32072, BHVP in-16 608621, AN F^{18}1360].

ROUSSEAU (Louise).
Author of children's books and works on *savoir-vivre*.

Histoire de chevalerie (légende, 4 acts). Co-authored by Alix Fournier.
Paris: Bibl. du théâtre des modernes, 1895.
Théâtre des Modernes, 27-2-95.
[RON Rf. 71.816, ARS GD 8° 38881, BHVP in-8° 616 619].

Papillons ! (1 act, verse, with music).
    Paris: Ollendorff, 1895.
    Institut dram. et lyrique, 1895.
    [BN 8° Yth 27222, ARS GD 8° 34791, AN F^{18}13 57].

Nos petits enfants.
    Institut dramatique et lyrique, 1895.
    [AN F^{18}1357].

Douce méprise (comedy, 1 act, verse).
    Paris: G. Dujarrie, 1902.
    Théâtre Mondain, 2-2-96.
    [BN 8° Yth 29990, RON Rf. 84.471, ARS GD 8° 27143,
    BHVP in-16 122021].

Le Pantalon trop raccourci (2 tableaux for youth).
    Paris: Nathan, n.d.
    [BN 8° Yth 28829, ARS GD 8° 30061].

La Première robe longue, Que dois-je faire ?, Sottise et désespoir de
Mathurine (monologues).
    Paris: Nathan, 1897.

ROUSSEIL (Mlle Marie-*Rosélia*-Suzanne).
    Niort, 1841 - ?
    Actress and poet.

Elza (drame, 1 act, verse).
    Paris: Lemerre, 1884.
    Théâtre du Vaudeville, 9-2-84.
    [BN 8° Yth 21421, ARS GD 8° 32566, BHVP in-16 607730
    (1), AN F^{18}772].

ROUSSEN (Jeane-Thérèse LAPEYRERE, Mme Léon de).
    Pseudonyms: Paul d'AIGREMONT, Pierre NINOUS.
    ? - 1907.
    Novelist.

Mère et martyre (drame, 5 acts). Co-authored by J. Dornay. Music by
H. Herman.
    Paris: Tresse & Stock, 1893.
    Ambigu-Comique, 27-1-1893.
    [BN 8° Yth 26289, BHVP in-8° 608450].

ROUXEL (Madame) (née ANTHONY).

> Le Nègre comme il y en a peu (vaudeville, 2 acts).
> Nîmes: Gaude, 1822.
> [ARS GD 8° 21448].

ROUY (Diaria).

> Un Bon petit diable (vaudeville, 1 act).
> Paris: Librairie théâtrale, 1859.
> Folies-Dramatiques, 24-11-59.
> [BN 8° Yth 17840, RON Rf. 47.482, ARS GD 8° 126, SACD
> PC 82, AN F^{18}1000].

> La Mère du condamné (drame, 3 acts, 4 tableaux).
> Paris: Michel Lévy, 1860.
> Théâtre Beaumarchais, 3-5-1860.
> [BN Yf 28 (10), RON Rf. 47.484, ARS GD 8° 39788 (pièce
> 11), BHVP fol. 402823 (8)].

> L'Ami du mari (comedy, 1 act).
> Paris: Michel Lévy, 1863.
> Second Théâtre Français (Odéon), 12-12-62.
> [BN 8° Yth 654, RON Rf. 47.485, ARS GD 8° 196, BHVP in-
> 16 607974 (3), AN F^{18}716].

> Qui perd, gagne (comedy, 1 act).
> Paris: Michel Lévy, 1863.
> Champs-Elysées, 7-2-63.
> [BN 8° Yth 15076, RON Rf. 47.486, ARS GD 8° 309, BHVP
> in-8° 611816, AN F^{18}1018].

> Une Méprise (comedy, 1 act).
> Paris: Libraire nouvelle, 1861.
> Champs-Elysées, 9-3-63.
> [BN 8° Yth 18512, ARS GD 8° 309, BHVP in-18 610019
> (10)].

> Les Profits de la Guerre (comedy-vaudeville, 1 act).
> Paris: Michel Lévy, 1864.
> Folies-Dramatiques, 23-5-64.
> [BN 8° Yth 14830, RON Rf. 47.487, ARS GD 8° 314, AN
> F^{18}1001].

Une Mère aux abois (vaudeville, 1 act).
Paris: Michel Lévy, 1865.
Folies-Marigny, 15-4-65.
[BN 8° Yth 18517, RON Rf. 47.488, ARS GD 8° 321, BHVP
in-18 611821 (8), SACD, AN F^{18}1121].

La Louve de Florence, ou Tocane en 1575 (drame, 5 acts).
Paris: Michel Lévy, 1865.
Théâtre Beaumarchais, 21-10-65.
[BN 4° Yth 2396, RON Rf. 47.489, ARS GD 8° 49024, BHVP
fol. 402823 (26), AN F^{18}1121].

Le Chasseur des Abbruzes (prologue).
Théâtre Beaumarchais, 21-10-65.

Allons Paris, debout ! (strophes).
Paris: Impr. E. Blot. n.d.
Théâtre de l'Ambigu-Comique, November 1870.
[BN Ye. 51568].

A l'oeuvre, femmes de France (strophes).
Lyons: Curard, 1872.
Grand Théâtre de Lyon, 26-2-72; Théâtre des Nouveautés, 14-
3-72.
[BN Ye. 51567].

ROYER (Mlle Anna).

Un Oncle qui s'ennuie (vaudeville, 1 act). Co-authored by G. Marot.
Théâtre Beaumarchais, 16-7-63.
[SACD ms. 103].

ROZIER (see PATON).

SABATIER (Jenny).
Pseudonym of Jenny-Caroline THIRCUIR, Mme Léon MALLAC.

Un Bon tiens vaut mieux que deux tu l'auras (proverb).
Paris: Dentu, 1863.
[BN 8° Yth 17841, RON Rf. 84.475, ARS GD 8° 31343,
BHVP in-12 609068, SACD].

SABATIER (Mme Louise).

> Le Revenant (comic opera).
> Salle Herz, 1865.
> [AN F^{18}1354].

SABINE (see MANCEL).

SABLIGNY (Mme de).

> La Vivandière (comedy, 1 act).
> Théâtre des Jeunes Artistes, 18-8-60.

SAFFRAY (see NAVERY).

SAINT-HILAIRE (Mme de) (Mme S.-M. de SAINT-H...).

> Marie Vander, ou le Siège de Leyde (comedy, 3 acts, verse).
> Théâtre de Cluny, 13-10-75.
> [BN ms. naf. 2951, AN F^{18}1031].

SAINT-JEAN (le comte de) (see RIOM).

SAINT-RENE (Mme).

> Blancs et noirs (revue).
> Cercle Pigalle, 24-3-93.

SAINT-SAUVEUR (Mme de) (see Eighteenth Century).

SAINT-SURIN (Marie-Caroline-Rosalie Richard de GENDRECOURT or CENDRECOURT, Mme *Rose* de Saint-Surin, then Mme de MONMERQUÉ).
Villefranche (Rhône), c. 1780 - ?
Author of novels, poetry, short stories and literary criticism.

> Miroir des salons (scènes du monde). Includes: "La Journée d'une jolie femme", "La Représaille", "L'Audience d'un ministre", "Le Vieux garçon", "Le Bal et le lansquenet".
> Paris: Maignard, 1831.
> [BN Yf 11536, RON Rf. 93.833, ARS GD 8° 1978, BHVP in-8° 11 510].

> Les Deux vendéens ou Angoulême le 16 août 1832 (scènes historiques, 2 tableaux).
> Paris: La France littéraire (tome IV), 1832.
> [RON Rf. 93.835].

SAINTE-MARIE (Mme de).
Pseudonym of Mme de PLAGNIOL.
Novelist.

Drame et conversations: "L'Amour du bien", "Dialogue pour la fête de Mlle L***", "Conversation pour une distribution de prix", "La Paralytique".
Paris: Gaume, 1839.
[BN Yf 11538].

Drames: "Le Pèlerinage [sic] à Notre-Dame-les-Infirmes" (drame, 1 act); "La Reine de mai" (drame, 1 act); "L'Amie jalouse" (drame, 1 act).
Paris: Gaume fr., 1840.
[BN Yf 11539, SACD P31].

Répertoire pour maîtresses, ou Drames pour jeunes personnes: "Le Château de Beaumont", "Une Chaumière dans les Alpes", "La Fête d'une mère", "La Correction mutuelle", "Un Jour des prix".
Paris: Gaume fr., 1850.
[BN Yf 11540].

SALLEZ (Mme Emilie).

Un Mariage compromis par le tabac (saynète, vers).
Paris: Journal de la Société contre l'abus du Tabac, 1880.
[ARS GD 8° 37105].

SALM-DYCK (see Eighteenth Century).

SAMSON (Caroline) (see BERTON)

SAMSON (Mme Jules).
Author of novels and an essay on education which received an award from the Académie française.

A Chambalud-les Eaux (comedy, 1 act).
Paris: Hennuyer, 1890.
[BN 8° Yth 23733].

Le Plan de Ninette (comedy, 1 act).
Paris: Hennuyer, 1890.
[BN 8° Yth 23785].

Le Choix d'une princesse (comedy, 1 act).
Paris: Hennuyer, 1893.
[BN 8° Yth 26236, ARS GD 26.543].

SAND (George).
Pseudonym of Aurore DUPIN, baronne DUDEVANT.
Paris, 1804 - *id.*, 1876.
Novelist.

Indiana (drame, 5 parts).
Théâtre de la Gaîté, 1833.

Gabriel (drame, 5 parts).
Paris: Félix Bonnaire, 1840.
[RON Rf. 34.004, SACD P31].

Les Sept cordes de la lyre (5 acts, prose).
Paris: Félix Bonnaire, 1840; Paris: Michel Lévy, 1869.
[BN Y^2 65286].

Cosima ou la Haine dans l'amour (drame, 5 acts, prose).
Paris: F. Bonnaire, Ch. Tresse, 1840.
Comédie Française, 29-4-40.
[RON Rf. 33.923, ARS GD 8° 19902, BHVP in-16 SAND 621
628, SACD R.D.C.P17].

Les Mississippiens (proverb, 1 act).
In Pauline.
Paris: Magen et Comon, 1841.
[ARS GD 8° 14203].

Le Roi attend (1 act, prose).
In Théâtre complet, volume 1 (see below).
Théâtre de la République, 1848; Comédie Française, 6-4-48.

François le champi (comedy, 3 acts). Adaptation from the novel of the
same name.
Paris: Blanchard, 1849.
Théâtre de l'Odéon, 23-11-49; Comédie Française, 22-9-88.
[RON Rf. 33.926, ARS GD 8° 20515, BHVP in-16 947 277,
SACD R.D.C.P17, TF 1 FRA San].

La Petite Fadette (comedy-vaudeville, 2 acts).
Paris: Michel Lévy, 1869.
Variétés, 1850; Opéra-Comique, 15-9-69 (new version comic opera, 3 acts).
[RON Rf. 33.994, ARS GD 8° 378, AN F^{18}698].

Claudie (drame, 3 acts).
Paris: E. Blanchard, 1851; Paris: M. Lévy, 1866.
Porte Saint-Martin, 11-1-51; Odéon, 1856; Comédie Française, 1-7-1904.
[RON Rf. 33.933, ARS GD 8° 7548, TF 1 CLA San, BHVP in-18 SAND 621 459, AN F^{18}713, TF ms. 1411].

Molière (drame, 4 acts).
Paris: Blanchard, 1851.
Théâtre de la Gaîté, 10-5-51.
[RON Rf. 33.940, ARS GD 8° 14257, BHVP in-18 SAND 621 513, TF 2 SAN Mol 1851, AN F^{18}921].

Le Mariage de Victorine (comedy, 3 acts).
Paris: Blanchard, 1851.
Théâtre du Gymnase, 26-11-51; Comédie Française, 7-3-76 (reprise 17-11-1926).
[RON Rf. 33.943, ARS GD 8° 49305, BHVP in-18 SAND 621 462, SACD R.D.C.P17, TF 1 MAR San, AN F^{18}829, TF ms. 1733].

Les Vacances de Pandolphe (comedy, 3 acts).
Paris: Giraud & Dagneau, 1852.
Gymnase, 3-3-52.
[RON Rf. 33.950, ARS GD 8° 18751, BHVP in-18 SAND 621 460, SACD R.D.C.P17, AN F^{18}830].

Le Démon du foyer (comedy, 2 acts).
Paris: Giraud & Dagneau, 1852.
Gymnase, 1-9-52; Odéon, 02-06-1904.
[RON Rf. 33.947, ARS GD 8° 8554, SACD R.D.C.P17, TF 2 SAN Dem s.d.].

En Baronnie de Muhldorf (drame, 3 acts).
Brussels: J.B. Tarride, 1853.
[RON Rf. 33.958].

Le Pressoir (drame, 3 acts).
    Paris: Michel Lévy, 1853.
    Gymnase-dramatique, 13-9-53.
    [RON Rf. 33.952, ARS GD 8° 16460, SACD R.D.C.P17, TF 2
    SAN O s.d., AN F^{18}830].

Mauprat (drame, 5 acts).
    Paris: Libr. théâtrale, 1854.
    Odéon, 28-11-53.
    [RON Rf. 33.954, ARS GD 8° 13826, BHVP in-8° 607 954
    (4), AN F^{18}711].

Flaminio (comedy, 3 acts).
    Paris: Librairie théâtrale, 1854.
    Gymnase, 31-10-54.
    [RON Rf. 33.959, ARS GD 8° 10670, BHVP in-18 SAND 621
    469, SACD PC 252, TF 2 DUM Dia 1853, AN F^{18}831].

Maître Favila (drame, 3 acts).
    Paris: Librairie nouvelle, 1855.
    Odéon, 15-9-55.
    [RON Rf. 33.961, ARS GD 8° 13275, BHVP in-18 SAND 621
    470, SACD PC 376, AN F^{18}711].

Lucie (comedy, 1 act).
    Paris: Librairie nouvelle, 1856.
    Gymnase, 16-2-56.
    [RON Rf. 33.966, ARS GD 8° 13001, BHVP in-18 SAND 621
    471, SACD R.D.C.P17].

Françoise (comedy, 4 acts).
    Paris: Librairie nouvelle, 1856.
    Gymnase, 3-4-56.
    [RON Rf. 33.968, ARS GD 8° 20520, BHVP in-18 SAND 621
    466, SACD R.D.C.P17, AN F^{18}832].

Comme il vous plaira (comedy, 3 acts). Adaptation from Shakespeare.
    Paris: Librairie nouvelle, 1856.
    Théâtre Français, 12-4-56.
    [RON Rf. 33.969, ARS GD 8° 7805, BHVP in-18 SAND 621
    468, SACD R.D.C.P17, TF 1 COM Sha, AN F^{18}679, TF ms.
    974].

Marguerite de Sainte-Gemme (comedy, 3 acts).
    Paris: Michel Lévy, 1859.
    Gymnase, 23-4-59
    [RON Rf. 33.970, ARS GD 8° 33367, BHVP in-18 SAND 621
    517, SACD R.D.C.P17, AN F^{18}834].

Le Marquis de Villemer (comedy, 4 acts).
    Paris: Michel Lévy, 1964.
    Odéon, 29-2-64; Comédie Française, 4-6-77 (revival 1894).
    [RON Rf. 33.978, ARS GD 8° 209, BHVP in-16 947 990, TF
    2 SAN Mar s.d., SACD R.D.C.P17, RON ms. 663, AN
    F^{18}717, TF ms. 1163].

Le Drac (drame fantastique, 3 acts). Co-authored by Paul Meurice.
    Paris: Michel Lévy, 1865.
    Théâtre du Vaudeville, 28-9-64.
    [RON Rf. 33.982, ARS GD 8° 213, BHVP in-18 607 707 (1),
    SACD PC 192, AN F^{18}763].

Théâtre. 3 volumes.
I. "François le champi", "Le Démon du foyer", "Maître Favila",
"Françoise".
II. "Claudie", "Lucie", "Le Pressoir", "Flaminio".
III. "Le Mariage de Victorine", "Comme il vous plaira", "Mauprat".
    Paris: M. Lévy, 1860.
    [BHVP in-18 SAND 621 520].

Marielle (comedy, 3 acts).
    In La Revue des Deux mondes, January 1860.
    [BN microfilm m. 800, RON Rf. 33.998, ARS GD 8° 42803].

Le Pavé (comedy, 1 act).
    Paris: Michel Lévy, 1862.
    Gymnase, 18-3-62.
    [RON Rf. 33.972, ARS GD 8° 34847, BHVP in-18 SAND 621
    515, SACD R.D.C.P17, AN F^{18}835].

Les Beaux monsieurs de Bois-Doré (drame, 5 acts). Co-authored by
Paul Meurice.
    Paris: Michel Lévy, 1862.
    Ambigu, 26-4-62.
    [RON Rf. 33.975, ARS GD 8° 31193, BHVP in-18 SAND 621
    516, TF 2 SAN Bea 1862, SACD R.D.C.P17, AN F^{18}955].

Plutus (nouvelle dialoguée).
In La Revue des Deux mondes, January 1863.
[BN microfilm m. 800, RON Rf. 34000, ARS 8° H. 26446,
SACD R.D.C.P17].

La Nuit de Noël (fantaisie, adaptation from Hoffmann).
In La Revue des Deux mondes, August 1863.
[BN microfilm m. 800, RON Rf. 34.001, ARS 8° H. 26446].

Théâtre de Nohant. Includes "Le Drac", "Plutus", "Le Pavé", "La Nuit
de Noël", "Marielle".
Paris: Michel Lévy, 1864.
[TF 2 San O 1864, SACD P31].

Le Lys au Japon (comedy, 1 act). Adaptation of Antonia.
Paris: Michel Lévy, 1866.
Théâtre du Vaudeville, 14-8-66.
[RON Rf. 33.989, ARS GD 8° 225, BHVP in-18 617 710 (2),
SACD R.D.C.P17, RON ms. 664, AN F^{18}765].

Les Dom Juan du village (comedy, 3 acts). Co-authored by Maurice
Sand.
Paris: Michel Lévy, 1866.
Théâtre du Vaudeville, 12-8-66.
[RON Rf. 33.986, ARS GD 8° 225, BHVP in-18 SAND 621
455, SACD R.D.C.P17, AN F^{18}765].

Cadio (drame, 5 acts). Co-authored by Paul Meurice.
Paris: Michel Lévy, 1868.
Porte St. Martin, 3-10-68.
[RON Rf. 33.990, ARS GD 8° 283, BHVP in-18 609 522,
SACD PC 92].

L'Autre (comedy, 4 acts).
Paris: Michel Lévy, 1870.
Odéon, 25-2-1870.
[RON Rf. 33.996, ARS GD 8° 244, BHVP in-8° 607 985 (1),
SACD R.D.C.P.17, TF 2 SAN Aut 1870, AN F^{18}719].

Le Bienfait n'est jamais perdu (comedy-proverb, 1 act).
Théâtre de Cluny, 7-11-72.
[AN F^{18}1028].

Une Conspiration en 1537 (1 act).
In A. Musset. Lorenzzaccio.
Paris: Imprimerie nationale, 1978.
[TF 2 MUS Lor 1978].

Théâtre complet (4 volumes).
Paris: Michel Lévy, 1866-1867.
[RON Rf. 33.921, SACD P31].

Théâtre complet (4 volumes).
Paris: Calmann Lévy, 1877.
[RON Rf. 33.922, BHVP in-18 SAND 621 521, TF 2 SAN O
1876].

SAPHO (Rachel).

A l'automne (comedy, 1 act, prose). Music by Francis Thomé.
Paris: Bibliothèque française, 1895.
Théâtre des Modernes, 18-1-95.
[RON Rf. 72.131, ARS GD 8° 36394, SACD PC 13, RON
ms., AN F^{18}1357].

SAVIGNAC (Mme Adélaïde-Esther-Charlotte DUBILLON, *Alida* de).
Paris, 1796 (or 1790) - 1847.
Author of novels and other books for children; wrote literary criticism
for several journals including the Journal des femmes and the Journal
des demoiselles.

Petits proverbes dramatiques: "Le Lutin, ou Tant va la cruche à l'eau
qu'à la fin elle se brise", "Bertrand Duguesclin, ou Bon chien chasse de
race", "Le Pâté de jambon, ou A bon chat bon rat", "Les Petites créoles,
ou le Soleil luit pour tout le monde", "L'Anniversaire, ou Avant le
saint ne chômons pas la fête", "Sancho Pança dans l'île de Barataria,
ou Tout ce qui reluit n'est pas or".
Paris: Gide fils, n.d.
[BN Yf 10623].

Théâtre de mes enfants. Three proverbs: "La Treille dévastée, ou
Bonne renommée vaut mieux que ceinture dorée", "Les Projets, ou
Pierre qui roule n'amasse pas de mousse", "L'Obligeant, ou Arrive qui
plante".
Paris: Gide, 1828.
[BN R. 50241].

Chacun son rôle, Le Médecin gourmand (comedy-proverb).
N.p., n.d. Listed in Bibliographie dramatique de Soleinne
(3601).

SAVORI (Pauline).

Divorce impérial, 1890
[AN F^{18}1353].

SEGALAS (Anaïs MENARD, Mme).
Paris, 1814 - *id.*, 1895.
Author of poetry, novels and children's stories.

La Loge de l'Opéra (drame, 3 acts).
Paris: Michel Lévy, 1847.
Second Théâtre Français (Odéon), 7-4-47.
[BN 8° Yth 10275, RON Rf. 47.961, ARS GD 8° 21065,
BHVP in-4° 402986 (25), OP LIV. 19/1288a, SACD PC 360,
AN F^{18}709].

Le Trembleur (comedy-vaudeville, 2 acts).
Paris: Marchand, 1849.
Second Théâtre Français (Odéon), 8-9-49.
[BN 4° Yth 4090, RON Rf. 47.964, ARS GD 8° 48621, BHVP
in-8° 12 617 (16)].

Les Deux amoureux de la grand-mère (comedy-vaudeville).
Paris: Librairie théâtrale, 1850.
Porte St. Martin, 18-11-50.
[BN 4° Yth 1108, RON Rec. 111, AN F^{18}898].

Les Absents ont raison (comedy, 2 acts, prose).
Paris: Librairie théâtrale, 1852.
Odéon, 7-5-52.
[BN 4° Yth 35, RON Rec. 111, BHVP in-8° 607948 (5), AN
F^{18}710].

Les Inconvénients de la sympathie (vaudeville, 1 act).
Paris: Marchant, 1854.
Théâtre de la Gaîté, 13-2-54.
[BN 4° Yth 2084, RON Rec. 111, ARS GD 8° 42310].

Deux passions (comedy, 1 act, verse).
>   Châlons-sur-Marne: Martin frères, 1893.
>   Galerie Vivienne, 26-4-92.
>   [BN 8° Yth 26482].

SEGUIN (Marguerite-Félicité).
Poet.

Les Orphelines polonaises (drame, 5 acts, verse).
>   Clermont-Ferrand: impr. de Perol, 1852.
>   [BN 8° Yth 13225, RON Rf. 76830, ARS GD 8° 21528].

SEGUR (Mme la comtesse de) (née Sophie ROSTOPCHINE).
St. Petersburg, 1799 - 1874
Author of novels for children and fairy tales.

Comédies et proverbes: "Les Caprices de Gizelle" (comedy), "Le Dîner de Mademoiselle Justine" (comedy), "On ne prend pas les mouches avec du vinaigre" (proverb), "Le Forçat, ou A tout péché miséricorde" (proverb), "Le Petit de Crac" (comedy).
>   Paris: Hachette, 1865 (numerous reeditions throughout nineteenth and twentieth centuries, most recent edition in 1992).
>   [BN Yf 11639, RON Rf. 86310, BHVP in-8° 727 334].

Le Petit de Crac (comedy, 2 acts).
>   Paris: Hachette, 1931.
>   [BN 4 Y^2 7536, RON Rf. 86514].

Les Caprices de Gizelle (comedy, 2 acts).
>   Paris: Hachette, 1937; Paris: Castermann, 1979.
>   [BN Yth 41471].

Oeuvres. Ed. Claudine Beaussant. 3 volumes.
Volume 2 includes "Comédies et proverbes" (see above).
>   Paris: Laffont (Bouquins), 1990.
>   [BN 16° Y^2 56374, ARS 16 Z 17529].

SEIGNEUX (M. de) (see VAN DE VELDE).

SEMEAC (la marquise de).
Pseudonym of la comtesse Jean de CASTELBAJAC.

Habile méprise (comedy, 1 act).
Théâtre Mondain, 16-1-97.
[AN F^{18}13 59].

SÉRAPHIN (Pauline).

La Perruque de Cassandre (pièce-féerie, 3 acts).
Théâtre Séraphin, 2-8-1846.
[ARS ms. Douay 1905].

SERY (Jean) (Henriette DANGEVILLE) (see Twentieth Century).

SIEFERT (Emilie-Georgette-*Louisa*) (Mme Jocelyn PENE).
Lyons, 1845 - Pau, 1877.
Poet and novelist.

Comédies romanesques. Contains: "Théophile" (comedy, 2 acts, verse),
"Le Recteur Bertholdus" (comedy, 1 act, verse), "La Bague" (drame
lyrique, 1 act, verse), "Le Retour" (comedy, 1 act, verse).
Paris: A. Lemerre, 1872.
[BN Yf 11662, RON Rf. 48.047].

Le Recteur Bertholdus (1 act).
In Revue des Deux Mondes, June 1870.
[BN microfilm m. 800, RON Rf. 48.048, ARS 8° H. 26446].

SIMONIN (see Gustave HALLER).

SIMONS (dame) (see CANDEILLE).

SKARIATINE (Mme Hélène de) (née comtesse SCHOUVALOFF).

Une Chaumière et son coeur (lever de rideau).
Paris: Michel Lévy, 1868.
[BN 8° Yth 18314, ARS GD 8° 37768].

Le Faune (vaudeville, 1 act).
Paris: Michel Lévy, 1868.
[BN 8° Yth 6543, ARS GD 8° 32805].

Satire et pari (comedy, 1 act).
Paris: Michel Lévy, 1868.
[BN 8° Yth 16137].

Théâtre de Mme de Skariatine. Contains: "Satire et pari", "Le Faune",
"Une Chaumière et son coeur".
Nice: Emp. E. Gauthier, 1868.
[BN Yf 11671, RON Rf. 84.483].

SOLDAINI (Mlle Argia).

Catarina (historical pantomime, 5 tableaux).
Théâtre Beaumarchais, 23-5-62.

La Flûte enchantée.
Théâtre Beaumarchais, 29-5-62.

SOLMS (see RATTAZZI).

SOUZA (Adèlaïde-Marie-Emilie FILLEUL, comtesse de FLAHANT, then
Mme de)
Paris, 1761 - *id.*, 1836.
Novelist.

La Duchesse de Guise, ou l'Intérieur d'une famille illustre dans le
temps de la ligue (drame, 3 acts).
Paris: Ch. Gosselin, 1832.
[RON Rf. 33.528, ARS GD 8° 20066].

STAEL (Mme de) (see Eighteenth Century).

STERN (Daniel).
Pseudonym of Marie de FLAVIGNY, la comtesse d'AGOULT.
Frankfurt, 1805 - Paris, 1876.
Author of political and historical essays; novelist and poet; held a
literary salon.

Trois journées de la vie de Marie-Stuart (scènes historiques).
Paris: Pillet fils aîné, 1856.
[RON Rf. 48.309].

Jeanne d'Arc (drame historique, 5 acts, prose).
Paris: Michel Lévy, 1857.
[BN m. 8° Yth 9428, RON Rf. 87.766, ARS GD 8° 12339].

Dante et Goethe (dialogues).
    Paris: Didier, 1866.
    [BN Z. 39724, RON Rf. 48.310].

Entre deux candidats (proverb).
    Paris: Schiller, 1868.
    [ARS GD 8° 36928].

Ninon au couvent, ou Il ne faut jamais manquer à ses amis (proverb).
    In Valentia.
    Paris: Calmann Lévy, 1883.
    [BN 8 Y^2 6488, RON ms. 737 Rés.].

STIRBEY (princesse) (see Gustave HALLER).

STOLZ (Mme).
    Pseudonym of comtesse Fanny de BÉGON.
    Author of children's novels.

Tante Marianne (comedy, 3 acts).
    Paris: C. Dillet, 1865.
    [BN 8° Yth 17050, ARS GD 8° 35791].

La Tulipomanie (comedy, 1 act).
    Paris: Périsse, n.d.
    [BN 8° Yth 29578, ARS GD 8° 26207].

Espérance (comedy, 3 acts).
    Paris: Bourguet-Calas, 1878.
    [BN 8° Yth 25419].

Les Petites misères de la vie (scènes dialoguées en deux actes).
    Paris: Bourguet-Calas, 1878.
    [BN 8° Yth 25508].

Qui est la Reine ? (allegorical comedy, 1 act).
    Paris: Bourguet-Calas, n.d.
    [BN Yf 13170, ARS Th. N. 16999].

Les Deux cousines (1 act).
    Limoges: Barbou, 1880.
    [8 Yth 25403].

Un Bouquet de fleurs (1 act).
    Limoges: Barbou, 1880.
    [BN 8° Yth 25575].

Rêves d'avenir (dialogue).
    Limoges: Barbou, 1881.
    [BN 8° Yth 20761].

Une Nuit blanche (scènes dialoguées).
    Paris: Bourguet-Calas, 1882.
    [BN 8° Yth 20650].

Le Cortège d'une jeune fille (scène allégorique).
    Limoges: L. Barbou, 1882.
    [BN 8° Yth 20742].

Honneur et profit (scènes dialoguées).
    Limoges: M. Barbou, 1882.
    [BN 8° Yth 20752].

Les Rosiers d'Elouard (scènes dialoguées).
    Paris: Bourguet-Calas, 1882.
    [BN 8° Yth 20646].

L'Amitié (dialogue).
    Paris: Haton, 1883.
    [BN 8° Yth 21200].

Economie et parcimonie (dialogue).
    Paris: Haton, 1883.
    [BN 8° Yth 21210].

L'Héritière (1 act).
    Paris: Haton, 1883.
    [BN 8° Yth 21281].

La Muette (2 acts).
    Paris: Haton, 1883.
    [BN 8° Yth 21225].

Les Oeuvres de M. Privas (2 acts).
    Paris: Haton, 1883.
    [BN 8° Yth 21227].

Recette contre la jaunisse (comedy).
Paris: Haton, 1883.
[BN 8° Yth 21231].

Simplicité (3 acts).
Paris: Haton, 1883.
[BN 8° Yth 21182].

Le Style, c'est l'homme (dialogue).
Paris: Haton, 1883.
[BN 8° Yth 21237].

Tout ce qui reluit n'est pas en or (1 act).
Paris: Haton, 1883.
[BN 8° Yth 21241].

Une Rencontre (2 acts).
Paris: Haton, 1883.
[BN 8° Yth 21244].

Les Droits de la femme (2 acts).
Paris: impr. de F. Levé, 1884.
[BN 8° Yth 24819].

Un Appartement sans inconvénient (comedy, 2 acts).
Paris: Bourguet-Calas, 1885.
[BN 8° Yth 21768, ARS GD 8° 26680].

Le Petit marmiton (comedy, 2 acts).
Paris: Bourguet-Calas, 1889.
[BN 8° Yth 23494].

La Famille Azote (comedy, 2 acts).
Paris: Bourguet-Calas, 1889.
[BN 8° Yth 23482].

Madame Ego (comedy, 2 acts).
Paris: Bouguet-Calas, 1889.
[BN 8° Yth 25463].

Tel maître, tel valet (comedy, 2 acts).
Paris: Bourguet-Calas, 1889.
[BN 8° Yth 23509, ARS GD 8° 26562].

Other titles listed on cover of above plays: "Une Amie dangereuse", "Une Reine absolue", "Quarante francs tombés du ciel", "Le Petit chevalier", "Le Coeur d'un père", "Le Petit doigt de Françoise", "Monsieur Pax".

SYLVIANE (Mme).
Pseudonym of Mme C. HUBAINE.

Noblesse du jour (comedy, 3 acts). Attribution uncertain. Possibly by Henri Conti.
    Galerie Vivienne, 22-2-96.
    [AN F^{18}1358].

TAGLIONI (Marie).
Stockholm, 1804 - Marseilles, 1884.
Ballerina at the Paris Opera.

Le Papillon (ballet pantomime, 2 acts, 4 tableaux). Co-authored by H. de Saint-Georges. Music by J. Offenbach.
    Paris: Jonas, 1860.
    Paris; Opéra, 26-11-1860.
    [BN 4° Yth 3136, ARS GD 8° 39173, BHVP in-8° 607376 (27)].

TALMA (Mlle Caroline VANHOVE, Mme PETIT, then Mme Joseph-François TALMA, and finally la comtesse de CHALOT).
The Hague, 1771 - Paris, 1860.
Actress, author of Etudes sur l'art théâtral (1836).

Les Heureux mensonges ou la Curiosité excusable (comedy, 1 act).
    Paris: G. Matriot, Barba, 1813.
    Théâtre de l'Impératrice, 19-11-13.
    [RON Rf. 36.312, ARS GD 8° 20759].

Laquelle des trois ? (comedy, 3 acts, prose).
    Comédie Française, 20-7-16.
    [AN F^{18}587].

Les Deux Méricour, ou la Double méprise (comedy, 1 act, verse).
    Comédie Française, 1-12-19.
    [AN F^{18}587].

TARWELD (Mathilde) (see BOURDON).

THENARD (Jenny) (also AZY).
Pseudonyms of Marie-*Jenny* VERNIN.
Paris, 1849 - ?
Actress at the Comédie Française and lecturer.

Une Présentation (monologue).
Paris: Librairie théâtrale, 1880.
[BN 8° Yth 25596, RON Rf. 83.808, ARS GD 8° 24895].

Un Scénario (monologue).
Paris: Librairie théâtrale, 1883.
[BN 8° Yth 20936, RON Rf. 83.807].

Ce cher docteur (monologue).
Paris: Librairie théâtrale, 1892.
[BN 8° Yth 25618, RON Rf. 83.802].

La Couturière (monologue).
Paris: Librairie théâtrale, 1892.
[BN 8° Yth 25759].

De Calais à Douvres (monologue).
Paris: Librairie théâtrale, 1892.
[BN 8° Yth 24959].

Le Voyage de noces (monologue).
Paris: Librairie théâtrale, 1892.
[BN 8° Yth 25672, ARS GD 8° 28699].

Five o'clock (monologue).
Paris: Librairie théâtrale, 1894.
[BN 8° Yth 26868].

Mon portrait (monologue).
Paris: Librairie théâtrale, 1894.
[BN 8° Yth 26909].

Réception (monologue).
Paris: Librairie théâtrale, 1895.
[BN 8° Yth 27042].

Le Monde (monologue).
Paris: Librairie théâtrale, 1896.
[BN 8° Yth 27643, RON Rf. 83.804].

Oh ! Le théâtre ! (monologue).
Paris: Librairie théâtrale, 1896.
[BN 8° Yth 27639, RON Rf. 83.805].

Les Soirées (monologue).
Paris: Librairie théâtrale, 1899.
[BN 8° Yth 28748].

En gare ! (monologue).
Paris: Librairie théâtrale, 1899.
[BN 8° Yth 28775].

Quoi ? (monologue).
Paris: Librairie théâtrale, 1899.
[BN 8° Yth 28747].

Indulgente (monologue).
Paris: Librairie théâtrale, 1899.
[BN 8° Yth 28677].

Timide (monologue).
Paris: Librairie théâtrale, 1900.
[BN 8° Yth 29275].

Les Vacances (monologue).
Paris: Librairie théâtrale, 1900.
[BN 8° Yth 29332].

Le Lézard (comedy, 1 act). Co-authored by J.P. Ferrier.
Paris: Librairie théâtrale, artistique et littéraire, n.d.
Hôtel des Sociétés Savantes, 9-12-1900.
[SACD].

Mon Rêve (monologue).
Paris: Librairie théâtrale, 1900.
[BN 8° Yth 29276].

La Rifla, fla, fla ! (monologue).
Paris: Librairie théâtrale, 1900.
[BN 8° Yth 29320].

Aidez-moi donc ! (monologue).
Paris: Librairie théâtrale, 1900.
[BN 8° Yth 29315].

Au concert (monologue).
Paris: Librairie théâtrale, 1900.
[BN 8° Yth 29316].

L'Avenir (monologue).
Paris: Librairie théâtrale, 1900.
[BN 8° Yth 29317].

Demoiselle d'honneur (monologue).
Paris: Librairie théâtrale, 1900.
[BN 8° Yth 29319].

Pas de politique (comedy, 1 act). Co-authored by Mlle J.-P. Ferrier.
Paris: Librairie théâtrale, 1900.
[BN 8° Yth 33614, RON Rf. 58.595, SACD].

Les Monologues.
Paris: libraire théâtrale, 1900.
[BN 8° Yf 1157, ARS GD 8° 2974].

Marie-Antoinette et son cercle (scènes du Petit Trianon).
Paris: Libraire théâtrale, 1901.
Théâtre du Palais de la Femme, World's Fair, 1900; also
performed in London for Princess Christian de Schlewig-
Holstein.
[ARS GD 8° 33505, BHVP in-18 121621, SACD].

Les Automobilisants (monologue).
Paris: Librairie théâtrale, 1905.
[BN 8° Yth 31202].

La Femme modern-chic [sic] (monologue).
Paris: Librairie théâtrale, 1905.
[BN 8° Yth 31198].

La Famille Piton (monologue). Other title: Chez les Piton.
Paris: Librairie théâtrale, 1905.
Arras, 09-04-1905.
[BN 8° Yth 31196, RON Rf. 83.803, ARS GD 8° 28493].

Sans cérémonie (monologue).
Paris: Librairie théâtrale, 1908.
[BN 8° Yth 32690].

Les Succès de Bébé (monologue).
Paris: Librairie théâtrale, 1908.
[BN 8° Yth 32689, RON Rf. 83.806].

En coup de vent (comedy, 1 act). Co-authored by Mlle P. Combier.
Paris: Librairie théâtrale, 1909.
Théâtre des Capucines, 23-11-1908 (performed by authors).
[BN 8° Yth 33268, RON Rf. 73.125, ARS GD 8° 29410,
BHVP in-8° 609213, SACD].

Pour son programme (comedy, 1 act). Co-authored by Combier. -
Paris: Librairie Théâtrale, 1911.
Théâtre des Capucines, 14-11-1909 (perfomed by J. Thénard).
[BN 8° Yth 34202, ARS GD 8° 29010, BHVP in-8° 609943,
SACD].

Consultation (comedy, 1 act). Co-authored by P. Combier.
Paris: Librairie théâtrale, 1911.
Théâtre des Capucines, 16-11-1909.
[BN 8° Yth 34192, ARS GD 8° 28798, BHVP in-8° 609942].

Pour un rond de cuir (comedy, 1 act).
Paris: Librairie théâtrale, 1912.
Paris, Théâtre des Capucines, 4-12-1910.
[BHVP in-18 123509, SACD].

THIRCUIR (see Jenny SABATIER).

THYS (Mme Pauline).
Composer.

Cri-Cri (féerie, 3 acts, 32 tableaux). Co-authored by G. Hugelmann, H.
Borssat and E. Fanfernot. Music by M. Joly.
Paris: M. Lévy, n.d.
Paris, Théâtre Impérial du Cirque, 15-8-59.
[ARS Th. N. 12331].

La Pomme de Turquie (operetta, 1 act).
Paris: Heugel, n.d.
Bouffes-Parisiens, 9-5-57.
[ARS GD 8° 39818].

Héritier sans le savoir (opéra de salon).
Performed at the home of M. Lefébure-Wély, April 1858.

La Perruque du bailli (opéra de salon).
Salle Herz, 17-8-60.

Quand Dieu est dans le mariage, Dieu le garde (operetta).
Performed at the home of the author, February 1861.

Les Trois curiaces (comedy, 1 act). Co-authored by de Saint-Germain.
Paris: Lévy fr., 1867.
Théâtre du Vaudeville, 20-11-66.
[RON Rf. 48.492, ARS GD 8° 226, BHVP in-18 607710 (7),
AN $F^{18}765$].

Le Passé (comedy, 1 act).
Théâtre du Vaudeville, 13-12-76.
[AN $F^{18}769$].

La Loi jaune (comic opera, 3 acts).
Liège, Pavillon de Flore, 8-12-1887.
[SACD ms. 3383].

Le Mariage de Tabarin (comic opera, 3 acts).
Paris: A. Lombardin, n.d.
[RON Rf. 77478, ARS GD 8° 33575].

L'Education d'Achille (saynète).
[SACD ms.].

TOMBELLE (Mme de la) (see BRUNO).

TOUZIN (Jenny).
Author of poetry, novels and a cookbook.

Cigale et Bourdon (operetta, 1 act). Co-authored by Jacques Maillet.
Music by A. Godefroy.
Paris: l'Alliance de Sciences, des Arts et les Lettres, n.d.
[ARS GD 8° 38463].

TRAMAR (la comtesse de).
Pseudonym of Marie-Fanny de LAMARQUE de la GARRIGUE,
baronne d'YSARN de CAPEVILLE.
Author of books for women on *savoir vivre*.

Les Bottines (comedy, 1 act).
Théâtre Pompadour, 17-11-99.

TRÉCOURT (Mlle Marie).
    Sedan, c. 1840 - ?
    Author of children's books.

    Travail et féerie (drame, 6 acts).
        Limoges: imp. Chatras, 1871.
        [ARS GD 8° 36686, SACD].

    Petits drames, poésies. Includes: "Après le siège" (drame, 1 act), "Le Coeur et la chaumière", "La Légion Thébaine" (tragedy, 2 acts).
        Paris: Leroy frères, 1878.
        [BN Yf 12027, RON Rf. 48.541, ARS GD 8° 3610].

    Un Cas de divorce (comedy-vaudeville, 1 act).
        Paris: impr. Jouast, 1880.
        Galerie Vivienne, 4-4-91; Salle Roussel 4-6-98.
        [BN Yf 13016].

    La Retraite (drame, 1 act). Co-authored by Mme de Chantal.
        Théâtre des Capucines, 30-4-84.

    Une Anglaise à Paris (1 act). Co-authored by Mme de Chantal.
        Théâtre des Capucines, 30-4-89.

    Scènes comiques pour la jeunesse: "Un Premier examen" (comedy, 2 acts), "Mlle Tant Pis et Mlle Tant Mieux" (comedy, 1 act), "L'Héritage" (comedy, 2 acts), "En décembre et en juillet" (proverb, 2 acts), "Anniversaire" (charade, 4 acts), "Les Deux interprètes" (comedy, 1 act), "Le Dernier jour des vacances, ou A chacun sa sphère", "Une Etrangère à Paris" (proverb, 1 act), "Un Déjeuner à la campagne", "Une Rencontre nocturne" (scène comique), "Le Nigaud, ou une Soirée chez le jeune Brémarchin".
        Paris: Jouve, 1885.
        [BN m. 8° Yf 160 (1), ARS GD 8° 3609].

    Scènes comiques et autres sujets pour la jeunesse: "Pour distribution des prix" (pièce historique et littéraire), "La Petite Marseillaise", "Les Deux jumelles", "Le Château et la ferme", "Une Journée de Miss Bridge", "L'Etourdie" (comedy, 2 acts), "Un Mauvais conseil" (dialogue), "Hortense la bourrue", "Les Suites d'un examen", "Un Vol", "Le Cheval de bois" (comedy), "Le Jeune conférencier", "Société contre les abus" (2 acts), "L'Anglais et le Monsieur complaisant".
        Paris: Piquet, 1893.
        [BN m. 8° Yf 160 (2)].

TRÉGAIN (comtesse de).

Les Porteurs de Bithynie (comedy, 1 act, verse).
Paris: Arnous de Rivière, 1876.
[ARS GD 8° 39298].

ULMES (Mme Tony d').
Pseudonym of Berthe REY
Novelist.

Monologues de salon. Co-authored by René Trémadeur.
Paris: Librairie théâtrale, 1895.
[BN 8° Yf Pièce 234].

Trop connu ! (monologue).
Bricon, 1895.
[BN 8° Yth 27291].

Le Toréador (monologue).
Bricon, 1896.
[BN 8° Yth 27608].

L'Echelle (comedy, 1 act).
Grand-Guignol, 5-11-98.
[AN F^{18}1217].

En tandem (saynète, 1 act). Co-authored by S. Mancel.
Grand-Guignol, 5-11-98.
[AN F^{18}1217].

Le Droit de tuer (drame, 1 act).
Grand-Guignol, 5-11-98; Mathurins, 6-6-99.
[AN F^{18}1217].

L'Hypnotisée (comedy, 1 act).
Mathurins, 17-6-1900.

Le Fou (drame, 1 act).
Odéon 1909; Nouveau Théâtre Indépendant, 12-7-1910.

Les Immortels (monologue).
Paris: R. Godfrey, J. Strauss, n.d.
[ARS GD 8° 38469].

UZES (see MANUELA).

VADIER (Berthe).
Pseudonym of Célestine Vitaline BENOIT.
St-Laurent (Jura), 1836 - ?
Author of novels, poetry, short stories, children's books, and a biography of H.F. Amiel.

Théâtre de famille: "Cendrillon", "La Belle au bois dormant", "Une Espièglerie de Louis XV".
Sandoz & Fischbacher, 1876.
[BN Yf 12047, RON Rf. 86387, ARS GD 8° 2990].

Théâtre à la maison et à la pension (10 volumes).
Paris: J. Hetzel, 1890.
[BN 8° Yf 500, RON Rf. 86388-86400].

La Revanche de Célimène (comedy, 1 act, verse).
Paris: A. Lemerre, 1906.
[BN 8° Yth 31998, RON Rf. 73.619].

Alkestis (5 acts, verse). Adaptation of Euripides.
Paris: A Lemerre, 1908.
[BN 8° Yb 935, RON Re. 803].

Dejanire (5 acts, verse). Adaptation of Sophocles.
Paris: A Lemerre, 1914.
[BN 8° Yth 35302, RON Rf. 73.620].

VALORY or **VALORI** (Mme de) (née Caroline TOCHON).

Greuze ou l'Accordée de village (comedy-vaudeville, 1 act).
Paris: Delavigne, 1813.
Théâtre du Vaudeville, 31-5-13.
[RON Rf. 36.201, ARS GD 8° 11196, BHVP in-8° 927084, SACD PC 275].

VAN DEN BUSSCHE (Mme) (see Marie EMERY).

VAN DER TAELEN (see Fernande de LYSLE).

VAN DE VELDE (Mme).
Pseudonym: M. du SEIGNEUX.
Born in Geneva.
Author of translations from English.

Léna (4 acts). Co-authored by P. Berton.
Théâtre des Variétés, 16-4-89.
[AN F^{18}813].

VAN DEURSEN or **VAN BEURSEN** (Mlle B.).
Pseudonym: WARD.

Le Clair de lune.
Théâtre du Panthéon, 24-11-38.

Les Exploiteurs et les exploités (comedy-vaudeville).
Théâtre Beaumarchais, 26-2-46.
[AN F^{18}1114].

Le Chat qui expire (vaudeville, 1 act). Co-authored by H. Vannoy and A. de Jallais.
Délassements Comiques, 28-9-50.

Un Duel aux pommes vertes (vaudeville, 1 act). Co-authored by H. Vannoy.
Théâtre Beaumarchais, 15-12-50.
[AN F^{18}1116].

Le Planton de la Marquise (comedy-vaudeville, 1 act). Co-authored by H. Vannoy.
Paris: Librairie théâtrale, 1851.
Porte St. Martin, 4-5-51.
[RON Rf. 49.013, ARS GD 8° 43740, AN F^{18}898].

Le Colporteur (comedy-vaudeville, 2 acts). Co-authored by Jallais and Vannoy.
Paris: Dechaume, 1851.
Délassements Comiques, 19-7-51.
[ARS GD 8° 41197, ARS 4° B.L. 3867].

Job en loterie (vaudeville, 2 acts). Co-authored by Vannoy.
Théâtre Beaumarchais, 13-11-52.
[AN F^{18}1116].

VANHOVE (Mlle C. M.).
Possibly the younger sister of Mme Talma.

Maria ou le Château de Dundayne (melodrama, 3 acts).
   Unpublished.
   Porte St. Martin, 1814?.
   [AN F^{18}598].

VANHOVE (Caroline) (see TALMA).

VARINE (Lydia).

L'Avocat timide (comédie de salon, 1 act).
   Paris: Tresse et Stock, 1884.
   [RON Rf. 84.525, ARS GD 8° 31115, SACD PC 55].

Chez la pâtissière (comedy, 1 act).
   Paris: Tresse, 1890.
   [SACD PC 121].

VARREUX (Célestine de).
Author of history books and poetry.

Les Bordas (tragedy, 3 acts).
   In Poésies.
   Paris: Maillet, 1864.
   [RON Rf. 48.684].

Clorinde (tragedy, 5 acts, verse).
   Versailles: Cerfer fils, 1875.
   [BN Yf 12053, RON Rf. 48.685, ARS GD 8° 29608].

VASILI (Paul) (see Juliette ADAM).

VELLONI della PONTE (Claudie LEGRAND, Mme).
   Lyons, 1861 - ?
   Author of one novel.

La Massue (drame, 1 act). Co-authored by L. Garnier.
   Paris: C. Lévy, 1899.
   Eldorado, 21-2-99.
   [BN 8° Yth 28731, RON Rf. 74.177, ARS GD 8° 33494,
   BHVP in-18 121288].

VENARD (Elisabeth-Céleste) (see CHABRILLAN).

VERNET (Mme Marie).

Bordelais et Marseillais (duo comique). Music by G. Meugé.
Paris: O. Bornemann, 1891.
[BN 4° Yth 5845].

L'Embarras de Mossieu [*sic*] le maire (scène comique). Music by Fr.
Wachs.
Paris: O. Bornemann, 1891.
[BN 4° Yth 5849].

Les Finesses de Geneviève (scène comique). Music by Fr. Wachs.
Paris: O. Bornemann, n.d.
[BN 4° Yth 5851].

Un Quart d'heure tragique (duo comique). Music by Fr. Wachs.
Paris: O. Bornemann, 1891.
[BN 4° Yth 5859].

Les Etrennes de Barbichon (1 act). Music by Ch. Pourny.
Paris: O. Bornemann, n.d.
[BN 4° Yth 6022].

Le Jour de l'an de Madame Durand (1 act). Music by Ch. Pourny.
Paris: O. Bornemann, n.d.
[BN 4° Yth 6023].

Almaïza, épisode de la prise de Grenade par Ferdinand le Catholique
en 1492 (drame historique, 5 acts).
Paris: Haton, 1893.
[BN 8° Yth 26646].

La Rose de la vallée (comedy, 3 acts).
Paris: Haton, 1893.
[BN 8° Yth 26663].

Marquise et normande (comedy, 2 acts).
Paris: Haton, 1894.
[BN 8° Yth 26866].

L'Oiseau de paradis (operetta, 1 act). Music by Georges Meugé.
Paris: Haton, 1895.
[BN 4° Yth 6365].

Petit Noël et Couds-moi des ailes (monologues).
Paris: O. Bornemann, 1896.
[BN 8 ° Yth 27980].

Le Château des Eglantiers (comedy, 1 act).
Paris: Haton, 1896.
[BN 8° Yth 27380].

L'Election de Madame Robineau (comedy, 1 act).
Paris: Haton, 1896.
[BN 8° Yth 27381].

Les Infortunes de la poupée (monologue, verse).
Paris: O. Bornemann, 1896.
[BN 8° Yth 28008].

La Loterie de Perquanco (opérette-bouffe). Music by Ch. Pourny.
Paris: O. Bornemann, 1902.
[BN 8° Yth 30044].

VERNIN (see THENARD).

VIARDOT (Michelle-Ferdinande-*Pauline* GARCIA, Mme Louis).
Paris, 1821 - *id.*, 1910.
Opera singer (until 1863) and composer; correspondence with George Sand.

La Soirée perdue. Co-authored by Marie Dumas.
Salle Herz?, 1873.
[AN F^{18}1348^B].

Au Japon (pantomime), written in 1896.

Cendrillon (comic opera, 3 tableaux).
Paris: C. Miran, 1904.
[BN 8° Yth 31053, BHVP in-12 615 734].

VIEU (Jane) (see Twentieth Century volume).

VILLETARD (Mlle Amélie).
Rouen, 1853 - ?
Author of one novel.

Nous sommes gens de revue (revue, 2 acts).
Salle des Familles (Théâtre Saint-Honoré), 20-5-75.

Monsieur Dorine (comedy, 1 act, verse).
Paris: Tresse et Stock, 1890.
Théâtre de l'Application, 15-1-90.
[BN 8° Yth 23850, RON Rf. 3.880, ARS GD 8° 33298, BHVP
in-18 120195, SACD PC 419].

Le Thème russe (comedy, 1 act).
Théâtre des Arts, 14-05-1904.

Le Septième jour (comedy, 1 act).
Théâtre des Arts, 29-04-1905.

VOIS (Maire-Louise).

Amour conjugal (scène de la vie triste). Co-authored by Ernest Vois.
Paris: E. Vois, 1898.
[BN 8° Yth 28603].

Le Bossu (drame, 1 act). Co-authored by Ernest Vois.
Paris: E. Vois, 1898.
[BN 8° Yth 28605, ARS GD 8° 30093].

La Bossue (drame, 1 act). Co-authored by Ernest Vois.
Paris: E. Vois, 1898.
[BN 8° Yth 28591, ARS GD 8° 37659].

Devant la mort (drame, 1 act). Co-authored by Ernest Vois and Alin
Montjardin.
Paris: E. Vois, 1898.
[BN 8° Yth 28606].

Institution libre (comedy, 1 act). Co-authored by Ernest Vois.
Paris: E. Vois, 1898.
[BN 8° Yth 28589, ARS GD 8° 37117].

La Môme Loupiotte (drame, 1 act). Co-authored by E. Vois and A.
Montjardin.
>   Paris: E. Vois, 1898.
>   [BN 8° Yth 28608, ARS GD 8° 27076].

VOUTE (Mme Alexandrine).

Le Mari prudent (comedy, 1 act).
>   Unpublished, before 1830.
>   [AN F^{18}582].

WALDOR (Mélanie de VILLENAVE, Mme).
Nantes, 1796 - Paris, 1871.
Novelist and poet.

L'Ecole des jeunes filles (drame, 5 acts).
>   Paris: Marchant, 1841.
>   Renaissance, 29-4-41; Porte St. Martin 15-6-42.
>   [BN 4° Yth 1329, RON Rf. 36.962, ARS GD 8° 41548, SACD
>   PC 199, AN F^{18}1262].

La Tirelire de Jeanette (comedy-vaudeville, 1 act). Music by M.
Delphin Balleyquier.
>   Paris: Librairie théâtrale, 1859.
>   Ambigu-Comique, 16-4-59.
>   [BN 8° Yth 17320, RON Rf. 30.964, ARS GD 8° 123, AN
>   F^{18}953].
La Mère grippetout (vaudeville, 1 act).
>   Paris: Librairie théâtrale, 1861.
>   Ambigu-Comique, 21-4-61.
>   [BN 8° Yth 11650, RON Rf. 36.966, ARS GD 8° 33913, AN
>   F^{18}954].

Le Retour du soldat (saynète patriotique). Music by Artus.
>   Paris: Michel Lévy, 1863.
>   Ambigu, 15-8-63.
>   [BN 8° Yth 15409, RON Rf. 36.967, ARS GD 8° 17099, AN
>   F^{18}955].

Paris au désert (cantata). Music by Borssat.
>   Paris: Librairie du Petit Journal, 1865.
>   Grand Théâtre Parisien, 15-8-65.
>   [ARS GD 8° 34679, BHVP in-8° 611821 (4), RON ms. 716].

Il n'y a plus d'enfants (scène de moeurs).
Salle Herz, 14-5-67.

Le Double piège (comic opera). Music by G. Douay.
Salle Herz, 8-6-68.

WAN-DEURSEN (Mlle R.).

C'était moi (drame-vaudeville, 2 acts).
Paris: Tresse, 1842.
Théâtre de Belleville, 6-10-42.
[RON Rf. 36.978, ARS GD 8° 41012, BHVP in-8° 610053
(7), AN F^{18}1304].

WARD (see VAN DEURSEN).

WEIL (Henriette).

Une Obligation (comedy, 1 act).
Paris: Morris père et fils, 1880.
3e Théâtre Français (Déjazet), 27-2-80.
[BN 16 Yth 25594, RON Rf. 49.027, ARS GD 8° 34551].

Hermance Walton (drame, 1 act, prose).
Guebviller, J. Dreyfus, 1882.
[BN 16 Yth 21477, RON Rf. 84.539, ARS GD 8° 33003,
SACD PC 288].

Les Deux fiancés (drame, 3 acts).
Guebviller, J. Dreyfus, 1882.
[BN 16 Yf. 921, RON Rf. 49.028, ARS GD 8° 32001].

WITT (May de).

Le Miroir (saynète).
Paris: Ollendorff, 1897.
[RON Rf. 84.540, ARS GD 8° 26473].

YSARN de CAPEVILLE (see TRAMAR).

ZENTA (Hermann) (see HOLMÈS).

Selected Bibliography

Albistur, Maïté and Daniel Armogathe. Histoire du féminisme français. Paris: des femmes, 1977.

Annales dramatiques, ou dictionnaire général des théâtres. 9 volumes. Paris: Babault, Capelle et Renaud; Treuttel et Wuttz; Le Normand, 1808-1812.

Barbier, Ant.-Alex. Dictionnaire des ouvrages anonymes. 4 volumes. Paris: P. Daffis, 1872.

Benezit, E. Dictionnaire des peintres, sculpteurs, dessinateurs et graveurs. 10 volumes. Paris: Gründ, 1976.

Bibliothèque du théâtre françois depuis son origine. 3 volumes. Dresde: M. Groell, 1768.

Biographie des femmes auteurs contemporaines françaises. Ed. A. de Montferrand. Paris: Armand-Aubrée, 1836.

Biographie Universelle. 45 volumes. Ed. Michaud. Paris: Desplaces, 1843-1857.

Blanc, Olivier. Olympe de Gouges : une femme de libertés. Paris: Syros-Alternatives, 1989.

Bonnifet, Nadeige. "L'Ecriture dramatique des femmes·: Histoire d'un échec ou pré-histoire d'une réussite ?" Mémoire de Maîtrise, Université de Paris III. 1985-1986.

---. "Répertoire de femmes auteurs dramatiques de la langue française du XVIe, XVIIe et XVIIIe siècle et de leurs oeuvres." Mémoire de D.E.A., Université de Paris III, 1987-1988.

Briquet, Mme Fortunée B. Dictionnaire historique, littéraire et bibliographique des Françaises et des étrangères naturalisées en France, connues par leurs écrits... depuis l'établissement de la monarchie jusqu'à nos jours. Paris: Treuttel et Würtz, 1804.

Brunet, Charles. Table des pièces de théâtre décrites dans le catalogue de la Bibliothèque de M. de Soleinne. Paris: Damascène Morgand, 1914.

Calame, Alexandre. Anne de la Roche-Guilhen. Romancière huguenote, 1644-1707. Geneva: Droz, 1972.

Campardon, Emile. Les Comédiens du Roi de la Troupe française pendant les deux derniers siècles, documents recueillis aux Archives Nationales. 1879; Geneva: Slatkine Reprints, 1970.

---. Les Comédiens du Roi de la Troupe Italienne pendant les deux derniers siècles. 1880; Geneva: Slatkine Reprints, 1970.

Catalogue général des ouvres dramatiques et lyriques faisant partie du répertoire de la Société des Auteurs et Compositeurs Dramatiques. Catalogue récaptulatif contenant tous les ouvrages représentés jusqu'au 31 décembre 1859. Paris: Guyot & Pergallo, 1863.

Catalogue général des ouvres dramatiques et lyriques faisant partie du répertoire de la Société des Auteurs et Compositeurs Dramatiques. Catalogue récaptulatif contenant tous les ouvrages représentés du 1e janvier 1860 au 31 décembre 1878. Paris: Typo. Morris, 1882.

Catalogue général des ouvres dramatiques et lyriques faisant partie du répertoire de la Société des Auteurs et Compositeurs Dramatiques. Catalogue récaptulatif contenant tous les ouvrages représentés du 1e janvier 1889 au 31 décembre 1898. Paris: Typo. Morris, 1900.

Catalogue général des ouvres dramatiques et lyriques faisant partie du répertoire de la Société des Auteurs et Compositeurs Dramatiques. Catalogue récaptulatif contenant tous les ouvrages représentés du 1e janvier 1899 au 28 février 1909. Paris: Impr. Cerf, 1910.

Cheliga, Marya. "Le Théâtre féministe." Revue d'art dramatique, October 1901.

Cioranescu, Alexandre. Bibliographie de la littérature française du XVIe siècle. Paris: Klincksieck, 1959.

---. Bibliographie de la littérature française du XVIIe siècle. 3 volumes. Paris: Ed. du CNRS, 1965.

---. Bibliographie de la littérature française du XVIIIe siècle. 3 volumes. Paris: Ed. du CNRS, 1969.

Conlon, Pierre M. Le Siècle des lumières. 11 volumes. Geneva: Droz, 1983-1993.

---. Prélude au siècle des lumières en Fracne de 1680 á 1715. 6 volumes. Geneva: Droz, 1970-1975.

Corvin, Michel . Dictionnaire encyclopédique du théâtre. Paris: Bordas, 1991.

Dictionnaire de Biographie Française. 17 volumes to date. Eds. Balteau, Barroux, Prevost. Paris: Lib. Letouzey, 1933-1989.

Dictionnaire de la musique. 2 volumes. Ed. Marc Honegger. Paris: Bordas, 1970.

Dictionnaire des lettres françaises. 5 volumes. Eds. Cardinal G. Grente, A. Pauphilet, L. Pichard, R. Barroux. Paris: Fayard, 1971.

Dictionnaire des littératures de langue française. 4 volumes. Eds. J.-P. de Beaumarchais, Daniel Couty, Alain Rey. Paris: Bordas, 1987.

Dictionnaire historique thématique et technique des littératures. 2 volumes. Ed. Jacques Demougin. Paris: Larousse, 1985.

Dictionnaire lyrique ou Histoire des Opéras. Eds. Félix Clément and Pierre Larouse. Paris: Administration du Grand Dictionnaire Universel, n.d..

Dominique Aury. "Les Femmes de lettres." Les Femmes célèbres. Ed. Lucienne Mazenod. Paris: Mazenod, 1960.

Gethner, Perry, ed. Femmes dramaturges en France: 1650-1750. Paris, Seattle, Tubigan: Papers on French Seventeenth Century Literature (Biblio 17), 1993.

---. "Melpomene Meets Women Playwrights in the Age of Louis XIV." Neophilologus 72.1 (1988): 17-33.

Gilder, Rosemond. Ces Femmes au théâtre. Trad. Brigitte Chabrol. 1931; Paris: Olivier Perrin, 1967.

Goldwyn, Henriette. "Femmes auteurs dramatiques au dix-septième siècle·: la condition humaine." Cahiers Du Dix-septième Siècle·: An Interdisciplinary Journal 4.1 (1990): 51-61.

Houssin, Monique and Elisabeth Marsault-Loi. Ecrits de Femmes. Paris: Messidor, 1986.

Jacob, P. L. Bibliothèque dramatique de M. de Soleinne. 5 volumes. Paris: Maradan, 1843-4.

Joannidès, A. La Comédie Française de 1680 à 1900 : dictionnaire général des pièces et des auteurs. Paris: Plon-Nourrit, 1901; Geneva: Slatkine Reprints, 1970.

Jordell, D. Catalogue général de la librairie française. 1886-1918. 16 volumes (XII-XXVII). Paris: Champion et Nilsson, 1892-1920.

Krakovitch, Odile. Les Pièces de théâtre soumises à la censure (1800-1830). Paris: Archives Nationales, 1982.

---. "Les Femmes dramaturges et la création au théâtre." Pénélope 3 (Autumn 1980): 29-36.

La Porte, l'abbé de. Histoire littéraire des femmes française. Paris: Lacombe, 1769.

Lancaster, Harry Carrington. A History of French Dramatic Literature in the Seventeenth Century. Part I: The Pre-classical period, 1610-1634. 2 volumes. New York: Gordian Press, 1966.

---. A History of French Dramatic Literature in the Seventeenth Century. Part II: The Period of Corneille, 1635-1651. 2 volumes. New York: Gordian Press, 1966.

---. A History of French Dramatic Literature in the Seventeenth Century. Part III: The Period of Molière, 1652-1672. 2 volumes. New York: Gordian Press, 1966.

---. A History of French Dramatic Literature in the Seventeenth Century. Part IV: The Period of Racine, 1673-1700. 2 volumes. New York: Gordian Press, 1966.

---. A History of French Dramatic Literature in the Seventeenth Century. Part V: Recapitulation, 1610-1700. New York: Gordian Press, 1966.

Lecomte, L.-Henry. Histoire des Théâtre de Paris : Jeux Gymniques, 1810-1812. Paris: Daragon, 1908.

Littérature française contemporaine (XIXe siècle). Ed. J. M. Quérard. Paris: Daguin, n.d..

Lorenz, Otto. Catalogue général de la librairie française. 1840-1885. 11 volumes (I-XI). Paris: D. Jodell, 1867-1887.

Lyonnet, Henri. Dictionnaire des comédiens français. 1902-1908; Geneva: Slatkine Reprints, 1969.

Manuel de bibliographie biographique et iconographique des femmes célèbres. Turin: L. Roux; Paris: Nilsson, 1892.

Millstone, Amy Blythe. "Feminist Theatre in France: 1870-1914." Thèse de Doctorat. University of Wisconsin-Madison. 1977.

Moulin, Jeanine. La Poésie féminine de Marie de France à Marie Noël : XIIe - XIXe siècle. Paris: Seghers, 1966.

Nouvelle Biographie Générale. Ed. Dr Hoefer. Paris: Firmin Didot fr., 1968.

Petite biographie des acteurs et actrices des théâtres de Paris. Paris: Lemoine, 1826.

Porel, P. and G. Monval. L'Odéon : Histoire du second Théâtre français. Paris: Alphonse Lemerre, 1876.

Prudhomme, L. Biographie universelle et historique des femmes célèbres mortes ou vivantes. Paris: Lebigre, 1830.

---. Répertoire universel, historique, biographique des femmes célèbres. 4 volumes. Paris: A. Désauges, 1826.

Quérard, J.-M. Les Supercheries littéraires dévoilées. 3 volumes. Paris: Maisonneuve & Larose, n.d.

---. La France Littéraire. 12 volumes. Paris: Maisonneuve & Larose, n.d.

Schneider, Louis. "Les Femmes auteurs chez Molière." Excelsior 21 janvier 1918.

Showalter, English Jr. "Writing Off the Stage: Women Authors and Eighteenth-century Theater." Yale French Studies 75 (1988): 95-111.

Talvart, Hector and Joseph Place. Bibliographie des auteurs modernes de language française (1801-1927). 22 volumes to date. Paris: Ed. de la Chronique des lettres françaises, 1928-1976.

Tissier, André. Les Spectacles à Paris pendant la Révolution. Répertoire analytique, chronologique et bibliographique de la réunion des Etats généraux à la chute de la royauté, 1789-1792. Geneva: Droz, 1992.

Travers, Seymour. Catalogue of Nineteenth Century French Theatrical Parodies. New York: King's Crown Press, 1941.

Vapereau, G. Dictionnaire des littératures. Paris: Hachette, 1884.

---. Dictionnaire universel des contemporains. Paris: Hachette, 1858.

Waelti-Walters, Jennifer. Feminist Novelists of the Belle Epoque. Indiana UP, 1990.

Wicks, Charles Beaumont. The Parisian Stage: Alphabetical Indexes of Plays and Authors. Part I: 1800-1815. Alabama: University of Alabama Press, 1950.

---. The Parisian Stage: Alphabetical Indexes of Plays and Authors. Part II: 1816-1830. Alabama: University of Alabama Press, 1953.

---. The Parisian Stage: Alphabetical Indexes of Plays and Authors. Part IV: 1851-1875. Alabama: University of Alabama Press, 1967.

---. The Parisian Stage: Alphabetical Indexes of Plays and Authors. Part V: 1876-1900. Alabama: University of Alabama Press, 1979.

--- and Jerome W. Schweitzer. The Parisian Stage: Alphabetical Indexes of Plays and Authors. Part III: 1831-1850. Alabama: University of Alabama Press, 1961.

Library catalogues consulted in their entirety:

Bibliothèque de l'Arsenal: Bound catalogues of the theatrical works contained in the *fond ancien* (B.L.), "Théâtre ancien" and "Théâtre Contemporain"; catalogue of the printed books of the Douay collection.

Bibliothèque Historique de la Ville de Paris: Section of card catalogue dedicated to theatrical works.

Bibliothèque Marguerite Durand: Catalogue of files containing a variety of information about authors (press clippings, biographical sketches, etc.).

Bibliothèque Nationale: Département des Arts du spectacle (located at the Bibliothèque de l'Arsenal): Catalogue of the Rondel collection; catalogue of manuscripts of the Douay collection.

Bibliothèque de l'Opéra de Paris: Card catalogue of librettos and manuscripts (LIV).

Société des Auteurs et Compositeurs Dramatiques: Catalogues of printed books and manuscripts.

Title Index

About the Compiler

CECILIA BEACH received a Ph.D. in French literature from New York University in 1993. In her dissertation, she examined representations of the maternal in works by modern French women playwrights. She is presently working on a checklist of works by French women playwrights in the twentieth century.

ISBN 0-313-29174-8

EAN

HARDCOVER BAR CODE